649
BEC

Beck, Joan

Best beginnings

DATE			
AG 11 '83			
OC 2 '84			
DEC 2 8 1985			
FE 27 '88			
JY 3 '89			
JE 6 '95			
NO 15 '96			

© THE BAKER & TAYLOR CO.

BEST BEGINNINGS

Other books by Joan Beck

How to Raise a Brighter Child

Effective Parenting

Is My Baby All Right?
(with Virginia Apgar, M.D.)

BEST BEGINNINGS

Giving Your Child a Head Start in Life

by Joan Beck

G. P. Putnam's Sons / New York

Permission to quote from published materials has been obtained from these
sources:
    The American Academy of Pediatrics for material from *Pediatrics*, vol. 68, July
1981. Copyright American Academy of Pediatrics 1981.
    Basic Books, Inc., for Helen Featherstone, *A Difference in the Family: Life with
a Disabled Child.* © 1980 by Basic Books, Inc., Publishers, New York.
    The Christian Science Monitor for Nancy Gail Reed, "Raising a Child to
Speak a Second Language." Reprinted by permission from *The Christian Science
Monitor.* © 1982 The Christian Science Publishing Society. All rights reserved.
    Prentice-Hall, Inc., for Cynthia S. Pincus, Leslie Elliott and Trudy Schlach-
ter, *The Roots of Success.* © 1980 by Cynthia Pincus, Leslie Elliott and Trudy
Schlachter. Published by Prentice-Hall, Inc., Englewood Cliffs, New Jersey
07632.

Library of Congress Cataloging in Publication Data

Beck, Joan Wagner, date.
    Best beginnings.

    Includes bibliographical references.
    1. Child development.   2. Pregnancy.   3. Infants—
Care and hygiene.   4. Children—Care and hygiene.
I. Title.
RJ131.B357   1982   649'.122   82-11311
ISBN 0-399-12683-X

Printed in the United States of America

Second Impression

For Christopher and Melinda

Contents

Preface

What does your child need most to develop best during the first six years of life? Today, there are new answers, beginning with conception and involving pregnancy, childbirth, early child care—and in particular, early mental development. Today, there are new ways to help make sure your baby will be born healthy and normal, blessed with the best beginnings in life possible. Today, there are new techniques for stimulating your child's mind to grow and flourish—easy, loving, happy ways of playing with him and caring for him that can make a lifelong difference in the level of his intelligence.

This book reports to you on the great mass of new research about child development from conception to age six. It translates the increasing fund of scientific data from biology, neurology, education, psychology, and pediatrics into practical information useful in day-to-day living with a young child. It goes far beyond the usual child-care instructions about burping, bottles, and bedtimes to explain why it is important to begin caring for your child nine months before he is born and how you can actually raise the level of his intelligence and increase his delight in learning during the early years of his life.

This book is not intended for every parent. It is for those who understand that only they can give a child the best beginnings in life and who want the most reliable, up-to-date information about how to do so. It is for mothers and fathers who plan to take having a child seriously, who can appreciate the fact that in raising a child—as in nurturing a career—the effort put into getting a good start makes everything else not only more successful, but easier.

Just knowing what's best for a young child isn't enough in an age when more than half of all women—including a majority of those with youngsters younger than age six—are employed outside the home for a variety of economic, social, and personal reasons. Can a mother who works full time away from home still see that her child gets the optimal care and mental stimulation that research now indicates makes for successful development? How much can a father or another caregiver or day-care center safely substitute for what mothers have traditionally done? What shortcuts can be made most safely, if there isn't time or energy for everything?

Answers to these questions are much less clear than the research on child development. Families are still trying to experiment their way to new patterns of living, to new ways of sharing the responsibilities and delights of living together with children. What works for one couple may not for others; what goes smoothly with an infant may not for a preschooler. Still, mothers and fathers cannot plan well until they understand fully the real needs of their children and the approximate priority of these needs. This book hopes to spell them out in ways that will help mothers and fathers find a happy balance between child care, careers, and other interests.

In a way it's ironic that the flood of new scientific data about the needs of young children—especially for individualized mental stimulation—comes just at a time when so many new opportunities are becoming available to women besides full-time mothering. Just when we can prove scientifically how important good parenting is to a child—especially to the development of his intelligence—women are being enticed out of the home by unprecedented opportunities for careers and undeniable pressures to earn money. In essence, the stakes have become higher, both for children and for mothers and fathers. Answers that worked a generation ago don't fit now. Child care needs to be different today, to give youngsters the benefit of new research. And often, it must be incorporated into family life in new ways, because family life has changed so much.

This book is divided into five sections, four of which cover the periods of (1) conception to birth, (2) the first year of life, (3) the years from one to three, and (4) the preschool years from three to six. Within each section, chapters will describe the growth that normally occurs and report on new scientific research about what is best for children during these developmental stages. A concluding chapter will suggest how these needs can best be satisfied within the framework of current life-styles. The emphasis on each section will be on the new scientific knowledge about the best possible beginnings for a child, with particular emphasis on his mental development. Routine information about children, about feeding, fevers, first aid, and family emotional problems, is amply available elsewhere.

This book is written for both mothers and fathers. To have a father actively involved in his care is one of the greatest advantages and evidences of love a child can have. To be so involved enriches a man—and a marriage—in more ways and to a greater depth than he anticipates before he becomes a father. "You" in this book, then, is intended to mean either mother or father. "She" is reserved for situations, like pregnancy, that are biologically female. So for contrast and convenience, "he" is generally used to refer to a baby or a child, although youngsters of both sexes are obviously intended.

In writing this book, I am functioning as a reporter, bringing to you a compilation of new research on prenatal development and on the growth of intelligence from birth to the age of six. The information comes from many sources: scientific meetings and seminars, professional journals and research reports, interviews, government studies, educators, psychologists, physicians, child-care professionals, and parents. I am grateful to all of these sources for help and in particular to the March of Dimes Birth Defects Foundation in White Plains, New York; to the Educational Resources Information Center (ERIC) for Early Childhood Education at the University of Illinois for computer searches for relevant research; and to the library staff of the American Medical Association in Chicago. Names of parents and children in most of the illustrative anecdotes and case histories have been changed to protect their privacy. And in the names of certain disorders, like Down's syndrome, the possessive form has been eliminated to conform to new medical terminology.

 SECTION I

Child Care from Conception to Birth

MARCIA is thirty-four and already listed in *Who's Who of American Women*. Her law degree is from one of the twenty best law schools in the nation. She was the first woman ever to become a partner in her Wall Street firm, a position she earned with no suggestion of sexist tokenism and holds with enthusiastic and competent work. Her income puts her among the top 1 percent of workingwomen and enables her and her husband, an editor with a New York publishing company known for its low pay scales, to live comfortably in expensive midtown Manhattan.

Now that she's reached the career goal she worked so hard to attain for more than a decade, Marcia is beginning, reluctantly, to realize she cannot continue to postpone indefinitely making a decision about having children. But she doesn't know how soon the biological clock will run out or what risks she and a baby might run if she pushes the biological deadline too closely. She's had almost no contact with young children for years, and while she can estimate the extra expenses a baby will bring, she has only the vaguest ideas about the satisfactions. She is used to thinking of herself as an attorney and a wife; she can't quite imagine herself as a mother. But if she and her husband decide to have a child, she wants to do it in her characteristic style. She wants to be fully informed about what's involved and plan ahead to make sure the undertaking turns out well.

Janet, twenty-seven, would refuse to have a child at all if it weren't for the efforts of her husband Bill to change her mind. Janet grew up with a mentally retarded brother and worries that someday she may inherit the responsibility for him that her parents now have. And she worries even more that if she had a child, he too might be mentally retarded. She can't bear to have her parents learn how deeply her brother's problems have affected her.

She can hardly admit it to herself. So she says, "Maybe later, I'm not ready yet" to Bill when he talks about a baby. And then she worries that she may lose him if she stalls much longer.

Stephanie had a baby three months ago—a happy, healthy, most-wonderful-baby-in-all-the-world baby, a wanted child, born close to the general timetable Stephanie and her husband had in mind for their lives. But now Stephanie's maternity leave is over. She is due back at her job in two weeks. The loving, capable, surrogate mother she intended to find to take care of the baby while she works nows seems as elusive as an Abominable Snowman. Before the baby was born, Stephanie had repeatedly justified her plans to return to her job by rationalizing that it's the quality, not the quantity, of parenting that counts with a child. But now she may have to choose between taking her baby to the home of a sitter who is already caring for three other small children or hiring an older woman with a poor command of English as a full-time baby-sitter at home. Or, she can quit her job and stay home herself. That raises other questions. Would staying home with the baby really be better for the baby, Stephanie wonders, or would she miss her outside business life so much she wouldn't really be a good mother or a good wife?

In recent years, several scientific fields such as pediatrics, genetics, obstetrics, neonatology, biology, psychology, and neurology—and new alliances between them, such as neurobiology, neurophysiology, and neurochemistry—have made important discoveries that can help parents and prospective parents increase their chances of having happy, healthy, intelligent children. In particular, this new information means:

1. More than half of all serious birth defects—including mental retardation—can be prevented if prospective parents learn how to safeguard their baby during the long months before he is born.

2. Parents can, by the amount of loving and individualized mental stimulation they provide in a child's environment, contribute substantially to raising the general level of his intelligence long before he starts formal schooling. By learning how to nourish his brain with sensory stimuli that help it grow, they can quite literally improve the quality of his mind for the rest of his life.

These new research findings are changing the specifics of child care, lessening its risks and increasing its rewards—for parents like Janet and Bill, Marcia and her husband, and everyone who wants to give a child the best beginnings possible in life. This new kind of child care that begins before conception and concentrates on the brain as well as the body isn't easy to synchronize with current life-styles, as pressures increase for women to combine a career with raising a child and as the number of single parents grows. But the stakes are so high—the optimal development of a new human being—that they may require even more adjustments in life-style and in the way both men and women manage their work.

Ideally, planning for a healthy, normal baby should begin before conception. Child care is a continuum, affected first of all by the quality of the ovum and sperm that unite to begin the new life and then by all that occurs during the first nine months of that life when body, and especially brain, grow more rapidly than they ever will again. What goes right during the nine months of prenatal existence is essential to a normal, happy, healthy life. If anything goes wrong, the results may be difficult to correct or to moderate for an entire lifetime.

Some babies have been born with physical or mental abnormalities since the earliest days for which we can find human traces. Until four or five decades ago, such mishaps were usually attributed to angry gods, old wives' superstitions, or blind mischance. But new research in genetics, biochemistry, and prenatal development in recent years has discovered many of the causes of birth defects: German measles and Rh blood factor incompatibilities in the 1940s; chromosome abnormalities and drugs like thalidomide in the 1960s; maternal drinking and smoking, plus dozens of genetic diseases and environmental factors in the 1970s and 1980s. We now know how to prevent literally dozens of serious birth defects—genetic diseases, malformations, mental retardation, chromosomal disorders, even mild learning problems and behavior disorders that don't show up until the school years.

About 7 percent of all infants are born with a serious birth defect that will substantially affect their lives—and the lives of their families. About 7 percent more are born with less severe abnormalities, like an easily corrected minor malformation or a moderate mental retardation that doesn't become obvious until a few years after birth. Like the miraculously complex chemical and biological sequences that turn an ovum and a sperm into a healthy newborn infant, the processes that cause a birth defect are complicated and few of them are completely understood yet. Some birth defects are caused by mistakes coded into infinitesimally small parts of genes inherited from either father or mother or both. Some are the result of errors in the number or structure of the chromosomes that string together the inherited genes. Some occur because something—virus, chemical, or radiation—reaches the unborn child in the womb and causes damage to a fragile bit of tissue. Some are the result of a combination of inherited vulnerability and hazard in the environment. For many more, there is still no known explanation.

But by beginning child care even before conception, by caring intelligently all through the nine months of pregnancy for their baby, prospective parents can greatly increase the odds that their child will start life healthy and normal. It takes, after all, much less effort than planning a career. And the stakes are infinitely higher.

1. Planning to Be Parents

A baby fits most easily and happily into his parents' lives at some stages than others. Ideally, he is conceived because mother and father decide that now is the right time—that their marriage is stable and secure, that they have sufficient income to stretch over his small needs, that they are emotionally mature enough to love him wholeheartedly, and that they are ready for this major step into adulthood.

It isn't as easy to find that time now as it used to be. Today, a woman may decide to postpone having a baby until she finishes graduate school or gets started in her career, or earns the next promotion, or until her husband's salary is so large the couple won't miss her earnings if she stops working. But the more successful she becomes in her job, the more she earns, and the more a couple comes to enjoy their child-free life-style, the harder it becomes to decide to have a baby.

It is easy to see the problems and costs of having a baby: the need for constant care, weekends and vacations included; the extra expenses; the daily diapering and feeding routines; the irreversible commitment to a different life-style; the sobering expectation that having a baby will seriously curtail a mother's career and possibly slow a father's; the open-ended commitment to another, unknown human being.

It is much harder to anticipate the satisfactions and rewards of having a child. Watching a friend take care of her baby isn't much help. You can't experience the same feelings she does about her baby any more than you understand why she fell in love with her particular husband. In fact, having a baby is a lot like falling in love, for it is essentially a love-and-be-loved relationship of great intensity, reinforced by biological forces so powerful they have ensured the preservation of the human race since its beginning. Begetting and nourishing an offspring is a basic part of life—a major experience too fundamental to be missed. Having children gives a balance to life that helps put into perspective, say, the importance of the balance sheet at Widget Sales Corporation or the promotion ladder at Smith-Lynch-Barney. A child gives you a link and a stake in the next generation. It makes you a family, with all its richness and caring and sharing and involvement. "When I first held my first baby, I had an almost tangible sense of my value system shifting on its axis," recalls a reporter on a big metropolitan daily. "I knew immediately I had made the right choice in deciding to have a child, no matter what it did to my newspaper career." She had not been sure at all before that minute.

Despite the obvious emotional, economic, marital, and career advantages of timing the birth of a baby carefully and despite a record-high use of contraceptives, it's estimated that about half of all pregnancies in this country are originally unintended. Almost one and a half million of the accidental pregnancies are terminated by abortion every year. Others may result in unwanted children who are neglected and abused. Some babies, especially the increasing number born to unmarried teenagers, not only start life at enormous disadvantage themselves, but also stunt the lives and future potential of their young parents beyond easy repair. Most of

the accidentally conceived children are accepted and loved, however—if not during pregnancy, then almost surely after they are
born.

But an increasing number of bright, caring young people now
plan their children as carefully as they do their education and
their careers—not only for their own sake but for their children's
benefit. Generally, such couples postpone childbearing until both
have finished their education and both have shown some initial
success in their jobs. If a woman has already demonstrated her
value to her employer, it may be easier for her to arrange for an
extended maternity leave, a part-time work arrangement, flexible
hours, a shared job, or simply extra time off in emergencies. If she
finds her baby so fascinating she opts for full-time mothering, earlier success in a job should make it easier to return to work even
years later if she wishes. Such planning now often pushes childbearing into a woman's early thirties.

This plan doesn't always work. Sometimes a woman finds her
job so satisfying and interesting she never gets around to deciding
the time is right to have a baby until time runs out biologically.
Or, she may decide at thirty-five or thirty-six to get pregnant, only
to learn of unsuspected infertility problems that require long treatment. (An estimated 10 to 15 percent of couples have difficulty
conceiving, but about 40 percent of them eventually do, with
medical help.) The increasing incidence of divorce may leave a
woman single in her early thirties, just when her timetable-for-
the-future called for having a baby.

Many women, of course, still have their children in their early
twenties, in a pattern common a generation ago. They may work a
year or two after they finish high school or college, then drop out
of the work force completely, perhaps never having had a strong
interest in a career and perhaps never intending to go back to a
job, even after their children are grown. Pregnancy and child care
usually come much easier for women who are not in the work
force because they aren't torn by the pressures of competing demands of home and job and have more time and energy for their
children. But a majority of women who followed this life-stages
pattern in the 1950s and 1960s are now returning to work, perhaps after some transitional college courses, because they don't

have enough to do at home, because of financial pressures, and because the women's movement has helped to open up more job possibilities. And today, many women who plan to be full-time mothers at home and have little interest in a career are still being pushed back into the labor market by financial need.

At least 90 percent of all women now spend some part of their lives in the work force. Social trends and economic factors make it inevitable that this percentage will continue to be high and that the proportion of adult years spent in the work force will increase. Women are going to college and graduate school in record numbers and holding an unprecedented number, variety, and level of jobs. The economic structure of at least half of our families and of the nation itself now depends on having women in the work force.

How and when to fit children into 1980s life-styles, then, has become a much more complicated matter than it used to be. Society has yet to reach a consensus on how mothers and fathers are to manage both jobs and child care. Most employers are slow to recognize that women workers who have young children may need adjustments in a nine-to-five workday and a forty-hour workweek set up for the convenience of workingmen, although such changes are now common in Western European nations. Debate about whether the care of young children of working mothers should be a public responsibility or whether state involvement in child care is an encroachment on family privacy and an unaffordable public expense still goes on, unresolved.

So today, in the absence of social consensus and in a time of transition, you have a wide—and sometimes confusing—choice of ways to fit children into your life. You can, for example, choose from five basic patterns of parenting, each with possible variations and each with its own particular set of advantages and disadvantages:

Traditional, with the mother assuming full-time care of the child and the father helping out occasionally, is still, by a slight margin, the most common pattern for families with offspring younger than school age. It offers close bonding between mother and child; can provide a child with consistent, quality-controlled parenting; frees a father to concentrate on his career; and usually takes less total family energy and involves less marital hassle than other arrangements. But it limits a family to a single income, curtails career opportunities and some kinds of personal growth for the mother, and for some women, may be intolerably restrictive.

Father as primary caregiver is just the opposite of the traditional family and is the most radical and unstable pattern of child care. But it is tried occasionally when a mother has a strong career interest and a father doesn't or when he wants to finish a thesis, write a book, or try free-lancing, or is between jobs and dependent on his wife's income. Except in unusual circumstances, it is temporary because of the difficulties imposed by social pressures to be more conventional. But it is still a viable option for a few couples and given the right father and a cooperative relationship between the parents who both work at child care, it can work well for young children.

Single-parent families increased 51 percent during the 1970s, up from 5.6 million to 8.5 million, and are now so common because of divorce and unmarried motherhood that it's estimated half of all children will spend some time in a single-parent home before they reach age eighteen. But going it alone puts enormous strain on a mother or a father, despite some enthusiastic advocacy from feminist groups. Studies show that children from single-parent homes have more academic and social problems in school and get into more trouble with the law than other youngsters. Single mothers make up the largest group of people receiving welfare. And single parents who work encounter all of the problems of working mothers without any support or help at all from a spouse.

Parents with full-time jobs are also increasing as a family style and 45 percent of married women with children under age six now hold jobs outside their homes. Many of these 5.5 million mothers have difficulty finding good child care for their 7.5 million offspring. About 1.6 million are put into a variety of public and private day-care centers of differing quality and 5.4 million are left with or taken to baby-sitters, sometimes relatives but more often not. How well they fare depends on the quality of the care they receive for the largest part of their waking day and on the quality of time parents spend with them when they are not working. In most of these families, the chief responsibility for child care still falls on the mother, with the result that she may be chronically tired and feel guilt about shortchanging both children and job.

The youngsters may, indeed, receive insufficient parenting and their mental development, in particular, might therefore not be optimal.

Parents with flexible working schedules are developing new ways of combining work and child care that may become prototypes for an increasing number of couples in the future. Women, especially, are seeking—and finding—part-time work, flexible hours, shared jobs, and extended leaves that make it easier to combine employment with child care. For women who want to keep up with a professional field or who must earn some extra money while still making their major commitment to their children, this can offer a reasonable compromise solution. In a few pioneering families, both husband and wife manage to have nonrigid work schedules and share child care on an egalitarian basis.

You also have several options for child care, depending on where you live, the age of your offspring, your income, and the amount of time neither parent can be at home. These include leaving your youngster with a baby-sitter in your home or hers, family day care, a day-care center, or a nursery school.

You probably won't know for sure what combination of job options and child-care choices—if any—will work out best for you until after your baby is born and you experience firsthand the whole new set of responsibilities, time and energy demands, and satisfactions that come with becoming a parent. Having a first child is a more wrenching adjustment and a bigger, more unpredictable transition than getting married or leaving school for a job. One study shows that 75 percent of pregnant employees who take disability benefits and plan to return to work after a maternity leave resign instead—a statistic that reflects not only the attractiveness of disability plans that include pregnancy, but also the major changes that new mothers experience in their priorities and pleasures after their baby has actually been born.

What is important during pregnancy—and even before conception—is knowing precisely what you should and shouldn't do to increase the odds your child will be born healthy and normal. After that, other decisions fall into place much more easily.

2. What Will Your Baby Inherit?

Will your baby have his father's brown eyes? His mother's curly hair? The shape of nose that marks so many members of your family? Will he be tall? Have teeth that need straightening? A tendency to be overweight? Will he inherit above-average intelligence? A sense of humor? Artistic ability? Most important, will he inherit good health?

The answers are partly written in complex packages of biochemical instructions called genes, which are linked together into strands called chromosomes, and are present in the nucleus of every cell of the body. It's been known since 1956 that every normal human cell contains forty-six chromosomes. One pair, called X and Y because of their shape during one phase of their activity, determine the sex characteristics of the individual. The other twenty-two pairs, called autosomes, direct all the other complicated activities of growing, maintaining the body's functions, and mounting its defenses against harm. New techniques developed in recent years now make it possible to identify each of the twenty-three pairs of chromosomes by slight differences in their shape and size and by the appearance of characteristic bands of coloration that appear when chromosomes are stained so that they can be studied in the laboratory.

No one knows yet how many genes are packed into each set of chromosomes. Estimates range from 100,000 (based on the number of biochemical functions genes are thought to control) to 2.5 million (assumed from the amount of genetic material—deoxyribonucleic acid, or DNA—contained in each cell). But scientists are learning to locate certain genes on specific chromosomes. Such gene mapping can already be of some aid in genetic counseling and may someday help make it possible to locate and correct an abnormal gene and prevent a hereditary disorder.

Every human being inherits half of his chromosomes from his father and half from his mother. Many of the genes on the chromosomes inherited from one parent are the exact duplicate of those from the other parent; for example, the chromosomes your child inherits may include a gene coding for brown eye color and one for the Rh blood factor from each of his parents. Your child is said to be homozygous for the particular traits coded in those genes and will have brown eyes and Rh blood factor.

But genes often exist in two or more forms, called alleles. Your child may receive a gene calling for brown eyes from one parent and a gene for blue eyes from the other; he will be heterozygous for eye color. The actual color of your child's eyes will be determined, then, by which gene is dominant and which is recessive. In the case of eye color, brown is dominant and blue recessive. An individual with one gene for brown eyes and one for blue (called his genotype) will have brown eyes (his phenotype). But he will also always carry the recessive gene for blue eyes on a chromosome. Should he, someday, marry a brown-eyed woman who also carries a hidden, recessive gene for blue eyes, these two brown-eyed people could have a blue-eyed child, even though blue eyes are a recessive characteristic. In fact, there is one chance in four in each pregnancy that a child will inherit the brown-eye gene from each of these particular parents, one chance in four he will inherit his mother's brown-eye gene and his father's blue-eye gene, and one chance in four he will receive his mother's blue-eye gene and his father's brown-eye gene; that makes three chances in four he will actually have brown eyes. There is also one chance in four he will get the blue-eye gene from both father and mother and therefore have blue eyes.

Similarly, if your offspring inherits a gene for the Rh blood factor from each of his parents, his blood type will be Rh positive. He will also have Rh-positive blood if he receives one Rh-positive and one Rh-negative gene from his parents, because the Rh-positive gene is dominant. Only if an individual inherits two Rh-negative genes will he lack the Rh factor in his blood. But a child can have Rh-negative blood, even if he has two Rh-positive parents—provided each of them has one Rh-negative gene and the child inherits them from each parent.

These are classic, simplistic examples of how traits governed by single genes are inherited. Many human characteristics result from combinations of genes and from genes interacting with their en-

vironment before and after birth. The effects produced by individual genes may also vary from one generation to another for reasons
scientists don't fully understand.

So exquisitely arranged is this process of inheritance that no
two individuals, out of the forty billion or so who have lived on
this earth, have ever had precisely the same assortment of genes
(except for identical twins, who develop as the result of a split in a
fertilized ovum after its genetic components have already been
fixed). In theory, if a couple could have millions of children, no
two would ever be exactly alike, even though they share the same
two parents and inherit their genes from them.

All of the ova, or egg cells, a woman will ever have are formed
months before her own birth, while her body is still developing in
her own mother's womb. By about the third month after conception, hundreds of thousands of specialized cells called primary
oocytes develop and begin to divide by a process that differs significantly from the usual kind of cell division. As is usual when a
cell begins to divide, the chromosomes in the nucleus duplicate
themselves and prepare to separate into two identical cells.

But in the oocytes, the duplicated chromosomes don't split
apart. Instead, they arrange themselves in matching pairs. Each
chromosome inherited from the unborn infant's mother lies precisely parallel to the matching chromosome from the father. The
segments of each chromosome pair split apart and change places,
or "cross over." A sticky substance seals the segments back together, forming new and distinctive chromosomes. Each still carries only the genes that the new baby inherited from her mother
and her father, but in new and unique arrangements that greatly
increase human genetic diversity.

About the fifth month of a baby girl's prenatal development,
this special process of cell division stops, never to occur again in
her body. By then—four months or so before she herself will be
born—about seven million oocytes are packed into her two ovaries. Some will remain there, their development suspended, until
she begins to ovulate at the age of eleven or twelve or thirteen. A
few will stay quiescent in the ovaries until ovulation ceases at the
age of forty-five or so. But even before birth, the oocytes, with
their unique packages of genetic coding, begin to disintegrate and
disappear. More than two-thirds will be lost even before the baby

girl is born. Only an estimated two million are left at birth; perhaps only three hundred thousand to five hundred thousand remain by the age of seven.

After puberty, every twenty-eight days or so at about the midpoint of the menstrual cycle, for reasons not yet well understood, the process of cell division begins again, usually in just one of the waiting oocytes. Each still contains forty-six doubled chromosomes, twice the normal load of genetic material. Now, the pairs of doubled chromosomes pull away from each other and move into two new cells, one much larger than the other, and now scientifically termed an ovum. The smaller cell begins to disintegrate and disappears.

The ovarian follicle which has sheltered the oocyte since months before the woman's birth now swells and stretches. Part of its wall thins out and the ovum is gently propelled into the fallopian tube where tiny hairs sweep it softly toward the uterus. Within hours—no one knows for sure, but probably about twenty-four—it, too, will disintegrate and die unless it is penetrated by an advancing sperm and, fertilized, begins to grow into a new human being.

As the ovum floats down the fallopian tube, it begins to divide once again, a process that will not be completed unless fertilization takes place. This time, the twenty-three remaining doubled chromosomes split apart and move into separate cells, again the ovum itself retaining most of the cellular material and the second cell, with half of the chromosomes, disintegrating. Now, the ovum contains only twenty-three chromosomes, ready to match the twenty-three chromosomes the fertilizing sperm brings from the father of what is now a beginning human life.

So it is blind biological chance that determines which of the seven million original oocytes will survive long enough to become one of the 350 to 400 which mature into ova during a woman's reproductive lifetime. And it takes two more shakes of the genetic dice to determine which twenty-three chromosomes of the forty-six doubled pairs in the oocyte will still be left in the ovum when fertilization occurs.

Blind biological chance also determines which of a father's genes will be carried in the sperm that meets the ovum in the fallopian tube to start the new life. Sperm production doesn't be-

gin until early adolescence, although the special cells which produce sperm can be found in the male testes early in prenatal life.
Sperm are formed in much the same way as ova, but the process is
much faster and takes only about sixty to seventy-five days. As
with ova, the chromosomes double but do not divide. Similarly,
they line up in matching pairs and segments of genetic material
are exchanged. But there is one exception. Male cells contain an
X and a Y sex chromosome, unlike female cells which have two
Xs. During sperm production, the X and Y line up end to end, not
parallel to each other, and no gene segments are exchanged.
These cells then split in two, each containing twenty-three doubled chromosomes, and then divide once more, to make four
sperm. Two will contain X chromosomes and if one fertilizes an
ovum, will produce a girl. Two carry Y chromosomes and if
one reaches the ovum first, will result in the conception of a boy.
All four have a different combination of genes. An estimated
300,000,000 to 500,000,000 sperm are ejaculated at one
time by a healthy, fertile male; he will produce an estimated
3,000,000,000,000 sperm during his lifetime. Again, it is blind
chance that determines which single sperm first meets the ovum to
begin a new life and which particular set of genetic instructions it
brings to the development of the new human being.

For all its basic simplicity, however, the human genetic code
still holds many unsolved mysteries for scientists—and many unanswered questions for parents and prospective parents. Many of
an individual's characteristics result from the interactions of several genes, probably located on different chromosomes, and on the
effects of the environment—beginning with the first days of prenatal life—interacting with the messages written in the genes.

How tall your child will be, for example, depends in part on
several genes—not only those that direct the growth of tissues, but
those that regulate and stop growth and those that initiate and
time the hormonal changes at puberty. It also depends on how
well nourished your child is, not only after birth but before, when
his body is growing more rapidly than it ever will again. Regardless
of what is written in the genes, a child who is severely malnourished may never reach his potential height. But improving nutrition may add inches to what seems to be genetically limited
height—at least among large groups of people over time.

Genes also determine much of what your child's basic body structure will be—whether your daughter will have the long, thin bones requisite for ballet dancing or your son the basic build for becoming a professional football linebacker. But again the role of environment is crucial—and obvious. Without training, practice, appropriate nutrition, motivation, and opportunity, no child will become a ballet dancer or a linebacker. Genetic factors may set the direction and limitations of a child's physical accomplishments, but they do not assure that he will reach his potential. And given optimal environmental conditions, there is some evidence that what was assumed to be genetically determined limitations may not be completely fixed. For example, with encouragement, opportunity, and motivation, women athletes in some sports are now setting records thought to be physically impossible two or three decades ago.

Intelligence, too, results from interaction between genetic potential and influences in the environment—in an even more complicated and less well understood way. It is difficult even to define intelligence precisely because it involves so many different abilities and skills. It is hard to measure; standard IQ tests take into account only a few aspects of intelligence and are inevitably influenced by economic status, experience, culture, health, learning opportunity, motivation, and other factors.

But whatever intelligence is and however it is measured, it does seem to run in families—both because of hereditary influences and because of the shared family environment. Controversy has raged for centuries about whether heredity or environment is the major determinant of intelligence. But we have no clear understanding yet of the genetic basis for "intelligence." We have no good scientific measures of "environment." And so the controversy seems destined to continue for decades more, at least.

The studies that have been done—primarily those which compared the IQ of identical twins reared in separate environments and those of adopted children with both biological and adoptive parents—suggest that heredity may contribute from 60 to 80 percent of a child's mental ability. But the studies have many flaws and limitations.

Geneticists have never found—and never expect to discover—a gene they can label "intelligence" and locate on a chromosome map. It seems likely that whatever hereditary basis does exist for intelligence lies, instead, in the genes that determine the structure of the brain, the mix of biochemicals essential to brain activity, and the efficiency of the sensory pathways from eyes, ears, nose, mouth, and skin to the brain. There may be a hereditary basis for the speed and efficiency with which the brain processes information, stores it, retrieves it from memory, and combines it with other data in "thinking." For example, one form of culture-free intelligence test simply measures the speed with which individuals can respond to a flash of light; a strong correlation was found between quickness and IQ.

There may be a genetic basis for the fact that some individuals have markedly superior or inferior auditory or visual perception. Some children find it almost impossible to learn to read, although they have normal or higher than average intelligence, because of visual perception difficulties. Perceptual problems and other kinds of learning disabilities are often found in family patterns suggesting a hereditary basis.

Most adults learn, eventually, to adopt their learning methods to take advantage of whatever sensory abilities are most efficient. Some people know they will learn more by listening to a lecture than by reading the same information. Others have discovered that if they want to remember a phone number or name, they have to see it written down so they can learn it through their eyes. Still others know that they learn best if they involve their kinesthetic senses and go through the motions of writing down what they want to learn. Such differences probably have a genetic basis, although they can be modified by teaching, practice, and motivation.

Genetic inheritance may also lay the foundation for exceptional abilities of several kinds. In particular, talent for music and for mathematics seems to have a large hereditary component; both are evident quite early in life and both seem to occur in family clusters. But there is some evidence to show that musical ability has a bigger-than-expected environmental component, however. New Japanese teaching methods that begin during the first years of life, for example, have produced an extraordinary number of fine young musicians.

But regardless of what is coded in the genes, environment does play a powerful role in the development of intelligence and of special abilities. There is increasing evidence that by providing optimal mental stimulation during the years when the brain is growing most rapidly, parents can substantially increase a child's intelligence and even foster the physiological development of the brain itself.

Considerably less is known about any possible hereditary basis for a child's personality traits. Some studies have been made with twins and with adopted children, attempting to find an inherited component in such characteristics as sociability, shyness, impulsivity, emotionalism, and vocational preferences. A few puzzling similarities have turned up in some recent research involving identical twins reared in separate homes; as adults some of these twins discovered they had a preference for the same colors, had married women with similar names, and had chosen similar names for their children. So far there is no good genetic explanation for such findings. It's curious, however, that research also fails to show clear associations between personality traits of children and those of their parents that can be attributed directly to factors in the environment. There is much more to be learned about what forms personality, or basic temperament, in children. And certainly, better research techniques are necessary to find reliable answers.

Evidence is accumulating, however, that severe mental illnesses, like manic-depression and schizophrenia, do have a genetic basis. Probably they are caused by an imbalance of biochemicals or by abnormalities in nerve function or in the neurotransmitters which regulate the flow of chemically coded information among nerve cells in the brain. If it could be established that these mental disorders are caused by faulty genes, it would open the way for finding biochemical treatments—lithium is already used with great success for certain forms of depression—and would relieve families and affected individuals of the feelings of guilt and shame so often associated with these illnesses.

Most current genetic research is not concerned with tracking normal hereditary characteristics, but with identifying genetic disorders and finding ways to prevent and treat them. What has already been discovered in the last two decades is of vital importance to parents who want to do everything they can to improve their baby's chances of being born healthy and normal. Michael and Nancy Goldberg, who live in a Chicago suburb, learned about genetic disorders in one of the most painful ways possible. Their first child, a son, is an exceptionally bright and handsome boy, whom they enjoy and love with enthusiasm and delight. They had every reason to expect that their second baby, a boy they named Jeffrey, would also be a joy.

But when Jeffrey was about five months old, Nancy began to worry that something was wrong. Their pediatrician, however, reassured the Goldbergs that their baby was normal—perhaps a little slow in developing, but normal. In the months that followed, the Goldbergs' concerns increased. Jeffrey was not only failing to develop the usual baby skills at the normal age, but he seemed to be regressing. Ten months, two pediatricians, an allergist, a therapist, and two neurologists later, the correct diagnosis was finally made, not only because of the baby's symptoms but because of a characteristic and unique cherry-red spot in the retina of each eye. Jeffrey had Tay-Sachs disease.

Tay-Sachs is a classic, textbook genetic disease. It occurs almost entirely in a limited population group: Ashkenazi Jews with ancestors in Eastern Europe. About one in every thirty of these Jews carries a single, recessive gene for Tay-Sachs disease—a mistake in a single piece of the genetic code. Each also has a matching normal gene, which is able to provide the missing bit of biochemical instruction in correct form. Such a carrier is clinically normal. But a blood test is now available that will diagnose his or her status as a carrier.

When two carriers marry—as happens in about one out of nine hundred couples who have Ashkenazi heritage—there is one chance in four in each pregnancy that the baby will inherit a normal gene from both of his parents. He will neither have Tay-Sachs disease nor be a carrier. He cannot pass on the genetic error to any of his descendants. There are two chances in four that the baby will inherit a normal gene from one parent and the defective gene from the other; he will then be a carrier, like his parents, but he will develop normally. He could, however, pass the defective gene on to his children.

There is also one chance in four in each pregnancy that the baby—like Jeffrey—will inherit the defective gene from each parent. Without a normal gene to supply the correct biochemical instructions, he will have Tay-Sachs disease. Such an infant appears normal at birth and for several months after; he is likely, in fact, to be a particularly beautiful baby. But because of the biochemical mistake, his body doesn't produce an enzyme called hexosaminidase A, or Hex A, which helps to dispose of excessive amounts of a fatty substance, a glycolipid. Without Hex A, the glycolipid begins to accumulate in the neurons of the brain and nervous system, making them swell up and die.

Late in the first year of life, such a baby's development begins to slow and then regress. Inevitably, he becomes unable to move about, to sit up, to see, or hear, or even swallow. He may have convulsions. Death eventually occurs by the age of three or four years, perhaps from choking or from frequent attacks of pneumonia. No treatment is known. By the age of twenty months, Jeffrey could no longer see or recognize his parents. He could no longer eat, but had to be fed through tubes in his nose. He had already suffered two serious bouts of pneumonia and had to have professional nursing care twenty-four hours a day.

At this point, both of his parents made decisions to help them bear the sorrow and pain of watching their baby's slow and inevitable death. Nancy decided to have another baby and Michael, a lawyer, filed a lawsuit against Nancy's doctor for not telling them that Tay-Sachs disease was a possibility for an offspring of theirs and for not letting them know that it could be diagnosed early enough in prenatal life for a safe abortion. Carriers of Tay-Sachs disease—like Nancy and Michael—can also be identified by a blood test, because they have only about 50 percent of the usual amount of Hex A, although they are otherwise completely normal. What Michael hopes to accomplish with the lawsuit is to remind physicians forcefully—by threat of malpractice suit—that they should warn their patients about possible genetic disease, that many carriers can be diagnosed before they become parents, and that prenatal diagnostic techniques may make it possible for them to have only children free of the disorder in question.

It was this medical assurance that she would not have to give birth to another baby with Tay-Sachs disease that gave Nancy the courage to risk another pregnancy. After she had been pregnant about three and a half months, Nancy had a test called amniocentesis (see page 38) in which a small amount of the amniotic fluid that surrounds an unborn infant in the uterus was withdrawn. This fluid contains some cells that have sloughed off from the baby's body and can be grown in the laboratory and studied. Three weeks later, Nancy was told that the genetic dice had come up wrong the second time. Her unborn baby also had Tay-Sachs disease. The Goldbergs decided to end the pregnancy. After several months, they tried again. This time, after amniocentesis, the report came back with good news. Nancy was carrying a baby free of Tay-Sachs disease. She later gave birth to a normal, healthy baby. One more pregnancy, again monitored by testing for Tay-Sachs disease has given the Goldbergs a third normal, healthy child.

Michael Goldberg's suit is still in the courts. But the point he wants to make—as do others concerned about helping babies be born free of genetic disorders whenever possible—is still of great importance: Prospective parents do need to know about the possibility of such illnesses and the ways they can use genetic counseling to increase the odds their child will be born normal and healthy.

Unfortunately, among our tens of thousands of genes, each of us has a few—perhaps three to eight—that are abnormal. These genes contain errors in the arrangement of the nucleic acids that form them so that they give garbled instructions to the cells for the function they are expected to direct.

More than two thousand genetic disorders have already been identified—serious and usually lifelong problems that occur because a mistake in a gene leads to a chain of biochemical consequences which prevent the body from functioning normally. Together, these genetic disorders now cause a big part of the medical problems in the United States. It's estimated that at least one third—probably more—of babies lost in miscarriages have a genetic or chromosome abnormality. An estimated 2.5 to 5.5 percent of all live-born babies have a serious genetic disorder, although it may not cause disease until later in life.

However, with an increasing number of specific genetic disorders, it's now possible to identify not only carriers of the abnormal gene but also affected unborn infants. By 1980, with the use of amniocentesis, tests were available to detect carriers of about forty-five genetic disorders and almost one hundred different genetic diseases and numerous chromosomal abnormalities in unborn children. The number of such tests is expected to increase in the 1980s.

Now it's important to make sure that information about genetic diseases gets into the hands of those who need it most so that they can protect their children from such serious medical problems even before they are born. This has not been as easy as public health experts thought it would be in the early 1970s when knowledge about genetic disorders and their detection began to accumulate.

Little mass screening of population groups is now being done to detect carriers of genetic diseases, although some states mandate that newborn babies be given blood tests to detect from one to a dozen or more genetic disorders. But genetic counseling services have been increasing rapidly since the early 1970s and are now widely available to prospective parents who seek them out. Most are affiliated with a teaching hospital and staffed by specialists who have master's degree training and work with physicians in identifying hereditary disorders, explaining to families the risks involved in having children, and advising them how these odds can be improved.

• *Prospective parents who suspect they might be at risk for having a child with a genetic disorder—either because someone in their family has such a disease or because they belong to a high-risk racial or ethnic group—should get genetic counseling before planning a pregnancy.*

One of the first things a genetic counselor does, often working with physicians' records, is to establish whether a disorder in a family member that is causing concern is actually a genetic illness. The retarded cousin may turn out to have suffered a lack of oxygen at birth, not a form of mental retardation that could be inherited. The aunt whose baby was born with multiple birth defects had German measles in early pregnancy, not a defective gene. On the other hand, the sister who has had three miscarriages and a stillborn baby may be passing along an inherited chromosome error that could also affect the offspring of the couple seeking counseling.

Once it's established that a couple could be running a risk of having a child with a particular hereditary disorder, the counselor spells out what these chances seem to be. Defective genes are inherited in three basic patterns, each with its own set of odds—just like other human characteristics.

Most common and difficult to predict are the genetic disorders caused by a recessive gene located on one of the twenty-two non-sex, or autosomal, chromosomes. Recessive autosomal disorders include sickle-cell anemia, Tay-Sachs disease, cystic fibrosis, phenylketonuria (PKU), albinism, thalassemia, and hundreds of other diseases, most of them very rare and some known to affect only certain family groups.

A child who inherits one recessive gene for a genetic disorder from one parent and one normal gene from the other parent will not have the disorder. The instructions coded in the single normal gene are sufficient to carry out the biochemical function the gene pair is supposed to do. But in some instances, biochemical tests can detect the fact that the child is a carrier.

When two carriers marry, however, there is one chance in four in each pregnancy that the child will inherit the defective gene from both parents. With no normal gene to provide correct instructions, a necessary biochemical substance will be missing and the child will suffer that specific genetic disorder. Should the child ever marry and have an offspring, he will pass on one of his defective genes to that child. If that youngster inherits a normal gene from his second parent, he will not have the disorder, but will be a carrier.

There is also one chance in four that a child of two carriers of the same abnormal, recessive gene will inherit the normal gene that each of his parents possesses. He will then not have the disorder. And he will not be a carrier. None of his children will be at risk, either.

Chances are two in four that the child will receive the normal gene from one parent and the abnormal gene from the other. He will be a carrier, but will not have the disorder. If he marries a noncarrier, odds are one in two for each of his children that they will also be carriers, but they will not have the disorder.

Like flipping a coin or rolling dice, genetic odds work independently in each pregnancy. It is not correct to assume that because chances are one in four that two carriers will have a child with a genetic disorder, they can safely count on having three normal children after they have had an affected youngster. Just as a coin can come up heads three or four times in a row, a couple can lose out more than once in four times with these particular genetic odds. The Goldbergs had one normal son, followed by two Tay-Sachs pregnancies before giving birth to a second normal baby.

All of us have three to eight faulty recessive genes, scientists estimate. But because most of these defective bits of genetic coding are rare, most of us never happen to marry a person who is a carrier of one of the same few incorrect genes. So the genes eventually die out. Or, they could be passed along from one carrier to other carrier descendants for generations—even for centuries—until one carrier happens to mate with another. Even then, if they have only two or three children and the genetic odds come out right, such couples may never even know the risks they have run.

The odds of carriers marrying, however, increase considerably with intermarriage among people who have lived in the same small geographic area for generations, or among the same ethnic group, or the same extended family. The rarer a recessive genetic disorder is, the more likely it is to be found in the children of those who have married close relatives. For example, a particular gene may occur in only one of every thousand people. If marriages were made on a completely random basis, there would be only one chance in a million that two carriers would marry and one chance in four million of having a child with the disorder caused by that particular gene. But if first cousins marry, the risks increase enormously. About one eighth of the genes of first cousins are identical. This means there is one chance in eight that two first cousins may have inherited the same, defective, recessive gene among the faulty bits of genetic coding every human is assumed to have—and one chance in thirty-two that each of their children could have a genetic abnormality.

Hereditary patterns are much easier to see in families if the defective gene is dominant and located on one of the forty-four non-sex, or autosomal, chromosomes. Such a gene will produce its effect regardless of what is coded in the matching gene inherited from the other parent. When a parent has a defective autosomal dominant gene, there is one chance in two in each pregnancy that the baby will inherit the defective gene—and have the disorder produced by its defective coding. There is also one chance in two the child of a parent with a dominant autosomal disorder will inherit his parent's normal gene. He will then not have the disorder and there is no possibility he could pass it on to his descendants.

More than a thousand genetic disorders have already been identified that are inherited in this autosomal dominant pattern, but many are very rare, and symptoms of the disorders they produce can vary.

The third pattern of genetic inheritance involves genes that are located on the X, or female, sex chromosome. No genetic information is known to be carried on the small male Y chromosome except that involving male characteristics. But the X carries instructions for much more than female characteristics. Faulty genes located on the X chromosome are inherited in two different ways, as a genetic counselor will explain to a couple concerned about an X-linked disorder, but are most commonly passed along from a carrier mother to an affected son.

Once a genetic counselor has established that a couple are at risk for a genetic disorder and determined the pattern in which it is inherited, there are other steps that can be taken to increase the likelihood that they can have a healthy, normal baby. Biochemical tests are now available that can identify the carriers of any of several dozen genetic disorders.

Tests can be used early in pregnancy to determine if an unborn child does, indeed, have a particular genetic disorder, or several other specific birth defects. The most common test, called amniocentesis, is done at about the fourteenth to sixteenth week of pregnancy. After the baby's position is ascertained by echosonography (ultrasound waves), a hollow needle is carefully inserted into the mother's abdomen, which is numbed by local anesthetic, and into the uterus. A bit of the amniotic fluid in which the unborn baby is immersed is withdrawn. Cells from the baby's body are constantly shed into this protective fluid and these cells can be grown in the laboratory and tested for genetic abnormalities. The process takes about three weeks. But the diagnosis can be made in time for the pregnancy to be terminated, if the couple decides to do so.

Cells obtained by means of amniocentesis also make it possible to look at the baby's chromosomes. They reveal whether the unborn child is a boy or a girl. And they will also show if he has any abnormalities that involve an entire chromosome or a major part of one of them. Usually chromosomal abnormalities are linked with the mother's age, or with the aging of a particular ovum that is fertilized at conception (chapter 3). But a small percentage are inherited, as can be determined by chromosome studies of parents and offspring.

Amniocentesis is considered medically safe for both mother and unborn infant. There are virtually no reports of injury to the mother. But there does seem to be a slight additional risk of spontaneous miscarriage following the procedure; it's usually estimated to be about 0.5 percent. Most couples worried about having a baby with a genetic or chromosome disorder think this additional risk of miscarriage is worth taking for the peace of mind that the test results can give. Often, the fact that a test exists gives couples at risk of a serious genetic or chromosome disorder the courage to go ahead with having children knowing that if the test results come up wrong, they can have the pregnancy terminated and try again. Ninety-seven percent of the couples who have had amniocentesis get good news; their unborn child does not have the disorder about which they are concerned.

Some congenital disorders result from a particular combination of several inherited genes or from an interaction of particular genes with influences in the prenatal environment. Physicians and geneticists cannot predict the occurrence of these disorders—they include spina bifida, cleft lip and palate, hydrocephalus, and clubfoot—as specifically as they can genetic and chromosome abnormalities. The malformations do seem to appear more often in certain families than in the general population and couples who have had an affected child or close relative with the problem have an increased chance—perhaps 3 to 5 percent or less—of having a baby with a similar birth defect. The most serious of these malformations, spina bifida, can now be detected before birth by a combination of tests (chapter 6).

The American Academy of Pediatrics' Committee on Genetics issued an official recommendation to pediatricians in 1980 advocating that a pregnancy should be monitored by amniocentesis when (1) the mother is more than thirty-five years old; (2) a previous child has had a chromosome abnormality; (3) either parent has a chromosome abnormality; (4) there is risk of a genetic disorder that can be detected by testing fetal cells; (5) there is risk of a genetic disorder that can't be specifically diagnosed prenatally but is linked to the X chromosome; (6) there is a possibility of a neural tube defect, such as spina bifida; and (7) there is risk of certain disorders that affect the blood.

A physician who fails to inform a couple who are in one of these categories about the possibility of a problem runs the risk of being sued for malpractice. Suits have been brought in the name of an afflicted child against medical laboratories which made an incorrect diagnosis and even against parents for letting a child be born with a serious handicap—what lawyers call a "wrongful life" or "wrongful birth." The legal concept of "wrongful life" is still a shaky one, but now has some small basis in case law. The idea that abortion is preferable to life with a handicap seems appalling to many people and so does using abortion to eliminate those who are less than perfect. It will be years before society reaches a legal—and moral—consensus on the subject.

Enormous progress has been made in recent years in genetics. Scientists have been developing startling new techniques for identifying genes on various chromosomes, for slicing chromosomes apart and splicing in new sections of genetic coding, and for incorporating into genetic material new genes capable of performing new functions. Although research is still limited to bacteria and to small laboratory animals, the astounding progress gives hope that someday it will be possible to provide missing genetic coding for humans who have inherited genetic disorders.

New means of visualizing unborn children are also being developed, along with new techniques for obtaining samples of fetal blood from the placenta for diagnosis. Doctors used to say in frustration that an unborn child lay just two inches away from medical help. That will be less true in the future, as new ways of getting medication to the unborn, new intrauterine surgical techniques, and new methods for correcting genetic errors are developed.

Genetic counseling can be obtained at most university teaching hospitals and medical centers. A directory of such services is

available from the March of Dimes Birth Defects Foundation, 1275 Mamaroneck Ave., White Plains, New York 10605.

3. Can You Choose Your Baby's Sex?

"I don't care whether it's a boy or a girl. I just want it to be healthy and normal." That's what most parents-to-be say, if asked if they are hoping for a son or a daughter. Some may even mean it. But many men and women do have a deeply ingrained preference for a boy or a girl, a wish so strongly held they may not even be able to admit it to themselves lest it somehow influence their luck with the genetic odds or color their attitude toward a baby who doesn't turn out to be their first-choice sex.

Historically, sex preferences have run heavily to boys—to sons who could inherit kingdoms or companies, be an economic asset, support parents in their old age, and carry on a family name. Sex preferences for males may be diminishing in recent years. Yet even couples who say they want both a son and a daughter usually prefer to have the boy born first. More couples stop having children after the birth of a son than of a daughter, indicating they have gotten their choice. And those who have tried to use modern medical techniques for determining the sex of an offspring usually are aiming for a boy.

There can be realistic medical reasons, however, for wanting to select the sex of an unborn baby. Certain genetic disorders, such as hemophilia and some forms of muscular dystrophy, are carried by genes on the X chromosome. Females who have a second X chromosome with normal genes will be protected from such disorders by this second set of genetic blueprints, even though they are carriers of the faulty X. But males, who have a Y chromosome along with a single X, lack such back-up protection and will be affected by any genetic mistake on the X. A mother who is a carrier of such an X-linked genetic disease can have healthy daughters, although odds are one in two that each of them will

also inherit the faulty X chromosome and be a carrier of the disorder. Chances are one in two that each of her sons will be a victim
of the disease.

Is there a way to select the sex of your baby? Yes—and no.

Sex is determined, of course, at the instant of conception, depending on whether the sperm that first penetrates the ovum carries an X or Y chromosome to unite with the X contained in the
ovum. Researchers who have tried to predetermine a baby's sex
usually aim to fix the race of the sperm through the vagina and
uterus toward the ovum so that the Y-bearing sperm gets there
first, if a son is desired, or the X-bearing sperm wins, if a daughter
is the goal.

There are several theories about how to fix the race. Some of
them are based on facts. Others still rest on assumptions. The
problem is deciding just how to tilt these factors to help either
the X-carrying sperm or the Y-bearing sperm to reach the ovum
first.

It is known that sperm carrying an X chromosome weigh about
3 to 4 percent more than those with a Y because the X chromosome is larger and made up of more genes. Dr. Landrum Shettles,
a pioneer researcher in human fertilization and sex selection,
claims he can identify the two kinds of sperm by their shape, using
a special microscope. Those with a larger, more oval-shaped head
contain an X chromosome, he says, while those with a smaller,
rounder head carry a male Y. But other researchers strongly dispute his observations. Sperm with a Y chromosome can be picked
out by using a special kind of staining technique; unfortunately,
the stain kills the sperm and they can then be used only for study,
not for fertilization.

Because the Y-carrying sperm are slightly smaller, it is assumed
that they can move faster in the race toward the ovum than X
sperm; some studies seem to prove that this is so, but others do
not confirm it. It is also assumed that Y sperm survive a considerably shorter time after ejaculation than do X sperm. The vaginal
secretions in which the sperm are swimming toward the ovum may
also make a difference as to which kind of sperm reaches it first,
researchers theorize—just as some racehorses do better on a muddy
track than do others. The mucus in the vagina, for example,

changes normally during the menstrual cycle. Generally, it becomes noticeable a few days after menstruation, when it appears thick and sticky. Then, two or three days before ovulation, the mucus thins out and becomes clear, slippery, and stringy. But attempts to race sperm through various kinds of sticky substances in laboratory tests haven't proved that there are clear differences in swimming preferences or abilities between X sperm and Y sperm.

Still another factor may be the acid-alkaline balance in the vagina, which also changes slightly during the normal menstrual cycle. Some researchers suggest Y sperm can survive and move faster when the secretions are mildly alkaline, while X sperm may live longer and do better in a more acid vaginal climate. But the acid-alkaline environment of the vagina changes quickly when ejaculation occurs and there is no clear evidence that trying to change the balance with a vinegar or baking soda douche before intercourse tilts the odds for either X or Y sperm. There's also no sound evidence for assuming that when a woman has an orgasm, it changes the secretions through which the sperm are moving in ways that affect X and Y sperm in different ways.

Even though these theories are scientifically shaky, the idea of being able to select a baby's sex is so intriguing that several researchers have put them together into boy and girl recipes for which they claim considerable success.

A couple who want to have a boy can increase the odds by following these directions, according to Dr. Shettles: (1) The couple should abstain from intercourse from the beginning of the menstrual cycle until the estimated time of ovulation, to increase the sperm count. (2) They should try to have intercourse as close to the time of ovulation as possible. In theory, this should position the faster-swimming Y sperm first in line to encounter the ovum as it is released at ovulation and begins to float down the fallopian tube. (3) Just before intercourse, the woman should use a baking soda douche (two tablespoons of baking soda in one quart of water) to make the vaginal secretions more alkaline. (4) The man should penetrate as far as possible into the vagina at the time of orgasm, so as to place the sperm at the cervix and shorten the race they must run toward the ovum. (5) The woman should try to have an orgasm before or simultaneously with her husband.

Dr. Shettles' recipe for a girl goes like this: (1) Intercourse should stop two to three days before ovulation, but there is no need to abstain before that time. In theory, the shorter-lived Y sperm will disintegrate before the ovum is released, leaving the field open to the X sperm. (2) Preceding intercourse, the woman should use an acid douche (two tablespoons of white vinegar in one quart of water). (3) The man should aim for shallow penetration at orgasm, to stretch out the course and presumably favor the tougher, more durable X sperm. (5) The woman should try not to have an orgasm.

Dr. Shettles claims that by following these directions carefully, chances of producing a boy run as high as 90 percent. However, he's basing his estimate on letters he's received since the publication of his book on sex selection—not on scientifically valid research.

One of the biggest difficulties in trying the Shettles formula—or any other—is learning to predict ahead of time precisely when the woman will ovulate. A few women regularly experience a sudden, sharp pain in the abdomen midway in the menstrual cycle that is thought to be caused by an ovum bursting out of a follicle. But most women have to rely on much less obvious clues and chart them over several months in hopes of finding a regular pattern. To be effective, such a chart must include the days of the menstrual cycle, the basal body temperature taken daily the first thing each morning before even getting out of bed, and daily changes in the texture and quantity of vaginal mucus.

Ovulation is thought to occur about fourteen days before the beginning of a menstrual period—regardless of how long or how irregular a cycle is. It doesn't happen precisely in midcycle, although it can for women who menstruate every twenty-eight days. Women who have an unvarying cycle can come close to anticipating the day of ovulation by counting back fourteen days from the day a period is scheduled to begin.

When menstruation starts, the basal body temperature—as taken immediately upon awakening in the morning—drops two or three tenths of a degree and remains low for about two weeks. Approximately a day before ovulation, it drops another two or three tenths of a degree, to the lowest point of the monthly cycle.

After ovulation occurs, the temperature rises—a half degree or more, usually—and remains relatively stable at the higher level until time for the next period to begin. (The first definite sign of pregnancy is the failure of the temperature to drop to signal the start of a menstrual period.)

Immediately following the end of a period, there is little cervical mucus in the vagina. Then six or more days before ovulation, secretions of a whitish, thick, gluey mucus appear, lasting three or four days. This changes to clear, slippery, elastic mucus during the period of maximum fertility—just before and immediately after ovulation. A day or so later, it decreases and almost disappears until the cycle starts all over again.

The Billings method of natural family planning is based on learning to recognize these changes in mucus secretions and to schedule intercourse, or avoid it, during the days when pregnancy is possible, depending on whether or not a pregnancy is wanted. Advocates of the Billings method claim most women can be taught to recognize and anticipate the time of ovulation.

Other researchers disagree with the Shettles formula. According to theories developed by Dr. Rodrigo Guerrero V of Colombia, South America, and popularized in the United States by Elizabeth Whelan, now director of the American Council on Science and Health, these are the instructions for having a boy: (1) The couple should have intercourse on the sixth, fifth, and fourth days before the woman experiences a rise in temperature that indicates ovulation has occurred. (2) They should avoid intercourse or use a diaphragm or condom until at least three days after the temperature rise. (3) If conception does not occur in three months, the schedule for intercourse should be shifted to the fifth, fourth, and third days before the expected rise in temperature.

The Guerrero-Whelan recipe for a girl goes like this: (1) A couple should not have intercourse until the third or second day before the temperature is expected to rise. (2) They should avoid intercourse or use a condom or diaphragm for two days or so after ovulation.

Whelan doesn't give much credit to the acid-alkaline douche theories but says the douches are harmless. She repeats the same directions Dr. Shettles gives: a baking soda douche for a boy, a vinegar douche for a girl. And she suggests there's no harm in following the Shettles instructions about orgasm.

Whelan is less optimistic about the success of these sex-choice techniques than Dr. Shettles is about his. She says couples aiming for a boy may tilt the odds to 68 percent by following her instructions, but those who try for a girl may increase the odds only to about 57 percent.

Is it worth the effort to try to determine the sex of a baby at the time of conception? Probably not, for several reasons. The evidence that the theories work is slight and generally unscientific. Much of it is based on enthusiastic personal reports from parents who happen to have a child of the sex they wanted. Research that makes a try at linking the timing of conception with the sex of the infant usually encounters several difficulties: Women rarely know precisely when they ovulate or which episode of intercourse resulted in conception, which makes it difficult for researchers to obtain accurate information, especially when they interview the women nine months later, at the time the baby is born.

The most precise research involves women whose pregnancy resulted from artificial insemination on a specific date, following months of medical monitoring to help predict the timing of ovulation. But no one knows for sure if artificial insemination may tilt the outcome of the race of sperm to ovum in ways that normal intercourse does not. And the results of this research often go contrary to studies of natural conceptions.

So because of differences in calculations about ovulation, the impreciseness of the research data, and the difficulties in comparing studies, it's impossible now to prove that any method of sex selection works—or offers better odds than another.

Couples who are tempted to try to pick their baby's sex at conception stand about an even chance of getting what they want in any case—with a slight edge for those hoping for a boy. Approximately 106 boys are born for every 100 girls. Even the sex-choice researchers who claim to have successful formulas aren't offering odds much better than the usual chances.

Suppose a couple really want a boy or a girl. Would it hurt to experiment with one of these formulas? Probably not—with two possible exceptions. A couple whose fertility is borderline may have difficulty conceiving at all if they persist month after month in restricting intercourse to the earliest days in the woman's monthly cycle when they calculate pregnancy may be possible in hopes of conceiving a boy under the Guerrero-Whelan formula. Their timing may be off just enough to miss the woman's fertile period completely.

A couple who wait to try to conceive until late in what they calculate to be the woman's fertile period may run a different risk. If fertilization occurs very late after ovulation, the ovum may be already starting to disintegrate, as it normally does if it is not fertilized. There is some evidence—primarily in animals—that if fertilization takes place at this very late stage, the cell division mechanisms in the fertilized egg may not work quite normally. The resulting baby could have a chromosomal abnormality that would be a serious birth defect. Almost always, however, this kind of faulty development results in miscarriage early in pregnancy.

If a couple really feel strongly about it, the sex of an unborn child can be determined by amniocentesis during the second trimester of pregnancy. In a few instances, prospective parents have resorted to abortion if tests show the sex of the unborn child was not what they desired and hoped that a subsequent pregnancy would turn out differently. Some families and physicians feel this practice is justified when the mother is a carrier of a genetic disease that affects only males. But even those who support the right of a woman to have abortion on demand cringe a little when abortion is used simply to eliminate a child who is not of the sex the parents prefer. Some physicians refuse to perform amniocentesis if they are told, or if they suspect, the ultimate purpose is to abort a child of the "wrong" sex.

4. Planning for Pregnancy

Along with economic and emotional factors that go into deciding when to have a baby, you should also consider several medical facts in planning a pregnancy. In recent years, medical research has made it possible to draw up several important guidelines that can give your baby an extra chance of being born physically healthy and normal:

• *The best ages for a woman to have a baby are those between twenty and thirty-five, although risks increase only slightly between eighteen and twenty and between thirty-five and forty, and most of these can be overcome with good prenatal care.*

Before the age of eighteen, a teenager's body is simply not mature enough to nourish an unborn child as well as it will be able to later on. Many teenagers have not yet completed their own physical growth. Many are poorly nourished. Most are not yet ready, economically, educationally, or emotionally, to become parents. And more than half of those who do give birth before they are eighteen are not married.

Because of the circumstances in which they become pregnant, teenagers often do not seek medical care early in pregnancy, adding to their physiologic risks. As a result, mothers under eighteen run a 35 percent greater chance of dying from the complications of pregnancy and childbirth than older women. Their infants are twice as likely to have a low birth weight as other babies and they have twice as high a death rate.

The 1980s are seeing new interest by women in having a baby after the age of thirty-five. Women who have been caught up in the excitement of a career, women who have postponed marriage, women who have been exploring nontraditional life-styles are now, in increasing numbers, deciding to have babies after the age of thirty-five. For many women, delayed parenthood may turn out to be rewarding and fascinating. But pregnancy after thirty-five does mean some extra hazards for both mother and child. And women who choose this option should know what these risks are and how to minimize them.

After the age of thirty-five—particularly after forty—a woman's body works somewhat less efficiently and well in nurturing and delivering a baby, especially if she has never given birth before. She is more likely to have toxemia of pregnancy, a disorder characterized by high blood pressure, rapid and excessive weight gain, and retention of fluid in the tissues. Toxemia can be dangerous, even fatal, to a mother and more often to her unborn infant, if it progresses. But with proper medical care, it can almost always be treated successfully. Older mothers also run a higher risk than other women of having a baby who is underweight or stillborn. And they are more likely to need a cesarean section to give birth.

Good medical care can shave all of these risks considerably, however. And the odds are still heavily in favor of the older woman—even the woman over forty—who wants to have a child.

The chief concern about the children of mothers older than thirty-five—and especially older than forty—is the increased risk of chromosome abnormality. As explained in chapter 2, all of a woman's ova are formed months before her own birth and lie dormant in her ovaries all during her lifetime. By the time she is thirty-five or forty, most of them have disintegrated and disappeared. Some of those that remain may have been slightly damaged by environmental factors that have affected the woman—perhaps by radiation, drugs, infections, or chemicals—or simply by advanced age. During the final process of cell division that should put twenty-three chromosomes into the egg as it is fertilized by a sperm to begin a new life, something goes wrong. One chromosome may lag behind as cell division is completed, leaving the fertilized ovum with one chromosome too few. With one exception, such a fertilized ovum cannot survive. No human being has ever been found—not even a baby lost early in pregnancy through miscarriage—who is missing one of the forty-four nonsex chromosomes. The only exception occurs when the missing chromosome happens to be an X and the defective ovum is fertilized by a sperm containing an X chromosome. Most babies who have only a single sex chromosome die before birth. But a few—perhaps one in every two thousand to three thousand live-born infants—have what is called an XO abnormality, or Turner syndrome. These females rarely grow to be taller than five feet, have immature sexual development, rarely become pregnant, and have other physical abnormalities.

An error during cell division, however, may put one chromosome too many in the ovum that is fertilized. The extra chromosome may be an X or a Y or any of the non-sex chromosomes. But this extra packet of genes distorts the biochemical instructions in the genes severely. In most cases, a baby with an extra chromosome does not survive. It's estimated that as many as half of all the ova that are fertilized by sperm contain a chromosomal abnormality. Almost all of the unborn children that develop from these ova die soon after conception—some so soon that the woman may not even realize she was briefly pregnant. The earlier in pregnancy a miscarriage occurs, the more likely it is caused by a chromosome abnormality. Only about 0.5 percent of such pregnancies survive until birth—and most of these babies have severe birth defects, usually including some physical malformations and mental retardation.

Most of the babies who do survive with an extra chromosome have an extra number twenty-one, one of the smallest of the non-sex chromosomes; they have a disorder called Down syndrome, or mongolism. Down syndrome is characterized by several abnormalities, including mental retardation ranging from moderate to severe, growth retardation, oriental-looking eyes, flat facial features, stubby fingers and toes, and, often, cardiac abnormalities. One child in every eight hundred is born with Down syndrome.

Older women are at a much greater risk of having a child with Down syndrome than younger mothers. Only one woman in two thousand who is younger than age thirty bears a mongoloid baby and only one in every six hundred between the ages of thirty and thirty-five. (Many of these women—or their husbands—have what is called a balanced translocation. One of their number twenty-one chromosomes is stuck together with another chromosome so that the parent has the correct total amount of genetic material. But it is arranged in such a way that the normal process of cell division can put an extra chromosome into an ovum or sperm, producing a child with Down syndrome.)

After the age of thirty-five the chances of having a child with Down syndrome increase sharply. Of mothers between the ages of thirty-five and forty, 1 in 270 bears a mongoloid baby. The risk jumps to one in eighty for women between ages forty and forty-four and to one in forty for mothers older than forty-four; the risk is even greater for women who are already beginning menopause and have what is called a "change-of-life" baby.

Down syndrome can be diagnosed by amniocentesis done at the fourteenth to sixteenth week of prenatal life, in time for the pregnancy to be terminated if parents choose to do so. For women who want to postpone having children until their late thirties, amniocentesis can remove some of the most serious risks, and it is routinely recommended for all pregnant women over thirty-five, unless the prospective parents are opposed to abortion regardless of any known disorders in the unborn baby. There is already some evidence that the use of amniocentesis is reducing the number of children born with Down syndrome.

Some researchers have concluded that all types of chromosome abnormalities are related to the age of the mother and are likely to occur more often in the babies of older women. But the link between age and extra sex chromosomes isn't as strong as the age factor in Down syndrome. Amniocentesis done to check for the possibility of Down syndrome will also detect other extra chromosomes or major chromosome abnormalities.

Sperm aren't stored for years in a male's body, as are a woman's ova, but are produced continually from early adolescence until well into old age. So sperm themselves aren't subjected to the same kind of deterioration as ova, although the cells that produce the sperm are formed during the male's own prenatal life. Defective sperm are also considered unlikely to win out over the millions of others ejaculated at the same time in the long race to reach the ovum first after intercourse. So most researchers have assumed that chromosome errors usually originate in the ovum.

But at least one study, based on careful examination of the chromosomes of mongoloid children and their mothers and fathers, has concluded that in about one fourth of the cases the extra chromosome that produced the abnormality came from the sperm.

A few studies show that the offspring of fathers older than age forty-five are somewhat more likely than those of younger men to be stillborn, or to have a birth defect, regardless of the age of the mother. But these risks, if any, appear to be quite small.

A more recent concern for career women who want to push childbearing into their thirties comes from a study made in France that suggests a woman's ability to become pregnant may decline markedly as early as age thirty. The research involved more than two thousand women, all married to men who were totally sterile, who were artificially inseminated during the time in the menstrual cycle when they were most likely to conceive, for a total of twelve cycles if necessary. Seventy-four percent of the women younger than thirty became pregnant. But only 61 percent of those between thirty-one and thirty-five and only 54 percent of those older than thirty-five conceived.

The semen used to inseminate the women was stored in frozen form and distributed by a central source. So the study eliminated poor quality sperm and poor timing of intercourse as reasons the women didn't become pregnant and made their age a more likely factor. But there's no good research yet to show whether a similar percentage of women older than thirty fail to become pregnant in normal circumstances.

• *Ideally, a mother should not begin another pregnancy until two years after she's given birth to a baby.*

It may be tempting for a woman with a strong interest in a career to plan to take off a few years to have children and to have two or three babies in quick succession, so she can concentrate her most intensive child-care responsibilities in the fewest possible years.

Such a plan does carry some risks—physical as well as psychological. Sibling rivalry tends to be greater when children are less than two or three years apart in age. The first child hasn't had enough time yet to be a baby, with his father's and mother's full parenting attention, until he has to share them with another infant. The second baby must compete, right from birth, with an older brother or sister who still has a baby's great and urgent need for mothering and fathering. Fatigue—physical and mental—can easily become a problem for parents, especially for a mother who has strong interests in a career outside the home, whether she tries to combine her job with parenting or gives up her career to stay home with her babies.

A woman's body does a better job of nourishing and sheltering a baby if there is at least a two-year interval between the end of one pregnancy and the beginning of another. Studies show that the closer together babies are born, the more risk there is of birth defects and obstetrical complications, and that the younger a mother is, the greater the hazards are in closely spaced pregnancies.

Large-scale, long-term surveys have also found that children who are quite close in age to older brothers and sisters generally have somewhat lower intelligence. The lower IQ may be the result of the inability of the mother's body to nourish the unborn infant adequately so soon after a previous pregnancy. Or it may occur because parents lack the time and interest to provide as much attention and enriching mental stimulation for a second baby as they did for the first. Probably it's a combination of these factors and their interaction.

• *Before a woman becomes pregnant, she should be sure she is protected against rubella (German measles) and other infectious diseases for which immunizations are available.*

When a woman has rubella during the first three months of pregnancy, even if her symptoms are so mild as to be virtually unnoticeable, her unborn baby runs great risk of severe damage. It has taken tens of thousands of human tragedies to learn this lesson.

One of those tragedies happened to Gene Tierney, the movie actress who costarred with Clark Gable, Tyrone Power, Rex Harrison, Henry Fonda, Spencer Tracy, Ray Milland, and others in dozens of movies made during the 1940s and 1950s. Early in 1943, Tierney was asked to help entertain servicemen and women at the Hollywood Canteen, as many stars did during World War II. She was then about one month pregnant. A few days later, she developed a mild rash that was diagnosed as German measles. In October 1943, she gave birth to a baby daughter, Daria, who weighed only two and one half pounds and had a cataract in one eye. Within a year it was discovered that Daria was severely retarded, visually impaired, and deaf. Eventually, she was placed permanently in a school for the retarded.

"Daria never improved," wrote Tierney in her 1979 autobiography, *Self-Portrait.* "She has never talked or seen clearly and has heard few sounds. We have never known the casual joy of sharing a letter or a mother-daughter phone call. But on my visits, she is always aware of my presence. She sniffs at my neck and hugs me." At the time Tierney wrote her book, she noted, "Daria has turned 35. She has the mind of a 19 month old child."

Tierney didn't learn that German measles occurring in early pregnancy could cause severe birth defects in an unborn child until months after Daria's birth when she read about the work of Dr. N. McAllister Gregg, an Australian ophthalmologist. Dr. Gregg made the first connection between rubella and birth defects when he linked the unusually large number of babies with cataracts among his patients with a 1940 rubella epidemic in Australia. This was the first time doctors realized that a virus in the mother's body could also infect an unborn child—often causing far more damage to the infant than to the mother.

The widespread 1964–65 German measles epidemic in the United States added more tragic evidence to implicate the rubella virus. Although almost half of the women known to have had rubella in early pregnancy during this epidemic had their pregnancies terminated, at least twenty thousand to thirty thousand severely damaged infants were born. Some of these babies—now almost young adults—are blind. Some are deaf. Many are mentally and physically retarded. Some have heart defects. Some have all of these symptoms and more. Most were contagious for months after their birth—with what is commonly known as "three-day measles."

Medical discoveries about rubella virus made in the 1960s led to the development of an effective vaccine, which first became available in 1969. Since then it has been part of the standard immunization schedule recommended for young children by the American Academy of Pediatrics, usually given at about the age of fifteen months along with vaccine for "regular measles" (rubeola) and mumps. But unfortunately, not every child has yet been immunized, and many women now of childbearing age missed out on the immunizations when they were young. Women are still exposed while they are in the early months of pregnancy, sometimes without being aware of it, and babies are still being born severely damaged by rubella virus.

Unless a woman who is planning to have a baby is absolutely positive she has had rubella or been immunized against it, she should check with her physician about getting the vaccine before she conceives her baby. It is extremely easy to be mistaken about having had rubella. The disease is often mimicked by other virus infections which produce a few mild symptoms and slight rash. In the past, doctors often didn't take the time to examine children in person when their mothers reported on the phone that they had German measles; they simply assumed this was so, especially if there were other cases in the community.

A simple blood test now makes it possible to tell for sure whether or not a person has developed antibodies to the rubella virus—a sure sign of having had the disease. Large numbers of women have been given this test and a surprisingly large percentage of them turned out to be mistaken about whether or not they had had German measles. Many were found to have had rubella in such a mild form it was not diagnosed. And almost as many others who thought they had had rubella apparently had had a different virus infection and rash and were still unprotected against a virus that could do great harm to an unborn infant.

If a woman isn't immunized against rubella either by vaccination or by the disease itself, she should be immunized at least two months before she plans to become pregnant. The vaccine itself does contain live German measles virus, greatly weakened by the manufacturing process so that the virus is just strong enough to trigger the body to produce protective antibodies against the disease but too harmless to cause the illness itself. It is theoretically possible—but unlikely—that such attenuated virus could still be strong enough to do damage to an unborn infant if the mother were given the vaccine early in pregnancy. Rather than take any such chances at all, most physicians refuse to give rubella vaccine to any woman of childbearing age unless they are sure she will use an effective contraceptive for at least the next two months.

Other diseases that harm unborn babies and can be prevented by vaccine include polio, mumps, and measles (rubeola). These diseases are linked primarily with miscarriage and stillbirth rather than with malformations and birth defects—probably because they do so much damage to an unborn baby that he cannot survive. A woman should be sure she is protected against all of these before she becomes pregnant. It is no longer necessary, however, to be immunized against smallpox, a disease so devastating to unborn children that even vaccinations during pregnancy could cause severe illness and death to an unborn infant. Fortunately, this fearful illness no longer occurs anywhere on earth; all smallpox virus have finally been destroyed everywhere, except for those in a few laboratories that are kept under strictest control for research purposes.

• *A woman planning to become pregnant should have a good physical checkup first.*

This routine precaution is aimed at assuring a woman she will be able to provide a safe and optimal environment for her growing infant and that her pregnancy will go as smoothly and pleasantly as possible for her. This is the opportunity to detect, evaluate, and minimize problems that could affect a pregnancy—heart disease, thyroid deficiencies, venereal disease, infections, diabetes, sickle-cell disorders, nutritional deficiencies, and anatomical abnormalities. Women who have such medical problems can—and have—given birth to healthy, normal babies, but the chances of doing so are much better if good medical care begins even before conception.

• *When a couple have decided they want to conceive a baby, they should have intercourse early and often during the several days preceding and during the estimated time that the woman ovulates.*

This precaution is aimed at making sure the ovum will be met by fresh sperm and fertilized as soon as possible after ovulation occurs, so that neither egg nor sperm will be what scientists call "overripe" when they join together to begin a new life.

There is considerable evidence now—in humans as well as in research animals—that when an ovum is fertilized during the brief, borderline time span when it first begins to age and disintegrate, its internal cell division mechanism may not work quite normally. Mistakes can occur as the fertilized ovum begins to divide and grow that put an abnormal number of chromosomes into the cells of the new organism. Most of these new lives are lost during the earliest days after conception. Some never implant successfully in the lining of the uterus and disintegrate with never a clue that conception occurred at all. Others die and are swept away during the first few weeks of pregnancy, with a delayed menstrual period sometimes the woman's only indication that she was, briefly, pregnant. Perhaps 1 percent of these infants survive to be born, babies who are usually severely handicapped by birth defects caused by chromosomal abnormalities.

Of all the precautions aimed at helping couples have healthy, normal babies, the way to guard against conception with an over-ripe ovum or sperm is the most interesting. Scientists recommend that a couple calculate the estimated time that the woman will ovulate (chapter 3) and plan to have intercourse at intervals of no more than twenty-four hours for several days just preceding and during this period. They should then avoid intercourse for the remainder of what they estimate to be her fertile period. This should ensure that fresh sperm will be present to meet the ovum when it is released and before it can begin to disintegrate.

Based on our current state of knowledge about conception and pregnancy, these precautions should considerably increase your chances of having a normal, healthy baby. They aren't a foolproof guarantee, of course; nothing is when children are concerned. But because the stakes are so high—nothing less than the best beginnings for a human life—it should be worth the extra effort and planning to give your baby an extra margin of safety.

5. *How Your Unborn Baby Grows*

FIRST MONTH

A baby begins so quietly and softly that no one can ever be sure precisely when life starts. At the instant of conception, an infinitesimal tadpole of a sperm plunges into the much larger ovum and immediately, by a process no one yet understands, the outer layers of the ovum turn into an impenetrable barrier, sealing out dozens of other sperm which reached the ovum only a second or a minute too late.

At that unknown instant, much becomes irrevocably fixed about the human-being-to-be. As the nucleus of the sperm moves into the nucleus of the ovum, combining chromosomes and pairing off for the first cell division of the new life, the baby is already irrevocably male or female. The genetic blueprint of his or her life is already completely encoded in the ovum's twenty-three chromosomes and the matching set of twenty-three from the sperm. Already, the new child's eye and hair color are set, his blood and tissue types determined, skin color and other racial characteristics fixed, and the potential for his height, intelligence, body type, longevity, and resistance to disease established. His environment—before and after birth—can moderate many of his inborn characteristics, but not all and only in some degree. Already, he is a unique being, with an immutable heritage.

The new life is marvelously protected and nurtured. Yet it is also fragile and vulnerable. For four or five days, the fertilized ovum floats slowly down the fallopian tube into the uterus, absorbing nutrients from the secretions surrounding it, dividing and doubling as it drifts until it looks like a lumpy mulberry of two dozen or more cells.

Now there is an urgency to its timing, a timetable that must be met if the new child is to survive and grow. If the baby is to be, the fertilized ovum must attach itself to the wall of its mother's uterus, ideally toward the top and back, away from the opening to the cervix. About the seventh day after conception, the little cell clump lands in the wall of the uterus, which is now spongy and soft with blood supplies and at the precise stage in the menstrual cycle when it is most receptive to a new life.

Quickly, the dividing cells send out little tendrils and roots that burrow into the uterine lining, tap into the mother's capillaries to obtain nourishment and oxygen, and begin to build a placenta— the unique organ that will sustain the growing child for the next nine months. The mother's body spreads a thin covering of cells over the nesting new life to create a blisterlike sheltering dome.

Timing is critical. Already, it has been about twenty-one days since the mother's last menstrual period. In about seven days more, the uterus is again scheduled to shed its lining, an event that would sweep the new life away unnoticed in the menstrual flow.

But now for the first time, the baby-to-be begins to exert an influence on the mother's body—even though it is yet no larger than the head of a pin. The developing clump of cells starts to produce a powerful hormone called chorionic gonadotropin, or HCG, which seeps into the mother's blood vessels and is circulated to her pituitary gland. HCG, in effect, signals this master gland to turn off menstruation for the duration of the pregnancy.

The failure of menstruation to occur as usual is one of the mother's first signals that conception has, indeed, occurred about two weeks earlier. If she has been taking her temperature regularly, she will also notice that it does not drop the half degree or so that is characteristic of the beginning of menstruation and the two-week first half of the cycle. This is another indication that pregnancy has begun (and one reason why pregnant women tend to feel somewhat warmer than usual). Soon, a third sign can also be detected. The HCG starts to show up in the mother's urine; the usual pregnancy test is based on whether or not HCG can be found in the urine. (Taken too soon after implantation, such a urine test can give a false reading of negative and may have to be repeated in another ten days or two weeks.)

Now the relationship between mother and baby becomes intricate as well as intimate, as the growing clump of cells directs the mother's body to respond to its needs. But the new child is not a part of the mother, despite its life-or-death dependence on her for shelter and sustenance. The baby has its own unique genetic heritage. It will manufacture its own blood and be responsible for its own circulation. If, after birth, a skin graft were attempted between mother and child, it would be recognized by either body as nonself and rejected. Yet for nine months, the mother's body tolerates the presence of the nonself child and the infant flourishes, nested in the womb of the nonself mother.

Already, the fast-dividing cells in the clump that has implanted in the uterus have begun to specialize. Although each cell contains the complete package of genes necessary to create a complete human being, some not-yet-understood mechanism switches off most of the genes in the cells and directs them to diversify into becoming bone or blood or brain or skin.

Part of the cells in the nesting clump now are diverted into creating structures to nourish and safeguard the growing infant. In the center of the blisterlike nest, the embryo itself is taking shape, stretching into an elongated form gently rounding at one end. Other cells begin to build a watertight balloon around it, a kind of inner-space capsule called the amnion. Gradually, it will fill with a waterlike substance called amniotic fluid which will protect the growing infant from bumps and jars—much like a plastic bag of water guards a goldfish as its new owner brings it tenderly home from the store. The amniotic fluid also provides a weightless, inner-space environment where the growing baby can easily exercise his developing body and keeps him in an even, warm temperature.

Wrapped around the amnion is still another sheltering structure, the chorion. From it grow the thousands of rootlike villi that burrow into the lining of the mother's uterus to obtain nourishment for the new infant. By the second week after implantation, tiny blood vessels begin to form inside the villi, soon connecting into three larger vessels that will make up the center of the umbilical cord. Away from the baby, at the other end of the cord, the blood vessels branch out to form the myriad little capillaries that become part of the placenta. Throughout the pregnancy, these blood vessels will deliver waste products from the new child to the placenta, where they will pass through the thin membranes of the villi into the maternal side of the placenta, where they are picked up by the mother's blood and excreted through her kidneys and lungs. Through the placenta will also pass several different hormones produced by the baby's body that influence the mother's body to make it receptive and nourishing to the infant. These blood vessels also pick up oxygen and nutrients from the mother's blood and bring them back, through the cord, to the infant.

Now, all the essential structures are in place for the new infant to grow and develop—growth that occurs more rapidly this first month after conception than it ever will again in the course of a human's life. By the end of the fourth week, the baby is ten thousand times bigger than the fertilized ovum and already a miracle of cellular organization.

As the dividing cells multiply and specialize, they also move at considerable speed through the new body, following precisely the instructions written in the genetic blueprint that is both common to all human beings and yet distinctly individual to this particular new life. In a way scientists do not yet understand, the new cells communicate with each other so that their specialization—into bone or eye lens or connecting nerve—depends not only on which genetic instructions are activated but where in the fast-growing body they are located.

The timetable of development is so exact that scientists can now tell—to the day—what structures are being formed and what the unseen child looks like. By the twenty-eighth day after conception, for example, the new child already has a primitive face, a mouth, and a throat. Under the mouth opening, six projections round out from either side, curving in to join into arches. Although they look a little like the gills of a fish, they are not a human counterpart, but simply the beginnings of a lower jaw and other structures of the throat.

What is also mistakenly called a tail is also visible now. But it is not a tail, merely the end of the baby's new spinal column, already forming around the new spinal cord.

Even though the new baby is only about half an inch long, the liver, digestive tract, and kidneys are already taking shape. The nervous system is developing, with the foundation of the brain, spinal cord, and nervous system already constructed. The circulatory system is sketched in. By the end of the fourth week after conception, the heart is already beating regularly sixty-five times a minute, pumping blood through an increasing number of arteries and veins. On the twenty-sixth day of life, a little clump of cells begins to organize on either side of the embryo, ready to form arms. By the twenty-eighth day, both upper and lower parts of the arms have taken shape and in three days more, what will soon become fingers are visible as soft, little paws. As the first month ends, buds for legs are developing, ready to grow at the same speed as the arms, but timetabled to follow by two or three days.

Although so much has already happened in the life of the new child, it is only two weeks since his mother first missed a menstrual period—scarcely time enough for her to do more than wonder if she might possibly be pregnant.

SECOND MONTH

If a time-lapse film could be made of an unborn infant during the second month of prenatal life, it would look almost as if an invisible sculptor were gradually shaping a human being out of a lumpy, curving little clump of embryonic tissue—and then reshaping and refining his work in ever greater detail. Cells are dividing rapidly, becoming specialized, and moving through the tiny body to sites ordained by their genetic instructions to combine with other specializing cells to form new organs and tissues in a precise sequence common to all mankind. So rapidly does growth proceed that a timetable for this stage of life shows at least one—sometimes three or four—major developments occurring every day. Yet already, individual differences can be detected in human infants—due largely now to variations in the genes they have inherited, but also to differences in their intrauterine environment.

An unborn infant grows about one twenty-fifth of an inch every day during the second month of prenatal life. He will be about one and a half inches long by the end of the eighth week, although he will weigh little more than one gram. For now, his head is larger than the rest of his body and almost as long. It bends slightly and gracefully forward, curving close to his chest and almost seeming to rest on it. The skeleton is already sketched in with silvery cartilage that can be clearly seen, after the sixth week, through the exceedingly thin and translucent skin. Gradually, the cartilage will turn to bone, with the first bone cells appearing on the upper arms on the forty-sixth to forty-eighth days of prenatal life.

Blood vessels, bright red with circulating blood, also glow through the translucent skin, the major vessels linked up in their permanent connections. During this month, new layers of skin gradually begin to cover the tiny body, giving it greater protection, and by the end of the month, the outer layers of skin will also contain oil and sweat glands and hair follicles.

The face is now becoming distinctly—yet uniquely—human. Just before the second month of prenatal life begins, the eyes start to form. Little bulges of tissue in the front part of the brain area begin to swell and grow on the twenty-fourth day, the cells specializing and changing to form most of the eye itself. Development is precisely timed to match the formation of the lens and cornea by other cells in the facial area of the unborn infant. By the thirty-third day, the eyes also contain retina and pigment and appear as dark circles, widely spaced in the little face. By the end of the second month, eyelids will be growing from little ridges around the rim of the eye and will be long enough to close halfway over the wide, dark eyes, giving the child a wise and sleepy expression.

During the fifth week of prenatal life, clumps of tissue on either side of the lower face begin to grow toward the center to form jaws. By the thirty-eighth day, they are ready to fuse in the center of the face. Now, the upper and lower jaws part, leaving the mouth slightly open. Two days later, the facial muscles start to grow. So do buds for the first set of teeth, The tongue takes shape on the forty-eighth day of prenatal life, growing from tissue on the floor of the mouth. The two sides of the palate grow together and close to form the roof of the mouth. On the forty-sixth day, the nasal passages in the nose are open. The neck grows longer and more distinct. Neck muscles develop, although they are not strong enough to hold the oversized head completely erect as yet. By the end of the second month, the head is still much larger, in proportion to the rest of the body, than it will be at birth. And the high forehead, large, dark eyes, and slightly open mouth give the unborn child almost the look of a caricature of a superintelligent humanoid from outer space.

The brain is also growing rapidly, along with the spinal cord and major nerves and branches, and by the sixth week, the nervous system is functioning well enough to direct and control the baby's muscles. Nerve endings and connections are multiplying to the eyes, the ears, the nose, and the mouth, laying the foundation for the development of the senses.

By the thirty-third day, for example, ear pits are appearing on the sides of the head; by the forty-fourth day, the ears have taken shape and the semicircular canals inside the ear have formed. Later on in prenatal life it will be easy to demonstrate that the unborn infant can definitely hear. His mother, by sudden activity may feel him react to loud or startling noises, and a physician can detect changes in his heartbeat in response to sound.

Nerve fibers from the nose link up with the olfactory area of the brain on the thirty-ninth day, establishing the connections for the sense of smell. Taste buds begin to form in the mouth at the end of the second month. The unborn infant will eventually have many times more taste buds than a newborn infant and evidence suggests that he does, indeed, have a keen sense of taste.

Most of the internal organs are roughed out and then further developed during the second month. Chambers are formed in the heart, whose regular beat grows stronger week by week; even by five and a half weeks, the baby heartbeat quite closely resembles that of an adult. The lungs develop, grow, and branch into lobes and then into minute tubes called bronchioles. The liver functions. The kidneys are already helping rid the tiny body of its wastes. The intestines and stomach take shape. The specialized cells that will produce ova and sperm are moving into place within the growing ovaries and testes. A rudimentary penis or clitoris is developing. Even the thyroid, thymus, adrenal, and pituitary glands have been formed and are beginning to work.

As the arms and then the legs gradually lengthen and their shape refines, the soft hand paws begin to separate into fingers on the forty-second day after conception. Not only are the baby's cells genetically programmed to multiply and grow, some of them are also instructed to disintegrate and disappear as they do between the separating fingers. At first, the lengthening arms stretch away from the infant's body. But they grow more graceful as they grow longer and begin to bend at the elbows, and by the end of the month, the hands usually are held relaxed and free quite near the sleepy face. By the end of the sixth week, the tiny fingers already are marked by their own unique fingerprints.

Legs, feet, and toes develop in the same rhythm as arms, hands, and fingers, lagging behind by only a few days, following the pattern of development that consistently flows from head to foot. By the sixth week, the soft foot paws show ridges which a few days later separate into individual toes. The heel takes shape by the end of the sixth week, and by the end of the second month, the lengthening legs and well-shaped feet are kicking gently. But they are still too small and the watery amniotic fluid too insulating for the movement to be felt yet by the infant's mother.

By the end of the second month after conception, the mother has only now for certain missed a second menstrual period and physical signs that she is, indeed, pregnant are still very few. For all his dazzling growth, the unborn child is still incredibly small— only about one and one-half inches in length and weighing only about one thirtieth of an ounce. But in the two months of his existence, he has grown a million times in weight and 240 times in length, his or her sex is clear, and, already imprinted on a pattern of development common to all human kind, is the stamp of individual identity.

THIRD MONTH

Now, the bones are hardening in the tiny body that will be three inches long and weigh one ounce when this month is completed. Gradually, the unborn child comes to have more substance, to take on more weight, to look more like a human baby. The nerves

and muscles are now working together more smoothly and pur-
posefully. As the amniotic fluid increases in volume and the uterus
grows in size, the infant moves, swims, kicks, somersaults, turns,
twists, and exercises at the end of his umbilical cord as gracefully
and easily as an underwater diver or an astronaut floating in space
attached to a life-support system. But he is still too small and too
weak for his movements to attract his mother's notice.

Before the third month of prenatal life comes to an end, the
unborn infant becomes able to move his thumb in opposition to
his fingers and to make a fist. He can bend his wrist. He can curl
his toes, and will in response to stimulation. If touched on the lips
(as shown in babies who are born too soon, but live briefly), he
will make rudimentary sucking movements.

Already, he can swallow and does drink some of the amniotic
fluid in which he floats. His functioning stomach and intestines
extract some nutrients from it and his tiny kidneys excrete occasional drops of sterile urine into the fluid which is cleansed and
changed in ways not yet clearly understood. The baby also
breathes some of the amniotic fluid into his lungs—something he
could not do after birth and survive. For now, his need for oxygen
is supplied by oxygenated blood from the umbilical cord and no
exchange of oxygen and other gases will take place in his lungs
until after birth.

As the sculpturing of the infant face progresses, it becomes
more attractive and comes to take on a kind of family resem-
blance, due in part to the genetically determined way the muscles
of the face attach. His face already bears a distinct individuality,
and expressions that suggest those of his parents cross his face. His
ears, at first low on his head, gradually move higher and settle at a
level about even with his eyes. His eyes move closer together. His
eyelids grow long enough to shut. They close over the developing
eyes during the ninth week and remain shut until the sixth month
of pregnancy, giving the baby a gentle, drowsy expression regardless of his increasing activity. The hard palate that forms the roof
of the mouth fuses firmly together. Glands that produce saliva
grow in the mouth. Baby teeth begin to form in the upper and
lower jaws, although they will not cut through the gums and become visible until months after birth. The vocal cords develop but

cannot produce sounds in the absence of air in the womb; the baby, though, is physically capable of making sounds long before his first cries at birth.

As the tentative skeleton of cartilage continues to firm into bone, the baby gradually becomes more obviously boy or girl. Genes trigger the production of male hormones that stimulate the development of the male child's penis and testes during the ninth week after conception; the girl's ovaries take shape during the tenth week and the external genitals become obvious during the fourteenth week.

Medically, the unborn infant is now called a fetus rather than an embryo. But there is also no doubt whatsoever that he or she is a unique and distinctly human individual.

FOURTH MONTH

With the unborn infant's body essentially well formed and the structures needed to sustain the pregnancy firmly established, the rest of the nine-month prenatal period is largely devoted to growth. During the fourth month of prenatal life, the infant stretches to eight to ten inches in length, almost half of the height he will be at birth. His weight increases sixfold, up to six ounces or more by the end of the month. As the development of the lower part of his body accelerates, his head seems less out of proportion and he continues to look more and more like a human child.

Ossification of the skeleton continues slowly, a process that won't be finally completed until almost 25 years after birth. The skin is still thin, red, and wrinkled, still translucent enough to let the red of the underlying blood vessels add to the reddish tinge of the body. Fingernails and toenails are developing; by the time he is born, they may be long enough to need trimming and his face may show tiny scratches where he has brushed his fingernails across his cheeks. Now he can suck his thumb and often does; some babies are born with little calluses on their thumbs as evidence of a habit already well established even before birth.

As the baby's body grows longer and stronger, he becomes more active in his intrauterine space capsule than he will be later on in pregnancy or for months after his birth. Now his kicks and turns become powerful enough to be felt by his mother—first, perhaps like a transient bubble or a gentle flicker, then unmistakably the movement of the unborn child. This awareness of the baby's activity is called "quickening" and in some legal traditions and folklore, it marks the beginning of the time the unborn infant must be considered to be a living being.

The heartbeat grows much stronger during the fourth month of pregnancy and can usually be detected by month's end by a physician with a stethoscope and perhaps even by a father who places his ear against the mother's abdomen in just the right spot. The infant's heart must do a prodigious job, pumping blood not only throughout the developing body, but also out through the umbilical cord, through the placenta with its branching blood vessels and villi, and back again to the baby's body. Although the placenta will continue to grow in size through the sixth month of prenatal life and the cord will enlongate as the baby grows in height throughout the pregnancy, both structures are now well developed and functioning.

The cord, during the fourth month, is about the same length as the unborn infant and will grow to an average of about twenty-four inches at birth, although in some cases it is much longer or shorter. It contains two large arteries and one vein, slightly coiled and encased in a gelatinlike substance. Like a garden hose stiffened and pulsing with the pressure of water, the pressure of blood pumped by the infant heart gives the umbilical cord a rigidity and tension much different from its sagging, collapsed state immediately after birth and helps keep it from tangling and kinking with the baby's intrauterine exercise. Blood, pushed through the cord at the rate of four miles per hour by the energetic little heart, moves through the two big arteries into the blood vessels in the placenta and then into the branching villi.

The placenta is shaped like a dish and is about three inches in diameter at the beginning of the fourth month of pregnancy; when it reaches its maximum size and its growth levels off during the sixth month, it will measure seven or eight inches in diameter, be about one inch thick, and weigh nearly one pound. It is a unique organ, made up of tissues from both the mother and the unborn baby. And it not only serves the infant by bringing nutrients and removing wastes, but it also influences the mother's body to help sustain the pregnancy and to prepare for the production of milk after childbirth.

Blood from the infant's body and blood from the mother's body never intermingle in the placenta. Instead, as maternal blood flows through the outer side of the placenta, it surrounds the millions of rootlike villi containing fetal blood which extend outward from the fetal side of the double organ. Complex fluid pressures and biochemical interactions occur during which waste products from the fetal blood pass through the villi and are picked up by the maternal blood, which carries them on to her lungs and kidneys where they are excreted along with wastes from her own body. At the same time, nutrients and oxygen from the mother's body seep through the villi to the fetal blood which carries them back to the infant through the single vein in the umbilical cord.

The placenta also functions to break down some substances brought by the mother's blood that are too big to pass through the walls of the villi. Some harmful organisms and materials in the mother's body are blocked from entering the baby's body by placental forces—but not all. It is still possible for viruses and some drugs in the mother's body to reach the infant through the placenta with exceedingly injurious effects. Antibodies, too, cross the placenta easily, so that for several months after birth, the baby benefits from the protection he has acquired to diseases to which his mother has developed immunity.

FIFTH THROUGH NINTH MONTHS

His body essentially formed and in good working order, little remains to be done during the last five months of pregnancy except for the unborn infant to grow in size and to practice the basic functions he will need to use immediately after birth as an independent human being.

His growth continues to be rapid, slowing down somewhat, however, during the last two months of his prenatal life as his body becomes more cramped in the sheltering uterus. During the fifth month of pregnancy, he will stretch out about two inches in length and add two or three more inches during the sixth month; by the time he is ready to be born at full term, he will average nineteen to twenty inches in length. He will weigh about two pounds when the second trimester of pregnancy ends, add two more pounds during the seventh month, about one and a third pounds during the eighth month, and reach an average of seven and a half pounds at the end of a full-term pregnancy if he has been well nourished by a well-nourished mother.

Brain growth is exceedingly rapid and important during these remaining months of pregnancy. At birth, the baby's brain will already weigh one fourth as much as that of an adult—far more, proportionately, than other organs which average about one twentieth of their full-grown size and weight.

As he grows in size, the unborn baby's red and wrinkled skin gradually fills out with fat. His appearance improves. The shape of his body becomes more refined. About midway through his prenatal life, the hair he will have at birth begins to grow on his scalp. His eyebrows and eyelashes develop. Temporarily, a kind of soft, silky hair called lanugo (a Latin word for wool) covers most of his body, but it will brush away and almost completely disappear before he is ready to be born.

More protection for the skin that still must spend months of time submerged in the watery environment of the uterus comes from vernix. A whitish, waxy cream formed by secretions from newly formed oil glands in the baby's skin, vernix coats and salves the body until birth, and afterward is gently washed away with the newborn infant's first cleansing.

Still marvelously adapted to his personal environment, the baby not only looks increasingly like a newborn child, but practices acting like one as well. He opens and closes his eyes, makes sucking and breathing motions, stretches, turns, kicks, exercises as much as his increasingly cramped quarters permit, and may even be detected to hiccup. Like a baby, he alternates periods of waking and sleeping, often seeming to time his sleeping to his mother's periods of greatest activity when he is rocked and lulled by her motions and to schedule his wakefulness when she wants to rest or sleep. Often when a mother lies down to sleep, she can feel the baby squirming around, perhaps exercising, perhaps trying to get comfortable himself. Like a newborn, an unborn infant also seems to have a favorite sleeping position. Sometimes, when a baby hasn't settled into the most favorable position for birth as the end of pregnancy draws near, a physician will try gently to manipulate him into place. Many of these babies stubbornly turn themselves right back to the position they prefer.

There is no question that an unborn infant can hear—not only the loud noises near his mother that make him startle, but also the sounds of her body, her heartbeat, and the gurgling of her digestive track. So accustomed does he become to the sound of a beating heart that after birth he can often be soothed to rest by a recording of a human heart played near his crib.

As pregnancy draws to an end, the growing infant becomes increasingly cramped in the uterus. His exercise is curtailed. He no longer has room to somersault or stretch out or even, at least, to turn. Normally, he settles into the position in which his growing body fits best in the pear-shaped uterus—head down, legs curled up, arms bent over his chest. As the time of birth approaches, his movements are further constricted by preliminary contractions of the uterus which tend to hold his head in the circle of pelvic bones surrounding the birth canal.

Pregnancy lasts, on the average, 266 days. But it varies widely within normal limits, and medical progress in recent years has made it possible for babies born much earlier to survive as normal, healthy children. New medical techniques and good nursing care have helped some infants born after less than seven months of pregnancy to live and develop normally. But the last two months of prenatal life are important, and every bit of normal weight a baby adds during those last weeks makes it easier for him to cope successfully with the hazards of the first days as an independent person. How much he weighs and how mature his respiratory system is make even more difference to his survival than his gestational age, physicians have learned. A pregnancy that goes full term, that ends in a normal birth activated by normal—although still mysterious—forces is by far one of the best beginnings parents can give a child.

6. *Taking Care of Your Baby During Pregnancy*

Paradoxically, an unborn baby is splendidly protected against hazards to his safety and development—and yet frighteningly vulnerable. His mother's body and the intricate layers of uterus, chorion, amnion, and amniotic fluid effectively cushion him from bumps and jolts and almost all other harmful physical contact from outside his mother's body. Until the late 1950s, it was also assumed that the unique system of exchanging nutrients and waste materials between the placenta and the mother's body also guarded the unborn infant from harmful substances from beyond the placenta. It took the startling thalidomide tragedy of 1960 and 1961 to convince the scientific world that the placenta was not the "barrier" medical textbooks called it and that there could be special and unforeseen hazards to unborn children in the drugs their mothers took during pregnancy as well as with radiation to which their mothers were exposed and infectious diseases their mothers suffered.

It is a fact prospective parents must face that about 7 percent of infants are born with problems serious enough to threaten their survival or to require special care from physicians, various kinds of specialists, family members, and sometimes teachers and others. At least that many more infants are born with lesser problems— difficulties that aren't immediately obvious and won't become troublesome until a child has difficulty learning to read in school, for example, or fails to mature normally as an adolescent. Birth defects cause a major percentage of children's health problems. More than 1.2 million youngsters and adults are hospitalized every year for illnesses linked to birth defects. Birth defects cause some of the most devastating handicaps children and adults ever have to face and often seriously affect the quality of life—not only for the individual himself, but also for his family.

There are hundreds of different kinds of birth defects. Some are malformations affecting the structure of the body itself, like cleft palate, spina bifida, and heart defects. Others are mistakes in the genetic programming of the body's chemistry, like sickle-cell anemia or cystic fibrosis. Still others are failures to grow normally during prenatal life.

About 20 percent of birth defects are now known to be hereditary, but more result from factors that harm the unborn infant during pregnancy, such as radiation, drugs, and viruses. Some are probably due to a combination of hereditary vulnerability and environmental influences. A few, like cerebral palsy, occur because of serious complications or injury during the process of birth. Others still can't be linked definitely to any specific cause.

But at least half of all birth defects or more can now be eliminated if all the knowledge we have accumulated in recent years about their cause and prevention were used—not just by physicians but particularly by prospective parents themselves. Parents-to-be can substantially increase the chances that their child will be born healthy and normal by following several specific precautions.

Linking environmental influences with damage to unborn infants has become a major investigative challenge in the last two decades. Several new teratogens (substances that cause birth defects) have been implicated beyond doubt. Many more are suspected. And probably even more still remain unknown for now, in part because they may only cause harm to a very small number of unborn children who have inherited a genetic susceptibility.

The unborn infant is most vulnerable to teratogens during the first three months of prenatal life, when his body is growing most rapidly and when his organs are in the process of formation. Damage to even a few cells during these critical days can do far more harm to an unborn baby than to a child or an adult, or even to an unborn infant in the last months of pregnancy. For the virus or chemical or radiation not only destroys the cells themselves, but also the whole line of other cells that these cells were programmed to produce.

Even a brief interruption of normal development during the early weeks of pregnancy when growth is proceeding so rapidly can have devastating effects. A palate that does not fuse correctly on a given day during prenatal life usually doesn't fuse later on and results in the birth of a baby with cleft palate. Cells that don't work together to close over the spinal cord at a given time can't do so later and another infant is born with the cruel handicap of spina bifida. There are critical days, for example, when hands are genetically programmed to separate into fingers, when valves are supposed to be formed in the heart, when the two sides of the upper lip are destined to join together. But even short, temporary interruptions in this swift and relentless timetable of development can mean the birth of a baby—months later—with crippled or missing fingers, with congenital heart defects, or with cleft lip. The same kind of interference earlier or later in prenatal life might have caused a different kind of birth defect, or perhaps none at all.

It took the thalidomide tragedy to teach this lesson to physicians—and to parents. And it is still probably the clearest case in point. Phocomelia, a birth defect characterized by severe malformations of the arms and/or legs, is extremely rare. One case occurs in about seventy-five thousand births. But suddenly, in Germany in the early 1960s, doctors began noticing what was an epidemic of phocomelia. As the number of damaged babies and grieving families increased, physicians began hunting frantically for the cause. Fortunately, several factors helped make detection possible in a relatively short time. The birth defect—unlike mental retardation, for example—was immediately obvious at the moment of birth. The epidemic had begun quickly, indicating the cause was something new in the German environment. And there were no cases among the thirty-two thousand babies born to families of American military personnel stationed in Germany during that time, quickly ruling out the possibility of a virus or a pollutant in the environment.

Still, physicians and other scientists were surprised when Dr. Widukind Lenz made the connection between phocomelia and the new drug thalidomide, which had just been introduced in Germany and was selling at the rate of twenty million tablets a month. Thalidomide was an exceptionally mild medication, thought to be even less potent than aspirin, and was sold without a doctor's prescription for about the same purposes as aspirin. Because it had not yet been approved by the Food and Drug Administration in the United States, it was not sold in American military post exchanges—accounting for the lack of phocomelia among American infants born in Germany.

Thalidomide taught physicians many vital lessons. They learned that mothers who took thalidomide on the thirty-fifth day after the beginning of their last menstrual period gave birth to babies who had no ears. Taking thalidomide between the thirty-fifth and forty-first days resulted in a baby without arms or with severe arm malformations. Similar deformities of the legs occurred in infants whose mothers used the drug between the forty-first and forty-fourth days. But after the fifty-second day, no harm apparently occurred to infants whose mothers used the drug. There was no evidence that thalidomide caused damage in unborn infants very early in pregnancy, although it is possible it could have caused recently fertilized eggs to fail to develop or the loss of newly formed embryos through unrecognized miscarriage.

The thalidomide tragedy carried the urgent message that substances which have exceedingly little effect on a pregnant woman can still do horrendous damage to her unborn child, that the placenta is not a fail-safe barrier protecting the developing infant, and that new rules for pregnancy are necessary to increase the likelihood babies will be born normal and healthy.

Unfortunately, most other teratogens are not as easy to detect and control as thalidomide. Some produce damage—like mental retardation—that may not show up for months or years after birth and may be attributed to other causes. In the 1970s, for example, the drug diethylstilbestrol was linked to abnormalities in cells in the vaginas of adolescent girls whose mothers took the medication during pregnancy years earlier. Sometimes a birth defect can be produced by more than one cause; phocomelia occurred in rare instances before thalidomide was developed and has been diagnosed since in a very few offspring of mothers who never took the drug. And some teratogens apparently only do harm to unborn infants who have a particular genetic susceptibility.

Research to link specific birth defects with environmental causes has been increasing since the 1960s. But it is difficult and often inconclusive. Animal tests have only limited usefulness, for pregnant animals do not always react as human beings do to viruses and chemicals. Thalidomide did not harm the offspring of the usual laboratory animals. Retrospective studies in humans require that a mother who has given birth to a child with a defect try to remember all that happened to her during the pregnancy, along with every bit of medication she took and every environmental pollutant to which she was exposed—a difficult if not impossible undertaking. Prospective studies require an enormous amount of cooperation from a large number of pregnant women so that their detailed records can be linked with particular birth defects if they occur at the end of pregnancy; even these prospective records of medications and pollutant exposure are not often completely accurate, samplings of such study participants show.

But based on the current state of scientific research, here are the chief precautions a pregnant woman should take to increase the likelihood that her unborn infant will be safe and unharmed during his prenatal life and will be born normal and healthy. The precautions are most urgent during the earliest months of pregnancy, when the unborn infant is most vulnerable. Some of the guidelines will turn out to be overly strict, as medical knowledge increases. Obviously, not all drugs, for example, harm every unborn infant. But because physicians can't yet be sure which ones are perfectly safe for every baby during every day of prenatal life, the only prudent solution at this time is the blanket ban against all medications not essential for specific medical reasons.

Not every pregnant woman who ignores or breaks one of these rules will automatically harm her infant—any more than every motorist who speeds through a red light will automatically be injured in a crash. But parents who care about the safety and health of a child should follow these precautions during pregnancy to safeguard their child during the first nine months of his existence:

• *Along with making sure she is protected against as many infectious diseases as possible by immunization before conception, a woman should try to keep herself in good health and avoid exposure to contagious diseases all during pregnancy—but particularly during the first three months.*

As with rubella, the harm that some virus infections can do to an unborn baby has little relationship to how sick they make the infant's mother—but more to the precise stage of prenatal development when they occur. New techniques developed during the past two decades for identifying viruses and antibodies produced by the body against them now show that a wide range of birth defects, miscarriages, and stillbirths are caused by inapparent virus infections early in pregnancy. Among those now identified with birth defects are cytomegalovirus (one of the herpes group) and some of the Coxsackie and ECHO viruses—all of which typically produce only mild, flulike symptoms in adults, the kind of illnesses that are usually brushed off as "what's going around right now" or have no symptoms at all. It's now estimated that from 0.5 to 1 percent or more of all babies are born with signs of having had a congenital cytomegalovirus infection, and follow-up studies show that a substantial percentage of these children have brain damage, subnormal intelligence, hearing impairment, or other physical problems.

A pregnant woman can't avoid all exposure to such viruses, of course. But when a virus infection is known to be spreading in a community, she should stay away from crowds where she could be exposed to the disease and should certainly avoid contact with individuals who are obviously ill. Keeping well also eliminates the need for medication during pregnancy.

• *A pregnant woman should not eat undercooked red meat or have contact with a cat that could have Toxoplasma organisms.*

Toxoplasmosis is another infectious illness that is far more harmful to an unborn baby than it is to an adult. In adults, the comma-shaped Toxoplasma organisms may cause fatigue, swollen glands, brief rash, and other coldlike symptoms—or none at all. But a baby who is infected before birth may be born with mental retardation, epilepsy, eye damage, hearing loss, and other problems. Only about one baby in a thousand is born with toxoplasmosis, but the effects can be devastating for a lifetime.

Adults usually acquire toxoplasmosis from one of two sources: undercooked red meat or the feces of a cat. So two types of protection are necessary. All the time she is pregnant, a woman should avoid eating raw or undercooked red meat, especially lamb or pork; Toxoplasma organisms are destroyed only when every bit of the meat is cooked thoroughly to at least 150 degrees F. And every time she handles raw meat in cooking, a pregnant woman should wash her hands immediately and thoroughly.

Precautions for avoiding an infection from cat feces are more complicated. Toxoplasma oocysts can live in the digestive system of a cat who has been infected by eating raw meat or mice or who has contact with infected cat feces. The cat then continues to excrete oocysts which can survive in moist soil or water for as long as a year or more after that. They can't be destroyed by the usual household disinfectants. A cat that doesn't hunt mice or eat raw meat or roam outdoors is probably not a hazard. But a woman shouldn't acquire a new cat if she is pregnant or plans to be soon. She shouldn't handle a cat that belongs to someone else, or even her own cat if it's allowed to roam and hunt freely outdoors. The cat shouldn't be fed undercooked table scraps or raw meat or allowed to hunt mice. Cats can be tested to make sure they pose no risk.

A pregnant woman should never clean a cat's litterbox; someone else should do it daily and wear disposable gloves in the process. And a pregnant woman should avoid a children's sandbox that could have been used as a litterbox by a cat or even gardening in an area that might have been frequented by a cat.

Helen Featherstone, assistant professor of education at Wellesley College, has written a heartbreaking, painfully self-analytical book about her son Jody who is blind, retarded, and has hydrocephalus, cerebral palsy, and epilepsy as the result of a Toxoplasma infection before birth:

"A child's disability flies in the face of much that families, school, and experience teach us," Mrs. Featherstone says. "We have not changed. We still work hard to meet our obligations to parents, children, employers, and friends. Suddenly disaster strikes our carefully constructed world. What could be more unfair?

"Even parents who feel obscurely responsible for the disability may feel angry. I believed that Jody's toxoplasmosis was my fault. While I was pregnant I had read an article that linked this obscure disease to birth defects, suggesting that infection might come through contact with cats or uncooked lamb. I had conscientiously overcooked my meat after that (I give cats a wide berth anyway), but as I searched for explanations I remembered an occasion on which I had slipped up. A friend had served us a rare, juicy shishkebab and I had gobbled it up hungrily, without a second thought. Perhaps I had gotten toxoplasmosis then—no one could be sure because, like many adults, I had never had any symptoms of illness. At any rate, I had gotten it somewhere and as a result Jody was handicapped.

"In retrospect, I felt I had not taken the threat of disease seriously enough (I knew toxoplasmosis did not affect one baby in a thousand). Even as I took precautions, I rebelled, thinking 'For heaven's sake, if you run around dodging meteorites, you'll end up in the funny farm.' I see myself as spontaneous and informal, poorly organized and forgetful—two sides of the same coin. The disease seemed a judgment on my life and character. So I felt responsible. I felt that Jody's disabilities had come about through my oversight or, even worse, as a natural consequence of the way I am. At the same time I was angry: perhaps I had been careless, but the punishment was wildly out of proportion to the crime."

• *Every pregnant woman who has had a genital herpes infection or a sex partner who has should tell her doctor so her pregnancy can be carefully monitored and precautions taken to protect her baby from serious harm during birth.*

Herpes, also known as the "love bug" and the "virus of love," is fast becoming the biggest venereal disease problem of the 1980s and is a serious threat to the unborn babies of infected mothers. No one knows for sure how many women of childbearing age have had herpes infections because it is not a reportable disease. But it is estimated that from five to thirty million adults in the United States have had herpes, and that the number of people infected with the virus has increased sixfold since the beginning of the 1970s. The Center for Disease Control in Atlanta reports that five hundred thousand new cases now occur every year and says it is spreading faster than any disease except influenza and the common cold.

There are five common types of herpes viruses which infect humans, including those that cause chickenpox, cytomegalovirus infections, and mononucleosis. Herpes simplex type I causes the familiar "cold sores" or "fever blisters" commonly found around the mouth. Almost everyone has had such an infection as a child, and the characteristic itchy, watery little blisters tend to reappear periodically, usually following an illness, a fever, or sometimes just exposure to strong sunlight.

Herpes simplex type II causes similar watery, itchy, burning blisters in the pubic and genital area, sometimes with fever, achiness, swollen glands, and general malaise. Like herpes I, the virus that produces genital sores is never quite destroyed by the body. The sores heal, but the virus remains dormant in the nerves near the lower spinal cord for as long as the person lives, periodically causing a new outbreak of sores, sometimes unpredictably and sometimes triggered by stress, fatigue, fever, sexual intercourse, or even menstruation. Herpes II is spread by sexual contact—usually with a partner who has an active infection, but sometimes also during an inactive period. Moreover, with the increase in oral-genital sex, infections caused by type II virus are being found near the mouth and type I sores in the genital area, or even both kinds of virus in the same part of the body.

Despite dozens of false hopes and new leads, it wasn't until 1982 that the Food and Drug Administration (FDA) approved a medication—acyclovir—for treating herpes. But acyclovir is not a cure. Used as an ointment, it merely speeds the healing of herpes sores, but doesn't affect the latent virus elsewhere in the body or prevent recurrences.

Besides the discomfort and embarrassment, genital herpes carries two serious dangers: Women who have had genital herpes are eight times more likely to develop cancer of the cervix than other women. And if a mother gives birth to a baby while she has an active infection, the infant may become infected during passage through the birth canal. Such a baby may develop sores all over his body, even in his eyes. The virus can damage his liver, kidneys, brain, or spinal cord. Fifty to 60 percent of all newborns infected with herpes die; 65 percent of those who survive suffer permanent brain damage. A majority of infections in newborns are caused by type II virus, but an estimated 30 percent are type I.

Like other viruses, herpes may cross the placenta during pregnancy and damage an unborn baby long before birth, although evidence that this occurs isn't conclusive. Miscarriage is quite common among women who have herpes infections during pregnancy, especially if it is their first outbreak of the disease. But it isn't certain whether the virus attacks the unborn child directly or whether the severity of the mother's illness brings about the loss of the developing infant.

A physician who is alerted to the fact that a woman has had a herpes infection—whether or not it is dormant—can usually prevent her baby from becoming infected during the process of birth. The doctor will monitor the woman's infectious state during the last several weeks of pregnancy, and if there are any signs of an active infection in the genital area when labor begins or when the baby is due to be born, the infant will be delivered by cesarean section rather than risk passage through an infected birth canal. It's important that monitoring begin early because mothers with herpes infections often go into labor prematurely. A baby can become infected during the process of birth, even if the mother doesn't have an obvious outbreak of sores, or even know she has the virus, a study showed. Because herpes can be difficult to detect, the American Academy of Pediatrics recommends that, all during the last several months of pregnancy, a pregnant woman avoid any sexual contact with a partner who has a genital infection. It's also possible for an unborn baby to become infected before birth if the membranes rupture four to six hours or more before delivery.

Despite these hazards, however, with vigilant obstetric care and cesarean delivery, it's estimated that only one in every sixteen babies born to a mother with herpes will have a neonatal herpes infection, with its terrible risk of death or serious brain damage.

• *A woman who is pregnant or thinks it is possible she could be should avoid exposure to unnecessary radiation or X ray.*

Fear of radiation made thousands of families flee the area around the Three Mile Island nuclear power plant near Harrisburg, Pennsylvania, when an accident occurred there in 1979. And it underlies much of the public protest and fear about further development of nuclear power. But given what we know now about radiation, these worries are greatly exaggerated.

It is true that radiation can cause miscarriage and birth defects. It was actually the first major teratogen to be discovered that did harm to unborn human babies. It can alter genes in the ovum or sperm, creating genetic abnormalities that may not show up for generations. It can cause miscarriage very early in pregnancy. And it can be responsible for brain damage, for malformations, especially during the early weeks of pregnancy, and for increased susceptibility to cancer that may not be evident for decades.

But the precautions against overexposure to known sources of radiation are also understood and generally followed routinely. X rays should be made only when strictly necessary, and then the reproductive organs of both men and women—and boys and girls—should be shielded to prevent damage to genes. X rays should not be taken of the abdominal area of any woman of childbearing age except during the first ten days after the start of a menstrual period, except in emergency. A woman who is pregnant or thinks it's possible she could be should tell her doctor or dentist if X rays are being planned for any purpose. And the possibility of pregnancy must always be evaluated if a woman of childbearing age requires radiation treatment.

Most of the radiation to which the average American is exposed comes from natural sources: cosmic rays; natural radioactivity in the ground, the air, and building materials; and other sources such as food, water, and the tissues of the body itself. Such exposure ranges from about 100 to 400 millirads annually, with an average of 125 millirads in the United States and from 80 to well over 1000 millirads elsewhere in the world, depending on altitude, radioactivity in the soil, and other factors.

By comparison, a person gets about 20 millirads from a chest X ray, while nuclear power plant operators average an annual exposure of 700 to 800 millirads. But only a very small amount of the annual exposure of Americans comes from other sources: perhaps 5 to 8 millirads total from the accumulated fallout from weapons tests; and 0.33 from color TV sets, eyeglass lenses, radium watch dials, some smoke detectors, and normal nuclear power plant operations. The average person who lived within a fifty-mile radius of Three Mile Island got only 1.4 millirads of radiation, and the greatest exposure possible closest to the plant over the entire six-day period of the emergency is thought to have totaled only about 70 millirads. There is no evidence that any human baby or any animals were born with malformations or other birth defects as a result of that incident.

It is true that radiation from the atomic bombs dropped on Japan during World War II did terrible damage to unborn babies whose mothers were in the explosion area. Almost all the pregnant women who were within one and a half miles of the blast center had miscarriages or stillborn babies or infants who died shortly after birth or were mentally or physically retarded. But they were exposed to hundreds of thousands of millirads in just a few minutes' time. There was an increase in the incidence of babies born with small head and brain size following exposure at Hiroshima to as little as 10,000 millirads during the first four months of pregnancy. And a majority of babies exposed to more than 150,000 millirads before birth were mentally retarded.

Scientists aren't absolutely sure, but there's no evidence that exposure to less than 10,000 millirads during prenatal life harms unborn children. And there is evidence that cells do have repair mechanisms that can cope with small amounts of radiation damage. So what are now routine precautions by doctors and dentists in using X rays should now eliminate the concern of prospective parents about this possible hazard to unborn infants.

• *A woman who is pregnant, or thinks she might be, should not take any drug unless it is absolutely necessary and specifically prescribed by a doctor aware of any possible effects on an unborn baby.*

Ever since the thalidomide tragedy first taught us that even a small amount of a drug taken by a mother could seriously damage an unborn baby, the list of substances known to be harmful to infants during prenatal life has been growing. It now includes not only some prescription drugs and some medications that can be bought over the counter, but also alcohol, insecticides, marijuana, and even diethylstilbestrol (DES), whose effects didn't show up in

offspring until almost two decades after it was taken by their pregnant mothers.

The problem is that the list of hazardous drugs isn't complete.
There are probably dozens more drugs and other substances that
damage unborn babies which haven't been identified. Some of
them may hurt babies only during a few, specific days of early
development, like thalidomide. A few may be more hazardous
later on in pregnancy when they harm the fast-growing infant
brain, or just before birth when they prolong labor or affect the
newborn's ability to cope with survival on his own without his
mother's support system. DES may not be the only time bomb
whose adverse effects don't show up for decades and therefore may
never attract attention and discovery. Some medications may hurt
only unborn babies with a special susceptibility. Others may cause
one kind of damage early in pregnancy and a different type of
harm a few weeks or months later during prenatal development.

It is extremely difficult for several reasons to pinpoint precisely
what drugs do what kind of harm to which unborn babies. Efforts
to link a birth defect discovered after a baby's birth with what a
mother does or eats or takes as medicine during every stage of
pregnancy have generally not been completely successful. It's too
difficult for women to remember such specifics months later. It's
even less accurate when the problem, for example, is a hearing
loss that doesn't show up until a baby is eighteen months old or a
learning disability discovered in first grade. Often women aren't
precisely sure what kind of medication they've taken even the previous day. In one study, three hundred women who had just had
babies were asked if they had taken any aspirin within the preceding twenty-four hours. None said she had. Yet concentrations of
aspirin were found in the cord blood of 10 percent of the infants.
On requestioning these mothers, researchers learned that they
were not aware that aspirin was contained in the products they
had used.

Not all drugs cross the placenta to the unborn infant directly.
Some are broken down into constituent parts first. But it may help
to make the problem clearer to understand that a pregnant woman
who takes a drug is usually also giving it to her unborn child—in
an adult dosage. Not only can the quantity be overwhelming to

the unborn baby, but his body may not be able to eliminate it as readily as an adult does. And its effect on rapidly dividing fetal cells may be different than on adult tissues. That's why there can be dangers in even the mildest over-the-counter remedies.

Tests on experimental animals are some help in compiling lists of drugs that are hazardous to unborn babies—but not enough. Human unborn infants simply don't react the same way to all drugs that unborn animals do. So this kind of research can't be counted on to identify all drugs that harm human children before birth—especially in instances in which a human baby may have an uncommon genetic susceptibility.

So, given the current state of knowledge about the effects of drugs on unborn infants, there is only one way to play it safe now and in the foreseeable future: to avoid taking any medication whatsoever all during pregnancy unless specifically prescribed by a physician for an urgent medical need. A woman who takes a drug regularly for a chronic medical problem should discuss its specific safety with her physician before she becomes pregnant.

The category of "drugs" that should be avoided during pregnancy includes many substances not usually considered as medications. A pregnant woman should avoid using ointments, salves, medicinal sprays, nose drops, douches, sleeping pills, anticonvulsants, pep pills, tranquilizers, reducing aids, baking soda for "heartburn" or upset stomach, aspirin, vitamin supplements not prescribed by a doctor, and all types of "home remedies"; insecticides, herbicides, and household cleaners commonly sprayed around gardens, homes, and garages; alcohol; cigarettes; and what are loosely considered to be "recreational drugs."

The Food and Drug Administration has been increasingly concerned about the possibility that caffeine may cause birth defects and issued a warning to that effect in September 1980. Experiments with rats have shown that those fed caffeine equivalent to what an adult would get from twelve to twenty-four cups of strong coffee a day produce offspring with an abnormal number of skeletal defects. Although the FDA has not yet decided to put warning labels on coffee, it has advised women who are pregnant to avoid caffeine-containing foods and drugs or to use them "sparingly." Not enough is known about the effects of caffeine on unborn human babies to know precisely what safe limits may be and what, precisely, "sparingly" should mean. No specific birth defects are yet linked directly with caffeine used by a woman during pregnancy.

A major study reported in 1982 by Harvard researchers which involved 12,400 women did find that heavy coffee drinkers (seven or more cups a day) had shorter pregnancies, low birth weight babies, and more breech births than other women. But many of the heavy coffee drinkers also smoked cigarettes, and when smoking and other factors were figured into the statistics, the effects of caffeine alone disappeared. Even though definitive answers aren't available yet about the effects of caffeine on unborn babies, the evidence from animal experiments does seem strong enough to justify the FDA's concern and to follow its advice.

One problem is that caffeine is contained not only in coffee, but also in tea, many colas, and some other soft drinks, some pain-killing drugs, wake-up pills, and other common medications. In smaller amounts, it is also found in cocoa and chocolate.

During the late 1960s, a few scare stories linked drugs like LSD and marijuana with chromosome damage and occasional instances of newborns with birth defects. But these reports failed to stand up under rigorous scientific examination. Now, however, evidence is accumulating that "recreational drugs" can and do affect unborn babies adversely and that women who are pregnant or think it's possible they could be pregnant should avoid them.

If a pregnant woman is addicted to a drug, it's likely that her baby will be born with a similar addiction and will suffer severe withdrawal symptoms during the days following his birth. Heroin addiction, in particular, is common among the newborns of addicted mothers. Follow-up studies of affected babies find evidence of neurological and psychological problems and of abnormalities in growth even years later. So devastating is exposure to heroin prenatally that in Michigan a woman was legally charged with child abuse for imposing heroin addiction on her unborn baby.

An increasing number of medical reports also link abnormalities in newborns with their mothers' use of methadone or angel dust. There is growing concern about the dangers pregnant women impose on their unborn babies by smoking marijuana—particularly because it is so widely used now. Animal experiments and some studies on human mothers suggest that smoking pot can increase chances of miscarriage and stillbirth. And because the tetrahydrocannabinol (THC) and other substances in marijuana can pass through the placenta and concentrate in the fatty tissues of the unborn infant—including in his brain—researchers say abnormal fetal development could result. Marijuana use during pregnancy is "very unwise" and "should be especially discouraged," the National Institute of Drug Abuse says in its 8th Annual Report to the U.S. Congress, *Marijuana and Health*. Reports also link pot smoking in both males and females with decreased fertility.

Almost all of the research on the adverse effects of drugs on unborn infants has concentrated on those used by pregnant women. With two decades of study, scientists are just beginning to understand some of the basic physiologic processes by which this damage can occur and how it can be prevented. Now, some preliminary observations are suggesting that perhaps drugs taken by a father prior to conception can also result in harm to the infant being conceived. There is some evidence in experimental animals that exposure of males to such substances as thalidomide, narcotics like morphine and methadone, caffeine, alcohol, and lead prior to conception does result in damage to some of the offspring which are then conceived. And preliminary reports do link some drugs used by human fathers to birth defects and growth retardation in their offspring.

So far, the possible mechanism by which such adverse effects could occur is not known. Perhaps the drugs may damage the sperm themselves. Perhaps they are simply present in semen and that in itself is enough to hurt the fertilized ovum in some way. Scientists also do not know how long before conception a male's exposure to a drug or chemical could have a harmful effect on a subsequent pregnancy—if indeed this is possible.

But some scientists who are doing research in this area now think it is "prudent" to warn prospective fathers that their exposure to drugs and chemicals prior to conception could hurt their children—even if such warnings must necessarily be vague and general.

• *A woman shouldn't smoke while she is pregnant.*
Although smoking isn't associated with specific birth defects, it

can have disastrous effects on an unborn infant. According to a 1980 report to Congress by the U.S. surgeon general, smokers have a 70 percent greater chance of losing a baby through miscarriage than nonsmokers and 25 percent more risk of giving birth to a stillborn child. Chances are 36 percent higher that a smoker's baby will be premature and 98 percent greater that he will have low birth weight, with its associated hazards and complications. The more cigarettes a woman smokes, the greater the dangers she imposes on her unborn infant—primarily through the nicotine that passes through the placenta into the body of the growing baby and by the high level of carbon monoxide in her blood which cuts down on the amount of oxygen that reaches her child. Other substances in cigarettes may also cause damage. And smoking may also decrease the flow of blood to the placenta, may damage the placenta, and may interfere with the transfer of necessary nutrients to the baby.

There is also increasing evidence that smoking during pregnancy is linked with long-term growth problems and stunted intellectual development in children, according to the surgeon general's report.

Subsequent research continues to turn up grim evidence that a mother's smoking during pregnancy endangers her child, not only before birth but after. Major studies show conclusively that growth retardation in unborn babies is due directly to smoking, even when the mother's weight gain during pregnancy, her nutrition, and genetic factors are taken into account. The incidence of dangerous complications of childbirth, such as too-early separation of the placenta, bleeding, and premature rupture of the membranes surrounding the baby all occur more frequently when mothers smoke.

Children of mothers who smoked during pregnancy continue to show some retardation in physical growth even up to age seventeen, according to recent research. They have more illnesses than the offspring of nonsmokers and are hospitalized more often for pneumonia and other respiratory problems. They also tend to lag behind in intellectual growth and have more emotional and behavioral problems. They are more irritable as babies and more hyperactive as children. Smoking during pregnancy is now considered to be a cause of hyperactivity in youngsters.

Many physicians are worried about the very low birth weight of babies born to smokers, particularly those weighing less than two pounds. Heroic intensive care now permits many of these endangered infants to survive. But medical costs are enormous and some survivors may have serious disabilities.

• *A woman who is pregnant, or thinks she might be, or plans to be soon, shouldn't drink anything alcoholic.*

In ancient Carthage and Sparta, laws forbade newly married couples to use alcoholic drinks lest they conceive a child while intoxicated. Reports in eighteenth-and nineteenth-century England linked weak and sickly children with alcoholic mothers. But it wasn't until 1973 that a scientific study in the United States first showed that alcohol used by mothers during pregnancy could hurt their unborn babies. That such an obvious possibility was completely overlooked as a cause of birth defects shows again how tardy physicians and scientists were to study the health and development of unborn infants.

The first studies on the effects of alcohol on unborn infants linked mothers who had a record of alcoholism with offspring who had what is now called fetal alcohol syndrome. Typically, these children look a lot like each other, more so than they resemble their families. They have smaller-than-normal head size. They usually have narrow eyes and a small nose that turns up slightly with a flatter-than-average nasal bridge. They are underweight at birth and are usually retarded in growth all during childhood. They are hyperactive and jittery, even as newborns. At least half of them have some heart abnormalities that may require surgery. And they are usually mentally retarded, with an average IQ of about 65, although it can range higher or lower. Fetal alcohol syndrome is now considered to be the third most common cause of mental retardation.

Since 1973, scientists have also found that moderate drinking by pregnant women can often be linked to less severe symptoms and lesser degrees of damage in their children. It's now considered likely that some unexplained hyperactivity and jitteriness in children, as well as some learning problems and borderline mental retardation, could be the result of mothers' drinking patterns during pregnancy.

Human and animal studies now make it clear that it is the alcohol itself that causes the damage to unborn infants—independent of cigarette smoking, other drugs, poor nutrition, life-style, poverty, mother's age, or child-care patterns after birth, although these factors may aggravate the damage from drinking. The alcohol that a mother drinks easily passes into her unborn baby's body, where it remains much longer than it does in the mother's system, seeping into the tissues and harming the baby's developing cells. The brain cells of unborn infants are particularly vulnerable to alcohol and many of the symptoms of fetal alcohol syndrome are caused by brain damage before birth.

Is there any safe level at which a pregnant woman can drink without hurting her unborn child? Scientists aren't sure yet. How much alcohol harms an unborn infant depends upon the stage of the baby's development when drinking takes place—the earlier in pregnancy, the worse the damage seems to be. It also depends on how quickly she consumes the drinks and on her individual metabolism, and whether the drinking occurs on rare occasions, such as one or two Saturday night binges, or is evened out over the pregnancy. Binge drinking at times when the unborn child is in a particularly vulnerable stage of development may be more harmful than a larger amount of liquor spread out over a long period of time.

It's now quite certain that a pregnant woman who drinks three or four ounces of alcohol a day—that is, approximately six or more cans of beer or glasses of wine or mixed drinks—runs a major risk of having a baby with some or all of the symptoms of fetal alcohol syndrome.

Risks are less for babies of mothers who drink less. But studies show that of women whose drinking averaged two or more ounces of alcohol daily, 19 percent had infants with some abnormalities. And 11 percent of women whose consumption of alcohol averaged only one to two ounces a day had children with some symptoms of fetal alcohol syndrome.

Drinking during the period immediately before a woman realizes she may be pregnant seems to be particularly harmful to the baby who is just beginning to grow.

In 1981, the U.S. surgeon general issued a flat warning that pregnant women should drink absolutely no alcohol at all because "alcohol consumption during pregnancy, especially during the early months, can harm the fetus." The report summed up research on the effects of a mother's drinking during pregnancy and noted that mothers who drink as little as one ounce of alcohol a day ran increased risk of having a baby with hazardously low birth weight and that one ounce of alcohol twice a week increased chances of miscarriage. The surgeon general also warned that women who are planning to become pregnant should drink no alcohol at all.

But some scientists aren't sure that such an absolute ban is necessary. In 1977, the March of Dimes Birth Defects Foundation warned, simply, "If you're pregnant, don't drink. If you drink heavily, don't become pregnant. If you can't stop drinking on your own, seek help before you become pregnant. Alcohol and pregnancy don't mix."

Subsequently, the foundation learned that this stern warning was causing considerable unnecessary anxiety and fear in pregnant women; a few who had had only a glass or two of wine before they discovered they were pregnant even considered having an abortion. The foundation has since modified its caution to spell out the dangers and simply tell women that fetal alcohol syndrome is a tragedy that they can prevent.

The American Council on Science and Health also takes a more moderate position on drinking during pregnancy. In a 1981 booklet, it say, "For those women who choose to drink during pregnancy, ACSH advises that they limit their daily intake to two drinks or less of beer, wine, or liquor. The alcoholic content of two twelve-ounce glasses of beer, two four-ounce glasses of table wine, or two mixed drinks each containing one and one-half ounces of 80-proof liquor is approximately the same; each contains about one ounce of 100 percent alcohol.

"Although no absolutely safe level of alcohol ingestion has been defined or probably ever will be, the health risks associated with the above level of consumption are apparently low, if they exist at all. These recommendations are intended only as guidelines, as there are substantial differences among women in their ability to tolerate alcohol."

However, three of the scientists who worked on the ACSH report added a dissent, urging that pregnant women not drink at all because no safe level of alcohol intake during pregnancy has been established, because the strength of drinks can vary, and because some unborn children may be unusually sensitive to alcohol.

Obviously, these answers aren't as definite as prospective parents need. But in deciding what to do about drinking during pregnancy, it may help to remember that what's at stake may be a child's health and mental ability.

• *A woman who is pregnant, or thinks she could be, should not take sauna baths or use a hot tub.*

Enough evidence of damage to unborn infants apparently caused by an increase in the mother's body temperature has now been found so that three cautions seem justified: In its newsletter about hot tubs, the U.S. Consumer Product Safety Commission warns pregnant women that soaking in water hotter than 102 degrees F. can cause fetal damage during the first three months of pregnancy and that they should make sure that the temperature of the water does not exceed that level. Other physicians are urging pregnant women to avoid hot tubs completely because of the difficulties in monitoring water temperature accurately. Pregnant women should also avoid long sauna baths for the same reason. And they should contact their doctor if they become ill and have a fever.

• *A pregnant woman who holds a job should be sure her workplace is safe for her baby.*

If a mother holds a job during pregnancy, it rarely poses any danger to her unborn infant. Except for fatigue and possible bouts of nausea in the early months, many women find it easier to work during pregnancy than to combine a job and child care afterward.

But a few workplaces may be harmful to unborn babies—a fact that has generated angry controversy among feminists, unions, employers, workingwomen, and government officials with the Occupational Safety and Health Administration (OSHA) and the Equal Employment Opportunity Commission (EEOC). Many women fear that the warnings by environmental health experts that some workplaces may be unsafe for the unborn will be used by employers as an excuse to ban all women of childbearing age from lucrative jobs unnecessarily and to return to the old sexist discrimination in employment.

There is still great uncertainty about what substances used in industrial workplaces actually can cause miscarriage or the abnormal development of the unborn baby of a pregnant worker. The case against working with lead is probably strongest. Organic mercury is also suspect. Female physicians and nurses who administer anesthetics in operating rooms, for example, have more miscarriages and babies born with birth defects than those who work elsewhere in hospitals. Questions have been raised about carbon tetrachloride, vinyl chloride and some substances in pesticides when exposure is heavy in industrial settings; but damage to human unborn infants is difficult, or impossible, to document. It's feared that there may be other substances in workplaces that are also causing miscarriages, birth defects, genetic damage, and stillbirths when mothers are exposed to them during pregnancy. But little is known preisely about what level of exposure to what substances is necessary to do harm to which unborn infants during what particular stage of pregnancy. As with other teratogens, it's assumed that damage to the unborn is most likely to occur early in pregnancy, especially during the first eight to twelve weeks, including the time span when a woman—and her employer—may not know for sure whether or not she could be pregnant.

To protect pregnant women and their unborn babies—and to guard against the possibility of being sued for causing a child to be born with abnormalities—some employers have banned all women of childbearing age, pregnant or not, from working in places where they could come in contact with harmful substances. Such rulings usually bring angry reactions from women's groups which charge that such a blanket exclusion is merely an excuse to keep women out of well-paying jobs. In a few highly emotional cases, women who felt they could not accept transfers to jobs with lower pay scales have had themselves sterilized.

Union leaders and EEOC officials have generally taken the position that workplaces should be made completely safe for everyone—men, women, and unborn babies. Undoubtedly, this is right. Many teratogens are also carcinogens; they can damage cells in ways that not only produce abnormalities before birth but also cause cancer in those who are exposed to them after they are born. But to guarantee that workplaces are safe for everyone is still a goal and not a reality, and it may take decades for animal studies and epidemiological data to provide complete reassurances.

Until then, as a practical matter, a woman who works in an environment in which she is exposed to suspect chemicals—lead, mercury, or other heavy metals—and who is pregnant, will have to take considerable responsibility for protecting her unborn baby herself. There are several sources she can go to for information: union leaders, the company medical staff, her own doctor, and the OSHA in her area or at 200 Constitution Avenue, N.W., Washington 20001. She may have to make a difficult choice between a job whose salary she needs and a risk to the welfare of her baby— with little accurate data on just how great that risk really is.

• *A woman should have a close-to-normal weight at the time of conception and eat a well-balanced, nourishing diet, gaining about twenty-two to twenty-six pounds during pregnancy.*

At birth, a baby should weigh at least five pounds and ideally closer to the average of seven and a half pounds for an optimal beginning in life. All of the nourishment that provides this growth comes from his mother's body—either from her diet during pregnancy or from nutrients stored in her body prior to conception. Both weight before conception and weight gain during pregnancy are related to a baby's weight at birth. Women who are chronically undernourished, perhaps even from their own prenatal life, and who are malnourished during pregnancy run a greater risk of having a baby with low birth weight. Low birth weight is often linked with a wide range of problems, from various kinds of slight learning difficulties and behavior problems during childhood to severe retardation, cerebral palsy, slow physical growth, and even stillbirth.

The link between what a woman eats during pregnancy and her baby's weight and health at birth isn't as precise in humans as in experimental animals; in animals, protein shortages in particular can be shown to cause faulty development in the brain. And low birth weight is also associated with several other interrelated factors such as, poverty, smoking, lack of good prenatal care, anemia, the mother's general health, mother's age, being pregnant with twins, and too short an interval between pregnancies.

On the basis of what is now known about prenatal develop-ment, the American Medical Association recommends that a woman gain 22 to 26.4 pounds during pregnancy, at a steady rate of a little less than 1 pound a week after the first trimester. Some physicians think an ideal weight gain may go as high as 30 pounds and aren't concerned if a woman begins adding pounds during the early weeks of pregnancy because of new evidence about how her body stores energy and nutrients for use during the later months of her baby's prenatal life. Only rarely now do doctors urge a woman to try to lose weight during pregnancy, or even to avoid gaining weight. It is much safer for a woman to diet to regain her own ideal weight after her baby is born than during pregnancy when she may risk doing harm to her unborn infant.

Ideally, a woman should eat an extra three hundred calories every day during pregnancy than the caloric intake that main-tained her weight before conception. Her body also needs extra protein, calcium, phosphorus, iron, and folic acid. According to the March of Dimes Birth Defects Foundation, a good daily eating plan during pregnancy includes the following:

Milk—Three cups daily for the first three months; four cups for the remaining six months

Protein—Three servings daily for the first trimester; four there-after. Two to three ounces of cooked lean meat, poultry, or fish, or ¼ cup of peanut butter, or one ounce of nuts, or one egg equals one serving

Leafy green vegetable—Two servings

Fruits and vegetables rich in Vitamin C—One serving

Other fruits and vegetables—One serving a day

Whole grain cereals and enriched bread—Three servings a day, counting one slice of bread, ¼ cup of rice or cereal or cooked pasta or one muffin, pancake, waffle, or biscuit, or ¾ cup of ready-to-eat cereal as a serving

A doctor may add a vitamin supplement or additional iron, but it should be taken only at his direction.

• A *pregnant woman should have good prenatal care supervised by a physician who is up-to-date on new medical research about the development of unborn infants, the prevention of birth defects, childbirth, and advances in newborn care.*

Ideally, prenatal care begins before conception, continues throughout pregnancy, and is coordinated with pediatric care after birth for the newborn child. A physician should confirm that pregnancy has, indeed, occurred; make sure the prospective parents understand what hazards to avoid during pregnancy and the importance of good nutrition; take a thorough medical history of both parents to identify any particular risks and to ascertain any need for genetic counseling; evaluate any indications for amniocentesis; monitor the progress of the pregnancy by regular checkups at three- or four-week intervals during the first seven months or so and at shorter periods thereafter; and complete arrangements for the birth in a hospital or alternative birthing setting with adequate protection for both mother and baby.

Complete prenatal care is so important for both mother and child that most obstetricians and family doctors include it in a package price along with medical services at the time of birth and follow-up checkups. Most health insurance policies provide for routine maternity care. And for those who can't afford private care or aren't covered by insurance, there is now a wide range of free and low-cost prenatal services available through hospitals, particularly those affiliated with medical schools, and neighborhood clinics, which are usually sponsored by voluntary health organizations or municipal or state agencies. Information about these prenatal services can be obtained from a local, county, or state health department; from the nearest office of the U.S. Department of Health and Human Services; or from a local Community Fund office or community referral agency.

Research in recent years has given obstetricians and family doctors several new medical techniques for safeguarding pregnant women and their unborn infants and for monitoring the progress of a pregnancy. For example, a new test made on a little sample of the mother's blood by the sixteenth to the eighteenth week of pregnancy can detect whether the unborn infant may have spina bifida (failure of the spine to close properly, permitting the spinal cord to protrude and resulting in permanent paralysis and loss of feeling below the defect) or anencephaly (absence of part of the brain, leading to stillbirth or inevitable death shortly after birth). Among the most common of birth defects, one or the other occurs in about two pregnancies out of every thousand—more often among families with British, Irish, Welsh, or northern European ancestry.

If an unborn baby has either of these conditions, an abnormal amount of a substance called alphafetoprotein (AFP) leaks into the amniotic fluid and into the mother's bloodstream, where it can be detected by a blood test. Unfortunately, to be sensitive enough to pick up the problem, the AFP test also gives an enormous number of false positive readings—perhaps as many as fifty for every one or two actual cases of spina bifida or anencephaly. A repeat AFP test eliminates almost half of these false positive cases from any further concern. For the others, doctors can use ultrasound to obtain a hazy picture of the unborn infant, perhaps actually showing a defect in the spine or skull, or more likely, demonstrating that the baby is older than assumed or that the mother is carrying twins (either possibility could account for the high AFP reading). If there is still doubt about a diagnosis, amniocentesis is done so that more tests can be made on the amniotic fluid itself—finally pinpointing the one or two cases of spina bifida or anencephaly out of the fifty pregnancies which originally produced a high AFP reading. Parents of these unborn infants then have the option of terminating the pregnancy or of making plans to have the baby born in a hospital equipped to give him the special care he will need.

Good prenatal care now can almost completely eliminate any worries that a baby will have Rh disease, once a much-dreaded cause of stillbirth, mental retardation, cerebral palsy, and other serious handicaps. Rh disease occurs because of an incompatibility in Rh blood factor between mother and unborn child. At the time of birth, as the placenta pulls away from the lining of the uterus, it's possible that some of the newborn baby's blood can seep into the mother's body through the uterine vein. If the mother has Rh-negative blood (as about one in seven women do) and her baby is Rh positive (as six out of seven people are), her body will react to the Rh positive blood as if it were a foreign substance and produce antibodies that destroy it. These antibodies remain in the mother's body and if she subsequently becomes pregnant with an Rh positive infant, these antibodies could reach the new baby through the placenta and begin to destroy his blood. As a result, the new child could die before birth or be born severely damaged.

When this problem became clearly understood in the 1940s, physicians attempted to help the unborn infants at risk by inducing early birth, in hopes of preventing the worst of the damage. This didn't help very much and added the hazards of prematurity to the dangers the babies already faced. In the 1960s, Dr. A.W. Liley used amniocentesis and a technique of intrauterine blood transfusions that made it possible to treat endangered infants even before they were born. And finally, the problem was largely solved by the development of an Rh vaccine, a gamma globulin substance containing a high concentration of anti-Rh antibodies. Given to an Rh-negative mother within seventy-two hours after the birth of an Rh-positive child, the vaccine attacks and destroys any stray Rh-positive blood cells in her body before they can trigger her immune system to produce her own antibodies. These acquired antibodies remain active for about four months and then die off. Should the mother become pregnant again, she will almost certainly have no Rh antibodies in her blood to endanger her new child.

It's an important part of prenatal care that a physician identify all pregnant women who have Rh-negative blood, to make sure they receive the Rh vaccine within seventy-two hours after giving birth, if their new baby is Rh positive. Every Rh negative woman should also receive the vaccine within three days of having a miscarriage or an abortion. The blood of an infant lost through miscarriage or abortion is rarely typed, but if it is positive, the abortion or miscarriage could trigger the mother's body to produce antibodies that could endanger a subsequent unborn child.

An Rh negative woman who developed antibodies from a pregnancy before the vaccine became available—or, in rare instances, from an accidentally mismatched blood transfusion earlier in life—can't be helped now by the Rh vaccine. Nor can the occasional woman who produces antibodies during a first pregnancy because a few of the baby's blood cells have seeped into her body. But once a generation of women has gone through the childbearing years protected by the Rh vaccine, Rh disease will become a great rarity.

One of the most important purposes of prenatal care is to prevent a baby from starting life with a low birth weight, with all of the associated risks of less-than-normal mental and physical development. Three out of four babies who die during the first few weeks after birth and half who fail to survive for the first year are born weighing less than five and a half pounds. Babies who are smaller than normal are more likely to suffer injuries during childbirth and from other birth complications. And low birth weight is linked to mental retardation, learning difficulties, physical awkwardness, and impairments of vision and hearing. The less a baby weighs at birth, the more problems he is likely to have, not only in surviving the first weeks of life but later on in childhood.

There are two major groups of babies who are born with a hazardously low weight. One group are the truly premature, born three or more weeks before the end of the normal 266-day prenatal life-span. Their weight and development are likely to be approximately normal for their gestational age. But they are endangered because their bodies, particularly the respiratory system, may not be mature enough to cope normally with independent existence. About three hundred thousand babies are born too soon every year.

The second group of low birth weight babies are born after a pregnancy of approximately normal length, but they are what doctors call "small for date." They may be less likely to have the serious respiratory problems of premature infants, but their small size may indicate other kinds of developmental problems.

There are many reasons why babies are born too soon and/or too small; many of the factors are interrelated and some can date back for more than one generation. Some low birth weight reflects a less-than-ideal prenatal environment—a mother who is ill (particularly with hypertension, toxemia, thyroid dysfunction, congenital heart problems, kidney disorders, or respiratory problems), is malnourished herself, lives in poverty, is carrying twins, is too young or too old, or smokes during pregnancy. Sometimes low birth weight is related to faulty growth of the baby; many too-small newborns are simply the hardiest survivors of conditions that usually result in miscarriage and a higher percentage of them have birth defects than do babies of average birth weight.

A study of 1.5 million full-term live births by the March of Dimes Birth Defects Foundation shows a direct relationship between prenatal care and a baby with low birth weight. Pregnant women who had the recommended thirteen or fourteen prenatal checkups had only a 2 percent chance of having a baby with low birth weight. Nine percent of those with no prenatal care at all had low birth weight babies. And between these extremes, the more visits a woman made for prenatal care, the less likely her infant was to have to start life outside the womb with less than normal size.

Medical techniques for protecting unborn infants and pregnant women have increased rapidly in the last few years. The most recent infant and maternal mortality statistics show dramatic drops that mean both mothers and babies are far safer now than ever before in American history. In part, the saving of babies' and mothers' lives is due to new technologies, like ultrasound, amniocentesis, and fetal monitoring devices that help physicians check up on unborn infants. And in part, they result from a growing awareness by prospective parents that they can—must—begin to care for their baby during the critical first nine months of life, the time when he grows faster and changes more than he ever will again.

Too many babies, however, are still being born with handicaps and genetic disorders and small neurologic differences that will become learning difficulties later on—some of them infants who in less medically sophisticated times would not have survived at all. Learning how to guard against these congenital problems—what to do and what not to do during pregnancy for the good of an unborn baby—is one of the most important things parents can ever do for a child.

Learning how to care for an unborn infant must of necessity involve explanations and warnings that can seem frightening and worrisome to prospective parents. Following some of the new rules and precautions can seem like a nuisance. But it's better to be able to take positive steps to increase the odds your baby will be born normal and healthy than simply to trust to blind luck, as every other generation has had to do. And when the stakes are so high—nothing less than your child's normal, healthy existence— no amount of planning and caretaking should be too great.

 SECTION II

The First Year of Life

YOUR baby is unique. Unless he is an identical twin, no one has ever had—or ever will have—precisely the combination of genes that provide the framework for his development. What kind of parent you are to him will have an enormous influence on the direction of his life and what kind of child, adolescent, and adult he will become. But he is not completely a blank slate on which you can draw any kind of individual you wish. His genetic heritage and his prenatal experiences have already endowed him with some basic characteristics, some fundamental temperament with which you must begin and which you cannot alter totally. He is already himself, already distinct in ways that even nurses in hospital new-born units can see. What you can do is help him to become the best Self possible.

It is an essential part of parenting to tailor child care, learning opportunities, daily routines, discipline, and other aspects of family life so they will work best for your particular offspring. But you must also help him fit into your life, to mesh his needs with yours in viable, sustainable balance. It isn't easy, but it can be endlessly challenging, fascinating, and rewarding.

Because your child is unique, not every bit of child-care advice will work equally well, or even at all. He won't develop, precisely, as the timetables indicate, but will spurt ahead here, perhaps lag behind there. It is an essential part of parenting to monitor the way your youngster responds to your child-care techniques and to let the feedback of his behavior shape your parenting.

For all the hundreds of books that have been written on child care, it is surprising to discover that much of what has passed for sound information in the past has been theory or assumption, often handed down from one footnote to another, from one bibliography to the next, until it is considered to have been proven. But the research basis for child-care theory is not very solid. Until recently, for example, there was little attempt to measure with any reliability or precision "environment" or its impact on youngsters. Little attention was paid to the brain, as the physical organ where learning and thinking take place. Few observers looked at babies and young children in their own natural habitat, at home with parents, for long periods of time, but only in doctors' offices or university-based day-care centers. Far more attention was paid to what was going wrong with children who were developing poorly than in identifying what helped bright and competent youngsters succeed.

That's one reason child-care theories have come and gone like fads. And it's another reason for paying great attention to your child and to his individual responses to your parenting.

There has been some better researh in child development in recent years. A few researchers have begun to look at babies and toddlers in their own homes over long stretches of time—and have made some unexpected discoveries. Brain scientists working in the new fields of cognitive neurophysiology are finding evidences of changes in the neurons and chemical workings of the brain to support the new theories about early learning. At least two scales that measure home environment have been developed to help researchers quantify influences on young children. And all of it backs the idea that parents can actually make a substantial difference in a child's intelligence by the kind of stimulating home and learning opportunities they give him.

7. How Your Baby Grows

The day your baby is born he is thrust from the sheltering, warm, cramped, dark environment of the womb into sudden light, sound, freedom to stretch and move, and the instant need to survive on his own, separated from the complex support system of his mother's body.

No matter how helpless he looks, he is marvelously prepared to cope with his new environment. Within minutes, his blood is rerouted away from the umbilical cord and through his lungs for the first time. His crying helps him to clear his lungs of accumulated mucus and fluid and pulls air into the expanding air sacs. If he is laid gently on his mother's abdomen, he will begin to push himself into position to nurse at her breast, and if helped to do so, his initial sucking will aid her uterus to contract and to limit postpartum bleeding. And already, he is learning—in ways that can be fostered by an environment rich in the right kinds of learning opportunities.

It will be a year of phenomenal growth. In the next twelve months, if all proceeds normally, he will triple his initial birth weight. His brain will increase in size proportionately, faster than it ever will again. He will learn to turn himself over, to hold his head upright without support, to sit, to crawl, to pull himself up on his own two feet, and to walk or be almost ready to do so. He will learn to distinguish and respond to several words, gain considerable control over his hands, and develop great expertise in manipulating his parents and others around him to respond to his needs and wishes. Never again will he learn new skills so rapidly. Never again will his growth and development be so obvious. And never again will he concentrate on learning with such total intensity.

To begin best, your baby needs good physical care, of course. Dozens of child-care books, pediatricians, grandmothers, and other parents can give you the specifics, so that information need not be detailed here. Your baby must also learn that he is dependably and nurturingly loved; understanding this bonding and attachment process is particularly important for two-career parents and for single parents. And he needs an environment full of learning stimulation carefully planned to match his particular stage in mental development and to encourage his brain to grow at an optimal rate. Parents who foster the growth of their child's brain in happy, loving ways can probably raise the level of his intelligence significantly—perhaps twenty to thirty points by the rough approximations of an IQ scale, researchers conclude. The increase in intelligence resulting from optimal parenting can easily make a lifelong difference in the school and career opportunities open to your offspring and in his ability to lead a satisfying life. How to foster mental development is the major focus of the remainder of this book.

The first days and weeks after birth are a time of adjustment for both newborn and parents. The process seems to be surprisingly easy with some infants, even for inexperienced, first-time mothers and fathers. But for other parents, getting used to a particular baby can mean months of rocky, fussy, sleepless anxiety. Sometimes, a difficult adjustment seems to be related to the circumstances of birth; a smaller-than-average infant, for example, usually requires more frequent feeding, may have trouble slipping into a schedule that's comfortable for parents, and may seem more irritable and tense than other babies. Sometimes, a mother or father can be nervous and anxious about job problems, money worries, marital troubles, or general unreadiness for parenthood, and those tensions can be picked up by the baby. But often, a normal, healthy, wanted baby born to experienced parents still can't be coaxed into sleeping through the night or getting over digestive distress, or relaxing into cuddling contentment for three or four months—for no obvious reasons parents or pediatrician can discover and remedy.

Learning the physical skills of parenting is much like learning any new set of moves—riding a bike or roller skating, for example. Once mastered, the techniques seem so obvious and natural you can't imagine why it felt so awkward and difficult to learn. First-time parenting also carries an awesome overlay of responsibility for a new life and the fatigue that comes with realizing this responsibility lasts twenty-four hours a day, every day, every week, every month. Add the exhaustion and shift in hormonal balance women experience after childbirth, and it's obvious why parents need to be patient and kind to themselves as they begin the loving process of adding a new member to their family.

Some babies take longer than others to adjust physiologically to life outside the womb. Their breathing may be uneven for weeks; if you are a first-time parent listening to a baby breathe, you can work up a panic unless you realize sighs and hesitancies, noisiness and startling are normal for infants. Although he can focus his eyes well at some distances, your baby's vision isn't adult-acute as yet and won't be for a few months; he may also have difficulty getting his eyes to track together and may occasionally look cross-eyed until he is a year old or more. Most troublesome, your baby's digestive system may not work smoothly. Many infants suffer acutely from what is usually called colic for two or three hours a day for the first three months or so of life. Although doctors don't agree on the precise cause or remedy, colic seems to be an acute abdominal distress that disappears automatically at about the age of three months, as a baby's digestive system matures. One physician says his research shows babies who have colic are more likely than others to grow up to be energetic, dynamic achievers and leaders—that may be some small comfort to you when you're wearily walking the floor with a miserable infant.

Genetic inheritance, prenatal experience, and environment after birth all work together to give your child his own individual pattern of development and his own unique temperament. You and the environment you create can do much to shape the person your offspring is and grows up to be. But you'll also discover, as you get to know your child better during the first weeks of his life, that he is not a lump of clay to be molded as you choose. The force of his temperament and personality will surprise you often, even when he is only an infant. Learning to take his temperament into account as you develop your parenting style is part of the art of caring for your child optimally.

Much of your baby's development during the first year of his life seems to be a natural unfolding of innate patterns. It's only when researchers study infants who have been seriously deprived of parents' loving care and of adequate mental stimulation in their environment that it becomes obvious how essential both of these factors are for normal development to occur. And only in recent years has new information in the fields of biology, psychology, education, medicine, and developmental neurophysiology been correlated to show parents how to provide a baby with optimal mental stimulation.

It takes the first year of life and a few months more for a baby to learn to move about independently, to use his hands reliably, to become adept at getting others to satisfy his needs and wants, and to obtain at least some of the information about the world around him that his brain so urgently requires. The general patterns of acquiring these skills have a genetic basis—he will learn to roll over before he crawls and become adept at crawling before he pulls himself up on his feet and discovers how to walk. But how fast he learns depends, in part, on the opportunities and encouragement in his environment. The interaction of genetic programming and environmental opportunity, along with his basic temperament, create a learning style that will influence the rest of his life.

BIRTH TO THREE MONTHS

Much of what a baby learns during the first three months of life is easy to take for granted: how to move his arms reliably, how to correlate what his various senses are telling him, that the demands of his body will be satisfied by loving adults around him, how to cry and suck to produce the food that relieves his hunger, and when he has had enough. But all of it represents complex learning. Even gravity takes getting used to for someone who has spent all of his previous existence afloat in a water-filled capsule.

But an infant is marvelously equipped to learn and survive. Some of the survival skills that he needs immediately, like swallowing and sucking, he practiced repeatedly before he was born. Others, like breathing, sneezing, crying, and blinking the eyes, come instinctively and immediately. Even the first day of his life outside the womb, even exhausted, battered, his head squeezed out of shape by the process of birth, he is ready to learn—and if given the chance, will show that he can use what he is learning and that he is fascinated and delighted with the process of learning.

Experiments with infants younger than twenty-four hours old show that a newborn can tell the difference between sweet and slightly sour liquids and prefers the sweet. He can distinguish patterns shown to him at about eight to ten inches away from his eyes and would rather look at a new design than one he has already seen. He can tell from what direction a sound is coming and shows a preference for some sounds over others. He can differentiate smells. And he can respond to soothing and to gentle human contact.

Even so, most of the first three months of life is a transition period during which an infant gets used to living independently outside the womb—accustomed, in fact, to being a baby—and his parents learn not only how to parent, but how to adapt the usual parenting skills to this particular child.

A newborn infant's head is disproportionately big for his body and needs to be supported whenever he is lifted. Learning to control it is one of his first developmental tasks. During the first weeks after birth, if you put your baby down on his stomach, he will barely be able to lift his head enough for his nose to clear the mattress. But between the ages of two and three months, his muscle control will improve enough so that he can hold his head up at a right angle to the crib. If you put him on his back, his head will usually be turned to one side or the other for the first several weeks of his life. After about six weeks, he'll begin to turn his cheek off the mattress, and after about three and a half months, he'll be able to move it a full 180 degrees while lying on his back.

If you hold your baby in a sitting position, supporting him under his arms, he'll be able to hold his head steady by the time he's three or four months old. If you put him on his back and gently pull him up by his arms, his head will lag behind until he's four to six months old.

Even before he is born, your baby may suck his thumb or his fist, as evidenced by ultrasound pictures, or even by little callous marks on his hand. He will probably begin to do so soon after birth, finding his mouth at first mostly by accident, but soon with deliberate intention. At first, your baby will show little other interest in his hands; they are too close to his eyes for him to focus on them clearly for the first few weeks of his life. But gradually, as his eyesight sharpens, he will become fascinated by his hands and their early random movements. If a hand accidentally bats a ball or makes a mobile stir, he won't understand the cause-effect connection at first. But by the time he's about three months old, it seems to occur to him that he and his hand can cause the sound or the movement to happen and he will start trying to aim his hand deliberately to produce the interesting effect again.

One of the first deliberate delights a baby discovers on his own is the fun of playing with both of his hands together. Most babies learn to bring their hands together in front of their face between two and a half and three months of age. By three months, your baby will probably be so fascinated with the discovery that he will be content to stare at his hands for five to ten minutes at a time, watching the fists open up into fingers and enjoying the astonishing sight of his two hands touching and feeling each other.

At first, your baby will instinctively grasp a pencil or rattle or finger or anything else pushed into the palm of his hand; he is more likely to keep his hands closed into fists at this age, in any case. But during the first few weeks of life, he will also let go randomly, without seeming to be aware that he has been holding something. After about two and a half months, he will begin to look at what's in his hand and try to push it into his mouth. Your baby's grasp will become more intentional about the end of the third month of his life. A few infants start to reach out toward an object—often unsuccessfully—by about two and a half months and most do so by four and a half months.

Your baby's eyesight improves remarkably during these first three months of life, and by the time he's three months old, he will have an intense interest and delight in simply seeing. Although soon after birth he can focus his eyes and see clearly only at about eight to ten inches from his eyes (about the distance from a mother's breast to her face, child development experts note), his ability to focus his eyes and see well at other distances increases rapidly and so does his skill at making both eyes track together. Once a bright object has caught his attention, a one-month-old infant should be able to follow it with his eyes if you move it slowly from one side to directly in front of him. By two and a half to three and a half months, he should be able to track an object for a full 180 degrees.

By three to three and a half months, your baby's vision will be almost as accurate as an adult's—better, probably, than that of most people older than forty. He will spend a considerable part of his waking hours obsessed with the joys of looking—at bright objects, at his own hands, at everything around him, and especially at human faces. A baby who is nursing or sucking on a bottle in his mother's arms will often stare intently at her face, almost as if he were trying to memorize every line and plane; after his first sharp pangs of hunger are eased, he sometimes seems more interested in looking intently at her than in sucking.

Your baby is born able to hear effectively—not only because his ear structures and the auditory areas of his brain are relatively mature at birth, but also because he has had considerable experience listening to sounds before his birth. For example, in one experiment, a hydrophone was tucked into a woman's uterus during labor and a recording made of what could be heard by the unborn child. On the recording were not only the sounds of the mother's heartbeat and body noises, but the muffled voices of both mother and doctor and, clearly identifiable, Beethoven's Fifth Symphony which was playing in the labor room.

Hearing also improves during these first months, and an infant learns quickly to discriminate between a variety of noises, such as crying, screaming, talking, and singing. Recent research shows that newborns in hospital nurseries can distinguish their own crying from that of other infants on tape recordings and are likely to quiet down and listen to themselves when given the chance. They can also be comforted, frequently, by regular sounds that mimic the human heartbeat they heard before they were born.

In the weeks right after birth, your baby is likely to startle and cry at loud noises. But by the end of three months, his hearing will be almost as acute as an adult's and he will be making progress identifying sounds and linking them with information he is getting from other sense organs.

To his own great delight, your baby will discover the fun of experimenting with producing sounds other than crying, probably during the second month of his life. Most babies learn to laugh out loud shortly before they are three months old and to squeal with joy at about the same time, or a few days later. Many babies even find it fun to make sounds deliberately with their own saliva and amuse themselves by doing so.

For the first three months of life, a baby is easily upset. His moods can shift abruptly, from sleepiness to screaming, from comfortableness to crying in fractions of a minute. He sleeps lightly and for shorter intervals than children or adults, rarely more than four or five hours at a time. He loses a few ounces of his birth weight before his eating patterns are established and it may take ten days or more to gain it back.

But by the end of three months, most of the transition from unborn to newborn to baby is complete. His sleep times now fall into a more regular pattern and, if parents are lucky, stretch into six hours or more at night. During the day, he is awake, alert, and in active contact with his environment for longer periods of time instead of drifting in and out of light sleep. He no longer seems distressed by the workings of his digestive system. His breathing patterns are more regular. He obviously enjoys being sociable with other people. And he has learned an essential social skill that emotionally enslaves everyone around him: how to smile.

Smiling usually begins between six and eight weeks of age, and by the end of the first three months of life, your baby will be happily, gleefully, excitingly smiling whenever he sees you. It's a wonderful reward for mothers and fathers who have endured a long pregnancy, the rigors of childbirth, sleepless nights, crying, endless diaper duty, and often a frustrating sense of their own inadequacies. And it marks the end of the first, most difficult months of caring for your baby.

THREE TO SIX MONTHS

The next three months bring an acceleration of your baby's fascination with being alive and in exploring his surroundings with his fast-developing sense organs and his increasing control over his own body. He looks more like a picture-book infant now, his wrinkled, wizened newborn appearance having vanished with his rapid gain in weight (most babies double their weight in the first five months after birth), his smiling excitement about being alive, and his delight in socializing with his family. He is easier to pick up and handle because his body seems more "together." He sleeps more soundly now and for longer stretches at a time, especially at night. When he is awake, he is more often alert and visibly interested in learning and exploring. Even his basic mood seems to have improved to a sort of eager geniality, although it is often disturbed by hunger, boredom, impatience, teething, or a need for fresh diapers.

In a way, your baby seems to be deliberately exploring his own body and his surroundings, deliberately sorting out and storing up visual, auditory, tactile, and kinesthetic information and combining the new data in ever more sophisticated learning. He still enjoys playing with his hands, but uses them now, too, to reach out to swipe or grab at something his eyes can see—an important and complex mental activity scientists call visual directed reaching. By the end of this three months, he will be reaching for objects accurately and routinely—a major step in development. He discovers that his feet make interesting playthings and takes new delight in kicking and pushing against a firm surface or object. Just as before he was born, the normal cycles of development begin with head, arms, and hands and are followed days or weeks later by similar progress with legs and feet.

Sometime between two and a half and four and a half months, your baby will discover that with great effort he can turn himself over—either from stomach to back or back to stomach. Usually, the accomplishment pleases him so much that he will fuss and cry until an adult turns him back so he can practice his new skill again and again. It takes another few weeks for him to figure out how to turn both ways with ease whenever he chooses. By the time he's six months old, he may be pushing himself up on his hands and knees, and a few babies will be starting to creep forward, usually pulling themselves by their arms while their legs drag behind. A few adventuresome types will also try to stand up, carefully holding on to a firm surface or a steady adult hand.

Because he's so interested in looking, your baby will be eager to sit up as much as possible in an infant seat, a high chair, or other safe spot. Most babies can balance themselves unsupported in a sitting position by the age of six months, and a few can maneuver themselves into sitting up in the course of rolling over. Because he can control his head reliably now and direct his hands with his eyes, your baby is eager to keep experimenting and learning all he can with these new abilities—and is surprisingly energetic in the efforts he puts forth and in his willingness to practice his skills repeatedly.

One new skill your baby will probably like to practice involves simply transferring a small object from one hand to the other and back again—a maneuver that helps him learn to coordinate one hand with the other and with his eyes and gives him a wealth of sensory information not only about the object in hand but about his own body. About half of all babies can transfer a small cube from one hand to the other at the age of six months if encouraged to do so and almost all can by seven and a half months. By six months, too, your baby will probably be trying to maneuver so he can get a toy that he can see just a little beyond his reach. Much of what a baby has in his hands he also explores with his mouth, of course, and you must be sure that nothing he can reach is small enough to swallow or make him choke.

By six months, your baby's interest in feeding himself is growing. He can pick up a cracker and eat it with obvious delight by the time he's six or seven months old. He may enjoy holding on to his bottle and deliberately pushing it in and out of his mouth once his first, powerful hunger is satisfied. He may also be able to hold a cup and have fun discovering that it contains milk or juice as well as being an intriguing plaything.

During the second three months of life, your baby will get better at linking what he hears with what he sees. He will reliably turn toward voices and noises and show signs that he is listening to music by cooing or stopping crying. Although he may associate the tone of your voice with certain events like feeding or bathing, he shows no sign of recognizing words as yet. But his own vocabulary of sounds is increasing and he seems to appreciate the sociability of listening to a voice and making sounds of his own in response. Not only will your baby cry and coo, but he will squeal, hum, giggle, laugh, grunt, and babble long strings of vowels and consonants at varying volumes and pitches. If you talk to him and then pause, he'll often babble back as if he were holding a conversation with you and squirming with joy at the fun of it all. Some studies show that girls tend to babble more at this age than boys and that both boys and girls babble more in response to a female voice than a male's. Your baby may say "Ma-ma" or "Da-da" by accident as he experiments with sounds, although fewer than half of all infants do regularly before the age of six months. But he won't learn to associate it with mother or father until his parents react to the syllables with so much excitement that he makes an effort to repeat the sound that got such an interesting reaction.

By six months of age, about half of all babies are ready to enjoy the sociability and great good humor of little games like peekaboo. Many infants will laugh aloud if you cover your face with your hands or with a piece of paper, then pull it away and say, "Peekaboo." Your baby will probably wriggle with delight at sharing a game with you and indicate by his body language that he wants

you to play again and again. He'll also be learning a little about
what scientists call object permanence—that objects and people
continue to exist even when he can't see them—and about how
time sequences from the present to the immediate future. Soon,
you'll notice that he tries to initiate the game himself, by covering
up his face with his hands or pulling something over his eyes—a
sign that his memory is developing and that he can also link past
events with the present.

SIX TO NINE MONTHS

Lured in part by all the fascinating things he can see just beyond
his reach and pushed by innate forces of growth, your baby will
spend much of this three months practicing at getting himself up
off his back and into motion. By the end of nine months, he will
have greatly widened his ability to move around and to gain new
information for his developing brain. And his increasing mobility
will force major changes in how you care for him and how you
help him learn.

By the time he's seven or eight months old, your baby will be
able to sit up without support and will balance himself well
enough so that he can free his hands to reach out for objects that
intrigue him. He can push himself into sitting easily and while
sitting, can twist, turn, bend over, and reach out without toppling
over.

He will become adept at crawling, too, after spending weeks
experimenting and figuring out how to push himself on hands and
knees and how to coordinate both legs and arms to propel himself
forward. At first, his arms work more accurately and powerfully
than his legs which, as usual, lag behind the upper part of his body
in development. But after several weeks of creeping, powered
mostly by his arms, he will manage to get his legs going in syn-
chronization with his arms and by the end of nine months he will
probably be crawling almost as fast as you can walk. He may even
be ready for variations, such as crawling while carrying something
in one hand or crawling up a few stairs.

Being able to crawl opens vast new horizons and learning opportunities for your baby, who until now has been bed-bound until

picked up by someone else and able to explore only those objects someone else put within easy reach. He will also begin to pull himself up to a standing position, although for a while he will need your help to plop back down again; during the weeks he's mastering this new skill, he may constantly demand that you lower him gently to a sit so he can pull himself up again and again, until one or the other of you is exhausted. Once he's standing firmly and confidently, he'll experiment with taking a few tentative steps while holding tightly to furniture or an adult hand— an accomplishment about half of all babies manage by the end of nine months and most of the rest by their first birthday.

Your baby's fascination with his hands continues and so does his skill at using them. Usually, at this age he shows no preference for being right- or left-handed and seems to take particular joy in using both hands together. He'll be able to bang two small blocks together accurately before he's nine months old. And he'll also become adept at picking up small objects using his thumb in opposition to a finger or two. Coupled with this ability often comes a special fascination for looking intently at very small objects, like raisins, crumbs, or even mites of dust. Not only is he intrigued with picking up objects of all kinds, he is equally interested in letting them go, especially when he can drop them over the side of a playpen, crib, or high chair onto a surface where they make a satisfying noise. Then he's likely to bend over to see what's happened to the object and noisily insist that someone hand it to him so he can repeat his experiment with gravity and impact sounds again.

Not only is your baby learning to use his hands in a new grasp-and-release operation and verifying for himself the constant effects of gravity, he's also learning with delight that he himself can cause something to happen by his own actions. This new interest in cause and effect—and joy in deliberately being a cause—is a major step in mental development and an explanation of much that your baby will be doing and trying to do in the next two years.

Most babies reliably say "Ma-ma" and "Da-da" by the time they are nine months old and understand what it means. Most will babble in imitation of speech if an adult talks to them and then pause, as if in conversation. Your baby will understand a few more simple words at this age and enjoys playing with the vast variety of sounds he can produce himself. He will come to associate words with the extremely simple games he likes to play, like pat-a-cake, bye-bye, and how-big-is-the-baby? But for the most part, he's far more interested in crawling and physically exploring his expanding environment than in talking.

Your baby's memory is also improving, with mixed results. He will recognize a sequence of activities that leads to eating, and will often quiet in anticipation of lunch when he sees the preparations you are starting. He will sometimes hunt for an object or a toy you've hidden under a cover while he watches you do it. And he will anticipate a romp with his father, if that's customary, when he hears him coming home from work. But sometime during these three months—most likely when he's about eight or nine months old—he will begin to react with considerable fear and fussing to people he now realizes are not part of his family. It may now be more difficult to leave him with a sitter than when he was younger, or even to put on a coat and get ready to leave him for a while because he is now able to associate your preparations with your temporary disappearance. But it is a sign that your infant is now securely and lovingly attached to you, even though the results can occasionally be a nuisance.

Even though he is working relentlessly to develop the physical skills that make it possible for him to move about independently and despite the difficulties and spills he takes in learning, your baby's mood will continue to be generally cheerful and full of good humor. Most of the time, he isn't daunted by the great amount of effort and practice it takes for him to learn a new skill, although sometimes he will lapse into frustration and tears, only to be comforted or distracted back into cheerful activity again with surprising speed. Most days, he'll keep working at his new skills until he collapses with exhaustion and needs to be soothed into relaxation and sleep. Even then, he can't seem to wait to get into motion again the minute he wakes up.

NINE TO TWELVE MONTHS

The same relentless, happy concentration on physical activity continues during the last three months of your baby's first year, as he discovers that he can balance himself well enough in an upright position to let go of his supports and then to lurch and wobble into taking a few steps on his own. About half of all infants can stand alone well by eleven and a half months and almost all by fourteen months. And half of all babies are walking well by their first birthday and most within another month or two. Achieving—and then experimenting with and enjoying—this marvelous new ability overshadows almost everything else in your baby's life, not only while he is developing this complicated skill, but for months after as he masters it and the novelty begins to wear off. It will be another six months until he is ready to shift his learning concentration to language.

Learning to walk is immeasurably exciting to a baby; many laugh out loud when they take their first independent steps, balancing with arms outstretched as they stagger a few feet and land with a whoop of joy in the waiting arms of a cheering mother or father. But even without a cheering section, your baby will continue to practice walking, with a concentration that leaves him little interest in anything else, even eating. By his first birthday, he'll probably be able to bend over to pick up an object and stand back up again without tumbling over. After a few weeks, he'll be balancing himself so well that he no longer needs to hold his arms to the side and can use them to carry small objects from place to place.

Along with walking, your baby's fascination with climbing begins. He'll discover that he can climb onto a low ottoman, onto a chair or sofa, or up any ungated stairs he can find and thus he'll need your active supervision to be safe.

Control over the muscles in his hands continues to grow during the last months of his first year. He continues to be intrigued with dropping things from high chair, crib, or his new upright position to see if they splatter or bounce or bang when they hit and, perhaps, to see what kind of reaction he gets from you. The action also gives him an idea of how far down the floor is from various heights and lets him enjoy being the cause of an effect he can now reliably produce by himself.

By year's end, more than half of all babies can participate in a simple game of ball, stopping the ball when it is rolled toward them and pushing it, or at least letting go of it in return. Some babies can use one hand to open a door or sliding panel and the other hand to reach in for a toy. Some can partially undress themselves by pulling off shoes, socks, and even pants and diaper. Some are beginning to show a preference for their right or left hand, more frequently using it to explore or handle new objects while the other hand is more often assigned simply to carry or hold on.

Most babies are now skilled at using the thumb-finger pincer motion and not only enjoy but often insist on feeding themselves by picking up bits of finger food on their own. At twelve months, more than half of all babies can drink from a cup well enough not to spill much. As interest in eating declines with your baby's concentration on mobility and with the beginning of the normal slowdown in weight gain, it's usually wise to let your child take the initiative in feeding himself from the finger food you select. It will probably be no messier than if you insist on spooning food into the mouth of a restless and balking baby.

Language development continues slowly during these months, with your baby learning to understand more words, but producing only a few, if any, words himself. Most of what he says will still be cheerful gibberish. He will understand "No" and what it means, although he will often find it funny to ignore and keep right on doing what he knows he shouldn't, perhaps even adding a comically woeful expression if he's discovered that can make you laugh. He may learn to say "No" himself and use it often, shaking his head from side to side as he repeats the word. For the most part, he's just enjoying the sound and the headshaking; it will be more than a year before he reaches a true negativism stage when he seriously intends to resist what you tell him to do.

Your baby's vision has been near adult level for months by the time he reaches his first birthday. But he still can't seem to get enough of looking. Scientists who monitor the activities of babies and toddlers on a minute-by-minute basis for hours at a time over periods of several weeks say that this kind of intent staring is one of a baby's most common activities. One researcher estimates that between the ages of eight and thirty-six months, children spend about 20 percent of all their waking time at what others have labeled "getting information—visual." What your baby is apparently doing is simply programming his growing brain with an enormous amount of information about the world around him— data he will use the rest of his life in highly complex thinking processes.

8. How You Can Help Your Baby Learn

There are at least four good reasons for deliberately increasing the amount of mental stimulation in your child's environment, starting from the first days after birth:

• You can substantially and permanently raise the level of your child's intelligence.
• Your child will be much happier if you surround him with appropriate learning opportunities, will be bored less often, fuss less, and be more fun to live with if his hunger for mental nourishment is satisfied.
• You will help your child achieve more of his innate potential.
• You will enjoy parenting more if you see yourself as your child's guide and companion in discovering the wonders of learning rather than primarily as a diaper changer, a spooner of cereal, a disciplinarian, or a baby-sitter.

Parents are the first and most influential teachers a child ever has. The quality and quantity of learning experiences you give your offspring during the early years of life will determine to a large extent how much of his innate capacity for learning will ever be realized. You are your child's teacher and guide through the most complex intellectual task he ever undertakes: learning the complicated symbol system that is his native language. What you do—and don't do—will actually affect the basic structure of his brain, its chemical functioning, and the ways it integrates complex information that make it "smarter." What you do—or don't do—can raise or lower your child's potential IQ by at least twenty or thirty points, research shows. You will have a major influence on the kind of permanent learning style your youngster develops,

and it will be largely up to you whether he starts his formal schooling ready and eager to succeed or already lagging behind and primed
to fail.

Astonishingly, parents' great and unduplicable influence on the
development of their child's intelligence wasn't recognized until
the 1960s, for several reasons. Child-care experts used to assume
that the development of young children was almost entirely genetically programmed, that it would proceed in regular stages, by
ages, regardless of external forces. They told parents that youngsters would acquire new learning only when they were "ready" and
that nothing a father or mother could do would speed up or slow
down this "readiness."

To do anything except wait for "readiness" to show itself would
be to push a child for the parents' own emotional gratification and
accomplish nothing except to cause frustration and possibly rebellion in the child, parents were warned. Give your youngster
emotional security, don't push, and leave the teaching to professionals when he is ready to start school, parents were advised.
Because so little research was done on child development from the
time infants left the hospital a few days after birth until they were
conveniently gathered together in groups in kindergarten and first
grade, the importance of early learning was overlooked. Parents
who did pick up signals of their youngster's enormous craving for
fresh mental stimulation and who talked about how bright and
eager he was to learn were simply put down as typical bragging
mothers and fathers.

As a result, parents got less information about how to nourish
their child's mind than they did about how to feed his stomach.
Much of what good parents did by instinct, tradition, and because
it made their child happy and easier to care for did turn out to be
fostering mental development. But it was like trying to feed a
child with no knowledge of vitamins, calories, or a balanced diet.

Then, in the 1960s, new discoveries were made and new data
developed in the fields of pediatrics, neurology, psychology, biology, and education that pointed up the vital role early learning
plays in the growth of the brain and the intellect.

That abundant learning stimulation early in life not only increased intelligence but could actually change the size and chemical composition of the brain was clearly demonstrated by resear-

chers like Dr. Mark Rosenzweig, professor of psychology at the University of California. In studies with laboratory animals, experiments showed that those receiving early learning opportunities had a heavier cortex (the outer layer of gray matter in the brain that stores information and "thinks") than did carefully matched animals reared in less stimulating environments. Their brains also had more interconnecting branches between cells and more of two important chemicals involved in brain activity. Similar controlled experiments and analyses of brain structure and tissue aren't possible with human children, of course. But thousands of studies on dozens of kinds of animals have confirmed the findings that appropriate, generous, early learning stimulation does help to build a better brain and the earlier in life the stimulation comes, the more effective it is and the brighter the animal becomes.

More recently, using a special electron microscopy method, Dr. Peter Huttenlocher, a pediatric neurologist at the University of Chicago, has discovered that the nerve cells in the cortex of the brain of newborn infants have about the same number of tiny branches (dendrites and axons) and interconnecting links (synapses) as adult brains. But they are immature in structure. During infancy, the number of synapses increases rapidly until, between the ages of one and two years, they reach a maximum that is about 50 percent higher than the average for adults. Their structure becomes more mature, until they resemble adult synapses by the time a baby is six to twenty-four months old. Then, apparently the synapses that are not being used begin to atrophy and disappear. Their density begins to decline until adolescence, remains constant from the age of sixteen to seventy-two, and then drops slightly after that.

This great abundance of synapses in early life may be an anatomic basis for what scientists call the plasticity of the brain in very young children. For example, young children can learn second languages much easier and without accent while adults cannot. And a child can often recover mental functions—such as speech—lost in an injury to the brain while an adult with similar damage cannot.

In the last few years, there has been an explosion of similar kinds of new information about how the nervous system is built and how early environment influences brain growth, according to

Colin Blakemore, professor of physiology at the University Laboratory of Physiology, Oxford, England. Using extremely sophisticated new techniques of brain research, developmental neurophysiologists are learning how and where information is coded and stored in the brain and how this process actually alters the brain's structure. They are discovering what sensory stimuli activate which neurons in the brain and how data can be filed away and recalled in related chunks in "expert thinking."

In particular, brain scientists are studying the plasticity of the brain during the early years of life, when its structures and capabilities are easily altered. They can demonstrate that the brain of a very young child requires an enormous amount of sensory stimulation during special, limited "sensitive periods" to develop well. And they can show that even genetically programmed brain development can be modified by environment—for better or worse.

Much of this new research seems to give neurological credibility to the early learning theories of Jean Piaget, Maria Montessori, Burton White, J. McV. Hunt, and others, who based their work on their observations of how young children learn. Other kinds of educational and statistical evidence are also piling up to support the urgent importance of early learning—and parents' crucial role in their children's mental development.

That changes in mental capacity are greatest during the early years of life when the brain is growing most rapidly has been documented by Dr. Benjamin S. Bloom, professor of education at the University of Chicago and a former president of the American Educational Research Association. Dr. Bloom correlated more than one thousand research studies and clearly showed that intellectual development does not proceed at a regular rate or increase after a child starts school. Instead, it decreases steadily, just as the rapid physical growth of the brain gradually slows down after birth—and just as the physical growth of the whole body decelerates, starting with the first year of life. (Although a baby doubles his birth weight by about five months after birth, it takes seven months to triple it. This rate of growth is never again repeated, even during adolescent spurts.)

Learning acquired early in life has a powerful, lasting quality that differs somewhat from learning acquired later on—probably because of the changing state of the developing brain—and that early learning is the foundation on which all later learning rests, Dr. Bloom emphasized. His research shows that if intelligence is considered to be a relatively stable characteristic in adults after about age seventeen, then 50 percent of that intellectual capacity is acquired by the time a child is four years old and 80 percent by the age of eight. After eight, according to Dr. Bloom's research, the general level of his intelligence can be changed only by about 20 percent.

This doesn't mean that your child will have acquired half of all his knowledge by the age of four, or that he can't learn more after he's seventeen. But by the time he's through high school, the level of his intelligence will be considered a stable adult characteristic. Whether he's bright, average, or slow, his intellectual level isn't likely to change very much as an adult. But, of course, he can use his intellectual abilities to learn more, or not, just as an adult can use his body in vigorous exercise, or not.

Just how a few simple early learning opportunities can make a remarkable difference in a child's interest and ability to learn was clearly demonstrated by Dr. Burton White when he was at Harvard University's Laboratory of Human Development. First, Dr. White measured the amount of time a group of infants, kept for the most part in white-sheeted cribs with white bumpers in an institution where they were awaiting adoption, spent awake and visually alert during the day and at what age they developed effective eye-hand coordination, so they could accurately reach out and grab an object they were looking at.

Then with other, comparable groups of infants, Dr. White added a few colorful objects for the babies to look at and reach for. He also made it easier for them to see what was going on around them. His measurements showed that the infants who had something interesting to look at were visually alert for a much greater percentage of the time than those who didn't. They were also able to make their eyes and hands work together effectively two full months sooner than the first group of infants. A baby who is alert and interested in what's going on around him and who can reach out accurately to touch and handle objects on his own can feed his brain much more learning stimuli than a baby who can't.

That's just a small sampling of the kinds of evidence that have been accumulating about early mental development in the last two decades. The research is far from complete. Much more remains to be learned about the structure and functioning of the brain, how it is affected by sensory stimuli, and what kinds of learning are most effective at what ages. Educators and brain scientists are just beginning to see how their work fits together and to develop practical methods for encouraging children to learn at an optimal rate.

Generally, the research supports these basic concepts that are useful to parents:

• Parents are the most important teachers a child will ever have. You can teach your youngster when he's most ready to learn, when his brain is growing and changing the fastest, and when his style of learning is being formed. You can help him learn individually, at the precise moment when his mind is most open to a particular kind of information, and at the rate most comfortable and encouraging for him. Because he loves you and wants to please you, there is no one with whom he would rather share the joy of learning.

• You can raise the level of your child's intelligence for life because the learning opportunities you offer him will stimulate the growth of his brain structure and change it in ways that improve its ability to "think."

• Your child has a built-in drive to learn that's as genetically based and fundamental as hunger and thirst. He has a basic need to explore, to investigate, to manipulate, to exercise all of his senses and to feed his endless curiosity. Satisfying this drive is as pleasurable to him as milk to a hungry infant.

• Your child also has a genetically based drive to become competent, a built-in need to handle, manipulate, investigate, try, and keep learning until he becomes expert and skilled. You will see your child repeat an activity again and again—pulling himself up, practicing sounds, trying to pick up objects, figuring out how things work—as he goes about developing his competency. Mastering a task will give him an inherent satisfaction and motivate him to learn more.

• The more new things your child has seen and heard and had the opportunity to do, the more he wants to see and hear and experience. The more learning stimuli that your child's brain has assimilated, the more his brain is able to take in and the more capable he becomes of learning from his environment and using the information to think.

• Presumably because of the way the brain develops and its changing needs for particular kinds of sensory stimulation, sensitive periods exist in your child's life when he seems to crave certain kinds of activities and when certain types of learning are most easily acquired. Although these periods are not as short-lived or immutable as similar phenomena in animals, they do help to explain some of the behavior of young children and give parents good clues as to what kind of learning experiences to provide.

• The most important intellectual task you help your child undertake is learning his native language, and so eager is he to do so that his mind soaks up the language clues in his environment and he will learn to talk and understand speech almost without your deliberate assistance. But you can speed the process—to his delight and satisfaction—by making it easy for him to pick up verbal clues, by responding appropriately to his efforts to communicate with you, and by using a vocabulary and grammar patterns that he can understand, yet offer him some new masterable challenge.

• Because your child's brain seems to have a special sensitive period for learning language in any form during early childhood, your youngster can learn to read and also to speak a second language more easily before he reaches the age of six than afterward.

Parents who have tried using some of these ideas with their youngsters almost always report enthusiastically about the results. They find that their children are more responsive and happier and that they obviously enjoy the opportunities to learn, especially when the companionship of a parent is involved.

There have been a few problems in using early learning concepts, however. Some manufacturers have been quick to label inappropriate, gimmicky toys as "educational" even though they offer youngsters less play value or learning opportunities than the pots and pans in the average cupboard. Overly gimmicked baby bedding and decorations for children's rooms have also been promoted as "mentally stimulating" when "gaudy" would be a more accurate description. Parents can usually guard against such sales

pitches by trying to evaluate precisely how their child would respond to the product and how he would use it.

Occasionally, the author of a child-care book or director of a
child-care center has misunderstood the purpose of early learning
and the ways in which very young children learn and has developed programs that are much too authoritarian and structured.
Children are compelled to sit quietly and learn; there is an emphasis on rote and repetition; and a sort of mechanical name-calling is
confused with real learning. By contrast, in true early learning, a
parent should act not as disciplinarian, but as guide and
cheerleader, setting the stage for a child to learn by his own discoveries. Learning shouldn't be forced on a youngster or dictated
by formal lesson plans, but should come, essentially, in response
to his own curiosity and initiative.

The younger the child, the more likely learning is to take place
on the run, in snatches of time no longer than a minute or two.
The curious assumption that children must sit down and sit still to
learn is one reason so many people thought youngsters weren't old
enough to learn much until they were old enough to sit in orderly
classes in school. But no one has yet been able to demonstrate
that thinking takes place in the part of the anatomy involved in
sitting.

A third problem is that the promoters of some day-care centers
have been quick to tack "educational" labels on their programs,
even though they are little more than traditional baby-sitting services with a few fancy trappings. Many of the Head Start programs, for example, have had little time for concentrating on early
learning activities. Some have taken only three- or four-year-olds
and lasted only a single summer. Many have been modeled after
traditional nursery school and the usual two- or three-hour schedule of outdoor play, finger painting, juice time, group games, and
housekeeping play has often left little time for trying out new ideas
for activities intended to raise the intelligence. Because so many
Head Start children have come from low-income homes, staff
members have often found that their needs for health care and
better nutrition were so overwhelming that they have had little
time for much else.

But even a small amount of attention to the early mental needs of young children pays off, Head Start research shows. Dozens of long-term studies on the results of Head Start and similar preschool learning programs for disadvantaged and other children have now been completed. Almost all of them show not only immediate gains in learning, but long-term payoff in school grades and other measures of mental development.

The findings of ninety-six such studies—all of which met rigorous scientific standards—were summed up at the annual meeting of the American Association for the Advancement of Science in 1978, and as Bernard Brown, of the U.S. Office of Child Development, put it, the statistics showed ninety-six successes to zero failures.

Not one of the ninety-six studies failed to show significant gains for the children involved compared to similar youngsters not in the program. Although the studies included a variety of summer-only, year-round, Head Start, Home Start (in which a visiting teacher goes to the home to show a mother how to help a baby learn), and other programs, all of them showed positive results, especially when measured over several years.

Not every child in every program did better than comparison youngsters without such opportunities. But as a whole, the children who had early learning programs had higher IQs than comparison youngsters—ranging from seven to ten points in most studies up to thirty to forty points in one report. When tested after several years of school, a much greater percentage of the children ranked at grade level or better in reading and math. Many fewer flunked—3 percent compared to 32 percent of classmates in one study. The most successful results came from the Home Start Programs. Even though Home Start teachers spend only an hour or so a week with a baby or toddler, the plan has two major advantages over Head Start: It reaches youngsters at an earlier age, usually during the first year of life. And it works through mothers, to change their parenting style and to add more learning stimuli to the home itself, rather than through a Head Start environment where a child spends only part of the day.

You need only a few simple guidelines when you set out to enrich your child's learning environment:

• The best way to tell if a learning experience or a plaything is appropriate for your child—what psychologists describe as being a "match" for his particular stage of development—is to watch his reactions. It's easy to tell when a youngster—even an infant—is fascinated with learning. He usually stares intently or concentrates with visible interest. Sometimes his whole body seems to become alert. If you are attuned to his learning processes, you can almost sense his brain recording and integrating new data. You can also tell rather easily when he is bored or overstimulated or not ready for a particular experience; he'll turn away, find a new interest, or fuss. An overstimulated baby will often seem to shut out excess noise and confusing stimuli by deliberately turning away and going to sleep. A toddler may suck his thumb, cry, act silly, cling, or whine.

But one of the skills you'll develop as a parent is sensing what your child is ready to learn and how to provide it.

• Your role in your child's learning may sometimes be to teach him directly, especially if you can analyze an activity he is trying to master and break it down into small steps he can handle one at a time. But more often, you can do your child more good simply as a director who sets up a learning environment with the elements he needs to make discoveries for himself and as a coach who cheers him on, gives him appropriate suggestions and feedback, and shares his excitement at his accomplishments.

• You can guard against any possibility of "pushing" your child in three ways: You can learn to detect from his reactions when he is being overstimulated (perhaps by a noisy roomful of strangers), remove him to quieter surroundings, and help him relax. You can avoid insisting that he stick to a task you've chosen when it is clearly too difficult for him and he isn't interested. And especially, you must never let him get the idea you won't love him if he can't perform up to your demands.

• Children learn best in a home where the atmosphere is warm and democratic, rather than cold and authoritarian, many studies have shown. You should make sure your child knows you love him, even when you have to tell him "No" to stop him from doing something he wants and even if you are away from him most of the working day. He should be allowed to make his own decisions when it is appropriate and convenient for you; a toddler can have a choice of whether to wear a red shirt or a blue one (but not to go outdoors without boots when it's snowing) or which game to play before bedtime (but not when he should go to bed).

• In teaching your child how to behave, you should reinforce his good behavior with attention and praise much more often than you scold him or punish him for inappropriate actions. Too often parents, especially those who are away from a child for long periods during the day, pay attention to a youngster only when he is naughty or needs correction. That makes him likely to misbehave even more because he wants attention so much, even if it means a scolding. By paying attention to your youngster when he's behaving or doing something of which you approve, you reinforce that activity and make him more likely to continue to act that way.

• You should help your child develop a positive self-image, by letting him know you consider him an individual capable of overcoming difficulties, of doing hard things, and of being considerate and good. You should avoid ever calling him "stupid" or "naughty" or "clumsy" or implying that he is, or making fun of his mistakes, or treating him as unnecessarily babyish. Children usually can't help but believe the labels parents hang on them and it's difficult for them to act otherwise. If you help your child see himself as capable, good, and caring, you greatly increase the likelihood he will behave as if he were capable, good, and caring.

You should also look carefully at situations in which you feel your child is misbehaving and be sure you have interpreted them accurately. Often your youngster simply hasn't been taught what correct behavior is for a particular situation. (The big, open spaces of a shopping mall may tempt him to start yelling if no one has ever told him it's a place for his "indoor voice.") Or he may lack the coordination and muscle control for something he's trying to do (get himself a glass of milk, for example). It's much easier on both of you if you treat such incidents as opportunities to teach him a bit (how to act, how to clean up a mess) than to scold him for being bad or awkward. He's more likely to learn something. And you'll both feel better about your relationship.

• One of the easiest and most successful ways to stimulate a youngster's mental development is to encourage him to share your own activities and interests. A family that talks about ideas and books with young children usually produces youngsters avid for ideas and reading. And curious, inventive, busy parents who find ways to include their young children in their enthusiasms usually produce enthusiastic, involved offspring.

• It is true that your child must often reach a certain level of biological development before his body and his central nervous system are ready for particular activities, such as walking and talking. Yet these levels have never been established with scientific accuracy, and recent research shows that appropriate stimulation in the environment can interact with the developing nervous system to speed up such "readiness." The traditional "readiness" stages taken as fact in child-care books for so many years can be wildly wrong for individual children. As one educator has suggested, "The only way you can tell when a child is ready for new learning is to give him an interesting chance to do it and see what happens."

• Child care is easier if you take into account your offspring's basic temperament. If you know that your baby is slow to warm up to new experiences, you can often give him time to sit on the sidelines for a while before you expect him to cope with a new situation. If you know he's easily distracted, you can shape his environment to cut down on confusion. If you understand that he's likely to feel scared and uncomfortable in strange situations, you can often plan to give him some loving support until he can overcome his distress.

These temperamental differences in children are likely to persist from infancy on, studies show. In fact, research on animals suggests some of these characteristics may have a genetic basis; it's possible, for example, to breed some animals to increase their innate aggressiveness. Even so, you can modify to some degree the temperamental traits you think might handicap your child—if he's too fearful or has trouble coping with frustration, for example—by gently and persistently responding to him in ways that encourage him to change.

Researchers have identified several measurable temperamental differences in young children. They include: Level of activity—how restless your child seems to be, how much he needs to be constantly on the go, how much he tosses around in his sleep. Sociability—how often your child smiles and laughs and seems to enjoy being with people. Rhythmicity—how easily he fits into a regular daily rhythm of eating and sleeping. Fearfulness—how slow he is to warm up to new stimuli and new situations and how afraid he seems to be of them. Soothability—how easily you can comfort your child when he's unhappy or irritable and how readily he can calm himself down when he's upset. Reaction to frustration—how distressed he becomes when he can't get something or do something he wants and whether he shifts his attention quickly to something else, persists in trying, or just screams. Ability to concentrate—how long he pays attention to a single object or keeps on with an activity when there are no distractions around.

One reason you can be such an effective teacher of your own child is that you can take these differences in temperament into account in the learning opportunities you give him. For example, if you understand that your youngster gets unusually frustrated and gives up too easily when he can't succeed at what he's trying, you can often show him, patiently and gently, how to break the activity down into two or three little steps he can manage. If he seems unusually apprehensive about new situations, you can give him extra emotional support and find ways to ease him into new activities slowly; with a preschooler, for example, you can playact a visit to the doctor or the first day of a new school ahead of time so it won't seem so unfamiliar and threatening to him.

With that general background, here are more specific suggestions for enriching your child's learning environment based, roughly, on the normal progression of development during the first year of his life.

BIRTH TO THREE MONTHS

Helping your newborn baby learn may not seem important when you first bring him home from the hospital. You're too tired. He's drifting in and out of sleep. You're still feeling awkward and anxious about the routine of his care. He's still trying to get comfortable with an immature digestive system—and a whole new world.

But there's a payoff for being aware of what his brain needs right now and finding relaxed and happy ways to satisfy it. He'll be more content and easier to care for—just as he is when you fulfill his need for food. And what he learns will smooth the way for a whole lifetime of learning to come.

One of your newborn's most basic needs is for tactile and kin-esthetic stimulation and providing it for him will probably feel so natural and right to you that you may not realize how much you are helping his brain to develop. Your baby needs to be stroked and patted—when you change his diapers, when you bathe him, when you gentle him back to sleep. He needs to be cuddled close against you, to feel your warmth and the strength of your body against his. He needs to be held upright on your shoulder, his head safely supported by your hand, so he can not only look around, but begin to learn how his body feels in a new position. Rocking a baby is another example of how providing appropriate learning stimuli can also help a baby feel content.

You can also give a tiny baby an enormous amount of tactile and kinesthetic stimuli by toting him around with you in a baby carrier, even when you're doing housework at home. He can listen to your voice, he can see more, he can feel the rhythms of your activity—and the experiences all foster the growth of a loving at-tachment between you.

American infants usually develop a little more slowly during the early months of life than babies in some other cultures—including primitive societies in Africa—because they have less physical con-tact with their mothers, studies show. Too often American babies are kept tucked away in cribs, like invalids, even when they are awake and, like any individual forced to stay in bed with nothing to do, they quickly become bored and fuss.

It's a good idea to place your baby on his stomach for at least a few minutes every day—longer if he enjoys it. This gives him a chance to practice controlling his head and changes his visual per-spective on the world around him. You can encourage him to practice developing his head control by putting a bright object where he can see it if he lifts his head.

You should talk to your baby whenever you are with him, be-ginning the first time you hold him. He'll be comforted by the familiar cadences and rhythms of your voice that he heard before his birth, and his brain will absorb the sounds and patterns of his native language. In turn, you should pay close attention to what he is trying to communicate to you and encourage his efforts by responding appropriately. As you get to know him better, you'll be able to detect a difference in the way he cries when he's hungry or wet or sleepy or hurt. When he begins to babble and coo, almost as if he were talking, you can help him understand the function of language by listening closely and then responding in words when he pauses. A baby's brain seems to require an enormous input of spoken language before it is able to produce language itself, and providing this input over the early years of your child's life is one of the most important ways you foster his mental development.

You should make music a part of your child's life, too, right from the beginning. He'll enjoy gentle lullabies that you sing or simple, clear melodies from a music box or record. By the time he's several months old, your baby will show by his behavior that he recognizes familiar music—even classical records—that he's heard you play many times before.

Even though your baby has little chance to practice seeing before birth, he can see surprisingly well the first day of his life. Even then, a newborn infant shows that he needs and enjoys visual stimulation. In tests made in newborn nurseries, day-old babies consistently prefer to look at more complicated patterns rather than at simple lines and they concentrate longest on drawings of the human face.

The development of the visual centers in your child's brain requires an enormous amount of visual stimulation, neurophysiologists are discovering. Although your infant will spend much of his time drifting in and out of sleep during the first three or four weeks after his birth, he will stay awake longer and pay more attention to his surroundings if there are interesting things he can look at. You should put a mobile over his crib—and change the objects on it every two or three weeks to renew his interest. It should be designed to look interesting from your baby's point of view, not yours. And it should be hung low enough for him to focus his eyes on it easily. There's no need to buy a toy-store model; you can make one yourself and keep changing it to renew his interest.

During the first few weeks of his life, an infant usually lies with his head turned to one side or the other, rather than looking straight up. So a good way to give him extra visual stimuli is to fasten two soft picture frames to the rails of his crib—one on either side at easy focusing distance from his eyes—and slip simple, bright pictures into them, changing them every week or two.

But the most important way to give your baby visual stimuli is to get him up out of his crib when he's awake so he'll have more to look at. You can put him in a safe, padded spot in the kitchen so he can watch you work and you can talk to him. You can carry him around the house with you in a baby carrier—and use a carrier outdoors instead of a baby buggy that buries him deep inside with no view except straight up. By the time he's eight or nine weeks old and has gained some control over his head, you can put him in an infant seat that gives him an upright view of his world.

Gradually, your baby will begin to combine the sensory information he gets from his eyes and ears and sense of touch into new learning. He'll associate the sound of your voice with your face, the tune he hears with the bright music box from which it comes, the fuzzy feel of his blanket with the way it looks. He's ready for the great jump in learning about the world around him that will come soon, when he can accurately direct his hands to reach out and grasp what his eyes are seeing.

THREE TO SIX MONTHS

Now that his body is functioning better and his life is less dominated by an urgent need for food, your baby seems more at home with himself and his world. He can see well at most distances, hold his head increasingly steady without support, and stay awake and alert during the day except for a morning and afternoon nap. He seems comfortable and trustful of the adults around him. His mood is generally upbeat. And he'll be learning so rapidly that you can measure the changes almost by the week.

One of your baby's major physical achievements during this three months is learning to roll over, a skill he's genetically programmed to develop but one he'll acquire more quickly and happily with a little help from you. If you can be understanding about what he's trying to do, patiently reposition him so he can practice his new accomplishment as much as he wants to, and cheer on his successes, you'll be making an important contribution to his learning—and setting a loving pattern for fostering future learning, too.

Your baby needs a place to exercise his new skills—a mat on the floor, a playpen, a crib with room for him to maneuver. But he shouldn't be left for long in a crib when he's awake; he's a growing child, not a convalescing invalid. A playpen is useful only when it puts him in the midst of family activities where there's lots to see and hear and gives him a firm floor for learning to roll over and push up. It shouldn't be used as a place to confine him safely, except in minor emergencies.

An infant seat is useful for your baby when he's three and four months old; it not only gives him a wider view of his world, but kinesthetic stimulation from the change in posture. But by five months of age, perhaps sooner, he'll be strong enough and active enough to tip it over and it should no longer be used. You can tuck him into a baby carrier or backpack, however, as long as he fits and isn't too heavy to tote; along with providing kinesthetic, visual, and tactile stimulation, it helps build a loving closeness too.

Daily exercise-play sessions with your baby also supply multiple learning opportunities. You can invent simple games to play with him, like counting fingers and toes, bicycling his legs gently, and touching parts of his body as you name them for him.

Your baby will greatly expand his ability to learn on his own during these few months when he discovers how to reach out accurately and grasp an object that he's looking at. Conscious control of his hands and the development of eye-hand coordination can be speeded up by several weeks or more—to your baby's great delight—by putting interesting objects within his reach to tempt him. You should hang a few bright, intriguing objects over the crib and playpen, positioned low enough for him to reach them easily. The best choices are those that ring or clang or squawk or move in an interesting way when he bats them with a fist or pulls on a handle or string. He'll activate them accidentally at first. But then he'll realize, in a sudden burst of excitement, that he can cause the action to happen and he'll try it again and again. Discovering that he can deliberately make something occur is one of the first big ideas a baby thinks up for himself. If you're watching closely, you can almost see his mind working on this concept and the pleasure he takes in testing it out.

You can also help your baby develop eye-hand coordination by putting small blocks or toys or colorful objects within his easy reach when he's sitting on your lap or lying on his stomach. He already knows that his mouth is a wonderfully sensitive source of information, and anything he can manage to hold on to he'll try to put into his mouth. So you must, of course, safety-check everything he can possibly grab.

There are other ways you can feed sensory stimuli into your baby's brain through his sense of touch. You can give him a baby blanket and stuffed animals with interesting textures. He'll almost certainly become strongly attached to one particular blanket or animal and insist on having it with him during the day and in his hand when he goes to sleep at naptime and at night. You can put an interesting variety of textures in his hands: pieces of crinkly paper, burlap, velvet, silk, fur, leather, and wood. You can touch his fingers quickly with snow or an ice cube or a slightly warm hot-water bottle and let him stroke a flower or, with careful supervision, pat a friendly cat.

Because your baby is so fascinated with human faces, one of the best visual stimuli you can give him is an unbreakable mirror, arranged so he can see his own face. Simple versions of peekaboo are another way to build on his interest in faces and enjoy your time together.

It's still too soon for your baby to say even a single word. But you should be helping him lay the foundations for speech in several ways. You should talk to him whenever you are with him, using words to comment on whatever he's paying attention to and whatever you are doing. By four or five months, he'll respond with a smile or by paying attention when you say his name, and in another month or two, he'll show that he recognizes several other words you're using.

Your baby's babbling will increase markedly during these three months and you'll notice that he often repeats vowel and consonant sounds again and again, almost as if he were playing with the sounds he's making. You can help him get the idea of what language is all about if you repeat some of the syllables he's been saying when he pauses, then wait for him to respond, and babble back as if you were having a conversation. Once your baby begins to say a few real words, you should stop any form of babbling or baby talk because you must be a good language model for him. It's only useful at this early stage in helping him grasp the concept of speech.

During this period, you'll notice that your baby enjoys repetition and at times almost seems to insist on it. He'll babble the same sounds again and again, watch his hands repeat the same movements over and over, and even try with his elementary body language to persuade you to keep on rocking him or bouncing him on your knee. Repetition serves three purposes for your baby. It gives him practice to help him master basic activities, such as reaching and grasping. It programs his brain with basic information about his environment. And it helps him learn about the consistency of the world around him—that objects always fall down, never up, for example, and that gravity must always be taken into account in moving about. You can help in this learning process by being patient with his need to do familiar things again and again and give him the opportunity to do so.

These months of experimenting with familiar activity also increase your baby's curiosity and drive to learn about new objects and activities during the next stages in life, experts on early mental development explain. The more activities with which he's familiar, the more he'll be intrigued with novelty and with new objects and activities, and the more he's learned, the more he'll be motivated to learn.

By the time your baby is six months old, he will already have laid the foundation for his future learning and begun to develop a learning style. His body is working much more reliably now and more under his conscious control. His vision is almost as acute as an adult's and he is increasingly aware of differences in depth and distance. He's delightfully social, happy with himself and his family, and ready for another big step in growing.

SIX TO NINE MONTHS

Your baby's ability to learn on his own and your relationship with him will change impressively during these three months because he'll become much more adept at handling objects and because he'll begin to move around independently. No longer will he have to stay just where others put him or be limited to what they put within his view or his reach. These heady changes seem to multiply his fascination with learning and his determination to explore every possible facet of his environment with intensity and delight.

One of the most important things you can do for your baby at this age is to let him spend a considerable part of his waking day on a clean floor in a warm, safe room where he can practice pushing himself up on his hands and knees and begin to propel himself forward by creeping or crawling. He should be barefoot and dressed in overalls with padded knees. And you should put a few intriguing playthings—a soft ball or fabric blocks or a toy that makes a noise when batted with a hand are good—within easy reach to lure him on and reward his efforts.

Everything that could possibly be broken, swallowed, pushed over, pulled off, slipped on, or tripped over should be put away. Stairs and doorways should be securely gated. Electrical outlets should be safety-capped and electrical cords put out of reach. The point is to let your baby move as freely as he is able without discouraging "Nos" and "Don'ts" from adults. You want to encourage him and cheer on his efforts to investigate and satisfy his curiosity—and not give him the idea it's wrong to explore and learn by scolding him. You will have to teach him the meaning of "No," the basic rules of safety, and respect for the property of others. But he's too young now to remember your rules reliably and his need for exploration and activity is so urgent that you cannot wait until he is old enough to pay attention to your admonitions.

You can add to the complex sensory stimuli your baby gets from crawling by varying the surfaces on which you let him move, putting him down on carpeted, wooden, and vinyl floors, even outdoors on the grass when the weather is suitable and you can watch him carefully.

Once your baby has experienced the heady freedom of moving about a bit on his own, he'll be increasingly impatient and restive about being kept in a crib when he's awake. It's good strategy from now on to consider him a person who doesn't need—or want—to be in bed except when it's time to sleep. If he associates his crib with sleeping, not playing, it will be easier in the future to coax him to go to sleep when it's time.

Your baby will probably be content to be in a playpen for a few more months—provided it's only for short periods, the playpen is close enough to family activity for someone to talk to him, and there are plenty of interesting toys to handle and experiment with. He may even welcome the handy playpen bars to hold on to when he wants to practice pulling himself up on his feet.

But restraining him more than necessary for safety will curtail his opportunities to learn and that is a steep price to make a baby pay for his parent's convenience.

Playthings are becoming increasingly important for your baby now that he can sit up, see well, and reach out accurately to grab objects that catch his attention. He needs a changing variety of toys and other objects to hold, to chew on, to finger, to pass back and forth from one hand to the other, to bang, push, drop, and retrieve. All of his toys—and the household objects that are equally fascinating to play with—must be big enough so he can't swallow them and at least some of them should be small enough so he can pick them up easily. They should include a variety of textures, weights, shapes, and colors and a few should have raised details his fingers can explore. Your baby also needs playthings he can use in the bathtub, such as sponge toys, boats, and pouring utensils. Objects that are almost but not quite similar—a blue block and a green block, or two red blocks of slightly different sizes—usually fascinate babies of this age. The slight discrepancies—something new combined with something familiar—are a major stimulus to learning for young children.

If you think about what your baby is learning from his toys—and it's the opportunity to learn that holds his attention and makes playthings intriguing to him—you'll have a good guide to the toys to choose. Not only is he interested in those that give him tactile stimuli, but those that let him experiment with cause and effect because they rattle or ring or turn or fit together or pop open when he experiments with them.

There's no need to spend a lot of money on toys, however. Your baby will have just as much fun, or more, with a nest of lightweight plastic mixing bowls, or a small cardboard box with another box inside, or a small pot with a lid and a block or two he can put in and take out.

Once your baby has learned to use his thumb and forefinger in a pincer grasp, he'll delight in pursuing bits of food around his high-chair tray and occasionally getting them into his mouth. You won't be able to feed him neatly in any case, so you might as well give him little pieces of fruit, scrambled egg, vegetables, cereal, and soft toast that let him practice his small muscle coordination and make him feel he's being a bit independent. With some patient help from you, he can learn to hold a small cup or plastic glass well enough to manage his orange juice and milk. But he can't get much food into his mouth with a spoon, although he'll often insist on trying while you do most of the actual spooning in yourself. It may help you to be patient during these messy months if you realize how much your baby is learning—and that the sensory stimulation he's feeding his brain is just as vital to his development as the nourishment he's getting from the food.

Your baby should now be able to recognize several words, usually including his own name, words for mother, father, bye-bye, cookie, and a favorite toy or pet. But he'll still need an enormous amount of language input before he'll generate any output of words himself. You can continue to help by verbally labeling objects to which he's paying attention ("That's your ball," "Toast," "Blanket") and by putting his actions into words ("You're putting the block into the box"; "Your arm goes into the sleeve this way").

You should also talk to your baby about simple cause-and-effect activities that involve him. You can show him how you let the water out of the bathtub, how you flip the switch that turns the lights on and off, how you wind up the music box. And you can set up experiences that help him grasp new ideas. For example, his memory is developing enough now so that he can understand that objects exist even when they are out of sight. You can help him experiment with object permanence by simple games of peekaboo and hide-and-seek and by hiding a toy behind your back or under a scarf and cheering when your baby persists in looking for it.

NINE TO TWELVE MONTHS

During the last three months of his first year of life, your baby will concentrate his energies and efforts into learning to move about independently. He'll become so adept at crawling that he can scoot out of your sight before you can catch up and he can get into dangerous trouble almost while you are watching. He'll learn to climb, too—up a single stair or two at first and then, within a month or two, up onto the sofa or onto the tabletop with the help of a chair or stool.

By his first birthday, he'll have learned to pull himself up on his own feet and to take a few steps holding on to a convenient hand or piece of furniture or even independently. Most babies are so fascinated and delighted with being upright that they work at this learning task relentlessly until they wilt with fatigue or scream in frustration and need to be rocked or soothed or diverted into resting. Some tactful, understanding mothers have even discovered that it's easier to feed a baby or even change his diapers while he's standing up than to persuade him to sit in a high chair or lie down for a few minutes.

You can't do much to show your baby how to crawl or pull himself up to start walking, but you can set the stage for him to learn how himself. That stage-setting role will become increasingly important in your relationship with your child during the next few years and is crucial to his learning. Even though it takes extra work and you have to put away some of your cherished possessions, your baby needs a big, safe space in which he can crawl, pull himself up, and start to walk in safety. He needs your steadying hand when he's ready to shove off from a handhold on the furniture. And he needs you to cheer him on and share his great glee at this major accomplishment.

If you have any doubts at all about your child's innate drive to learn and the tremendous joy it gives him to master a new skill, watching him teach himself to walk should resolve them. No matter how many times he tumbles, no matter how many bruises he gets, no matter how long it takes for body and brain to learn to work together, he keeps on trying. Later on, when he understands language well and is frustrated about some other difficult learning tasks, you can remind him how hard he worked at teaching himself to walk and how he never stopped trying, and that he's just the kind of person who can tackle hard jobs and keep at them until he succeeds.

The safety precautions that were adequate for a crawling baby aren't enough to protect a toddler, especially the type with the instincts of a mountain climber combined with no concept of danger whatsoever. He does need constant, unobtrusive supervision— a job that will get harder and take more energy in the two years just ahead.

Although you can't actually teach a baby physical skills like walking, you can show him a few basic moves that will prevent some tumbles. You can actually move his body through the motions of turning over on his stomach and sliding off a low bed or sofa feet first, rather than risking a fall. You can show him how to back down the stairs if he starts up and can't reverse direction. And if he's learned to pull himself up but not yet how to let go and sit down again, you can gently push him through the motions.

Your baby's ability to use small muscles is increasing now and with it his interest in manipulating every kind of object he can get his hands on. He is using his hands more precisely, often just the thumb and finger to pick up a small item, and releasing what he's holding easily and smoothly. As his concentration and strength grow, so does his delight in learning with his hands. Staring intently, in deep concentration, he'll experiment with holding a block or toy in each hand, then gravely putting one down to pick up a third or banging them together to see what kind of sound he can create.

He's old enough now for a simple game of rolling a ball back and forth to you, catching it between his outstretched legs, and learning important lessons in releasing and pushing and in cooperative play. He'll follow your lead in dropping clothespins into a plastic bottle or little pail and pouring them out to start all over again. He'll also enjoy investigating stacking toys, nesting objects, small blocks to push and stack, fit-together toys, and easy pegboards with big pieces. If you introduce him to the baby in a full-length mirror, he'll be fascinated. If you put several interesting small objects in a shallow box and let him rummage around, you may be surprised at how long he'll spend fingering them and looking at them intently.

What your baby is doing isn't "play" as adults usually use the word—but "play" in the sense scientists mean when they say they are "playing around" with ideas or writers when they "play around" with words. Your youngster is actually teaching himself dozens of important ideas, learning through all of his senses, and creating concepts that he can't put into words but show that he is beginning to understand. He drops a small block into a box and takes it out again—teaching himself about "inside of" and "outside of." He stacks one small block on top of another or beside it and begins to think in terms of "in back of," "in front of," "on top of," and "under." When a big block won't fit into a little box, he tries again and again and gradually formulates the concept of "bigger" and "smaller."

You can't teach your baby these concepts in words, of course. But you can help by making sure he has the playthings in his environment that set him up to learn these ideas by fascinating experiments. When he does seem to grasp a new idea, you can share his enthusiasm and put his exciting new finding into words for him.

Your baby's language is still largely a matter of input, not output, although most babies can say "Ma-ma" and "Da-da" to mean their parents and perhaps a word or two more by their first birthday. Your baby will understand much more of what you say to him now, however. He will probably begin to follow simple instructions like "Wave bye-bye," and "Pull off your socks." If you play a little game of naming the parts of his body as you give him a bath, he'll soon be able to expand the game to point to each one as you ask him to.

Along with friendly talk, you can stimulate your baby's interest in language by sharing with him the fun of simple rhymes and songs. It's also time now to start your child on a lifetime love of books and reading. You should choose a simple picture book with realistic illustrations, wait for a time when you are both relaxed and he isn't in a fervor over walking, cuddle him close, and introduce him to the idea that pictures can represent familiar objects in two-dimensional form and that black marks on the paper can be translated into words. He may not understand all the words you read to him. But he will recognize familiar things in the pictures. If you make reading a regular part of your daily lives, he will make a lifelong association between reading and feeling good and he will have warm, comfortable associations about getting new ideas through books.

Your baby has come a long, exciting, marvelous way in twelve months. Already, the learning opportunities you have given him show up in the rate of his progress and in his eagerness to learn in the future. If he's had optimal mental nourishment for his fast-growing brain, he will generally seem content with life, pleased with himself, and endlessly hungry for new experiences. You may be tired, but watching your child develop so astonishingly fast in the year since his birth should be an unforgettable reward and give you an enormous sense of pride and joy.

SECTION III
The Years from One to Three

"As early as the age of three, striking differences in the intellectual and social development of children can already be observed. Some three-year-olds are alert, curious, highly motivated to learn and highly skilled at creating intellectual stimulation for themselves. They attend carefully to what is going on around them; they eagerly seek out opportunities to learn from others; they clearly enjoy mastering new skills and assimilating new information and often do so on their own without depending on adults to get them started or keep them going. They are pleasant to be with and interesting to interact with because of their zest and responsiveness.

"By contrast, other three-year-olds seem already apathetic and 'turned off.' They flit from task to task, seldom staying long enough with an activity to really learn from it. Or they cling to adults, badgering them for unnecessary attention. Their behavior seems altogether unfocused and unorganized, or if patterned, it seems guided more by habit than by the intention to master skills or to understand or create. The people around these children find it more strenuous and less rewarding to provide learning experiences for them. Their inattention, their apparent lack of interest in learning, irritate and frustrate all but the most dedicated of parents and teachers. And so a vicious cycle starts, which, widening year by year, may envelop the child's whole future.

"Let us follow these children for a moment into first grade. How will the teacher react to their obvious differences in knowledge, skill, work habits and motivation to learn? Typically, within the first few weeks the teacher will segregate these children into different reading groups, math groups, and the like where they will spend a substantial part of every school day. There they will experience very different teacher expectations, standards, and styles of interaction; there they will be exposed to very different sets of classmates, and there they will use very different materials and move at a very different pace. Once assigned to a given group, the typical child has little chance of moving out of it. His performance in such groups will largely determine his academic record in first grade and this record in turn will be the 'objective' evidence on which the second grade teacher will make her decisions about him. And so on, up and out.

"In this way, the differences we discerned at age three cast their shadows well into the future and have deep, cumulative, longlasting consequences."

This particular evaluation of the importance of the years between one and three comes from the late Jean V. Carew, a Harvard University educator. It's based on minute-by-minute observations of interactions between parents and children in their own homes during five sampling periods between the ages of twelve and thirty-three months and the correlations between these activities and IQ scores of the youngster at the age of three.

Even though they are working from different kinds of observations and research data, an increasing number of educators, psychologists, and neurologists are coming to the same conclusion: The time span between the ages of one and three may well be the most critical in an individual's life for the development of intelligence. Major, lasting differences between children show up clearly by age three, but aren't significant at age one. What produces these critical differences in competence and intelligence during these two years are home environment and the specific ways in which caregivers interact with a child, the research makes clear.

Only a few families, perhaps 10 percent, manage to get their children through this two-year span as well educated and developed as they can be, one specialist in early childhood education emphasizes. In part this may be because parents are hurried and harried with other concerns and are at a particularly difficult stage in their own young adult lives. But it's also because child development experts themselves are just beginning to understand the critical importance of this period and to help show parents what their youngsters need so urgently.

9. How Your Toddler Grows

A youngster's first birthday comes amidst a great burst of learning and for most children marks a gradual transition from baby to toddler. During the next two years, your child will essentially complete his growing mastery over his own body; he will be able to walk, climb, run, stoop, manipulate, draw, and feed himself without having to pay much close attention to make sure his brain and muscles work together smoothly. With the dexterity and mobility to satisfy his unbounded curiosity, he will be exploring his environment with an awesome intensity. Now that he is upright and mobile, he will have a new view and a fresh fascination with handling objects of every kind. And once his walking is under firm control, he will turn his attention to language; by the time he's three years old he will understand most of the language he will use the rest of his life, although he won't be able to reproduce all the words himself by then.

By the age of three, it will be quite apparent what kind of individual your offspring will be. Physically, he will have changed from a baby into a child, slimming down, shaping up, eating less as his overall growth slows down from the breakneck pace of the first year of his life. His personality and learning style will seem to crystallize, too, into distinctive characteristics that reflect not only the experiences you provide for him, but his innate temperament and heredity as well. Tommy, you can expect, will throw himself headlong into everything he wants to do with reckless, bruising enthusiasm. Billy, you know, prefers to sit on the sidelines, quiet and observant, until he feels he's ready to take on a new activity and do it well. Betsy will continue to learn on the run, too busy to sit still except when she's corralled for meals. Nancy is more thoughtful, less sociable, but learns just as fast in her own less rambunctious way.

Despite the increasingly apparent differences in children and their rate and style of development, growth between the ages of one and three years still follows some common patterns and occurs in identifiable stages. Here, on the average, is what you can expect to see happening to your toddler between his first and third birthdays, although the age spans are only approximate and your child will probably spurt ahead in some areas and lag behind in others:

TWELVE TO EIGHTEEN MONTHS

It takes several months of the second year of your child's life for him to master the basics of walking, until he can take this form of locomotion for granted and enjoy the delights of being upright and mobile without having to concentrate on every step and change of balance. Now, he still lurches and staggers about, feet wide apart and arms outstretched for balance, his face either grim with concentration or laughing with pride and joy. Even well into the second year of life many toddlers still resort to crawling occasionally, no matter how well they can walk, when they want to get somewhere in a hurry, or just for fun.

But by fifteen months, at least, your toddler will be off and running—usually from earliest morning until he wilts from fatigue at night, except for one long, daily nap. He trots, he climbs. He can walk backward and perhaps upstairs, one foot at a time. He insists on pushing his stroller instead of riding in it. He fights against being cooped up anywhere, not only in playpen or crib, but often just in a parent's loving arms. There's just too much to do, to handle, to explore, to learn about. He's also discovering that he can say "No"—or at least act it out—and now that he can walk easily, he's determined to assert every bit of independence he can muster.

Your toddler's increasing control over the muscles of his hands and fingers makes possible many new ways to explore and have fun by himself and with others. He delights in pushing a ball back to you after you've rolled it toward him. He may try to dust a table with a cloth, to copy you. Given a pencil or crayon and paper, most youngsters will scribble spontaneously. Almost all toddlers can build a tower of two blocks by the time they are eighteen months old; half can pile four blocks on top of each other successfully, although a few can't do so until age two.

Most toddlers enjoy pulling off their own clothes and most can manage to get off at least a shoe, a sock, or a jacket by the age of eighteen months. Most toddlers can feed themselves without spilling much by then, too.

Between twelve and fifteen months, toddlers still spend an enormous amount of time looking intently at objects or "gaining information—visual" as researchers put it. But gradually, their attention shifts from looking at and handling objects to experimenting with the objects and with trying to master simple skills. Your child can probably turn the knobs of the TV set and likes to make the volume blast louder at his command. He can flip the pages of a book, although he may take two or three at a time. He can pull open drawers and cupboards, use a stick to help reach something he wants, unzip a zipper, string big beads on a cord, put pieces into a simple inset puzzle, and fit shapes into an easy sorting box.

Your toddler's growing ability to use his hands, however, combined with his increasing mobility, his drive to be independent, and his insatiable curiosity can get him into trouble or danger unbelievably fast. His urgent need to learn about the world around him still propels him to handle everything he can reach, to poke, to investigate, to push and pull, to experiment, to experience, to try. He'll be harder to keep safe during the next two years, but he'll be more intelligent and attuned to learning by the age of three if he has great opportunity to explore and investigate now.

Most young children don't make much obvious progress in learning to talk during this six-month age span. They seem to be too busy acquiring more control over legs and arms, hands and feet. It's an unusual toddler who can say more than ten words clearly and understandably by the age of eighteen months; these words usually include the names of people in his family, a name for himself, and words like "cookie," "ball," and "no." But most youngsters do an increasing amount of vocalizing during this age span, producing more consonant sounds in their jabbering, and increasingly using gestures and pointing to communicate. Young toddlers enjoy "conversations" with adults and older children, talking earnestly and happily with inflections and speech patterns that imitate adult talk but include few or no recognizable words. Such pretend talk continues to be important, however, in helping a toddler grasp the concept of speech and giving him practice for later on.

Your child's ability to understand what you say is growing much faster than his ability to talk. About half of toddlers can point to at least one part of their body when asked to do so. Almost half can name one or two pictures in a book, and about the same percentage can follow two directions if you give both at the same time.

With his great preoccupation with objects that accelerates after his first birthday (one-year-olds spend 88 percent of their time interacting with objects and only 12 percent with people, a Harvard study found), a toddler also seems to push for a close working relationship with his mother, or whomever his primary caregiver is. He's beginning to figure out for himself that he can use an adult as a resource person to answer his questions, tell him the names of objects in which he's interested, and generally make learning opportunities available that help to satisfy his driving curiosity.

One researcher has described a toddler's incessant following of every move his mother makes as "shadowing." This intense interest also shows up in imitative play and in his eagerness to share his new discoveries and fascinations with her, bring her objects he's playing with, and pull on her to come and see what he's found.

A toddler also seems to work out a sort of social contract with those around him, especially his mother, during this year. He'll gradually come to understand and accept house rules about what he is permitted to do and what not and to figure out the boundaries of acceptable behavior, perhaps even more accurately than you intend. He'll learn what to expect from you in response to his actions—that you'll consistently forbid him to maul the cat or play with the water in the toilet, for example, but that you'll sometimes let him get away with turning on the TV or pulling the pots and pans out of the kitchen cupboard.

EIGHTEEN TO TWENTY-FOUR MONTHS

The next big step in your toddler's development will be learning to talk, one of the most exciting and difficult mental accomplishments of his lifetime. When he's eighteen months old, you'll probably be able to list—or count on the fingers of both hands—the number of words your child can say clearly enough to be understood by those outside of his immediate family. But sometime during this six-month span, you'll probably realize you've lost count of the words he can say, that he's learning new ones faster than you can keep track.

Most toddlers learn to put two or more words together into a phrase or sentence some time before their second birthday, although some do not. But much of what your almost two-year-old says is still impossible to understand—a difficulty that occasionally makes him burst into tears of rage and frustration because he's not able to make you understand what he wants. Sometimes an older child can do better than an adult in interpreting the jargon and deciphering what your toddler is trying to tell you. Often you can help your youngster communicate by suggesting he show you what he wants or by trying to supply him, tactfully, with the words he needs—words he can understand even if he still can't say them himself: "You want to take your teddy bear with you in the car?" "You want me to read you the story again?" "You can't find your ball?"

Your toddler's skill at using hands and eyes together continues to grow during this age period and he takes great delight in manipulating his toys and putting parts of things together. During this learning process, he may concentrate for a surprisingly long time on a toy with fit-together pieces, putting it together and taking it apart again and again. This kind of repetition is an important way your child learns and gives him a feeling of mastery over a small part of his environment which he enjoys. A plaything that gets this kind of concentrated attention from a child makes what some psychologists call a match with the youngster's need for a particular kind of mental stimulation at a particular point in his development.

Your child will continue to gain more mastery over his body in the months before his second birthday. About half of all toddlers learn how to jump in place before they turn two and one out of two can pedal a trike or kick a ball. About half of just under two-year-olds can wash and dry their own hands and put on their shoes. Nearly all can "help" around the house by putting toys away or getting a familiar object on request. Your toddler's walking skills will improve. He will climb more and higher and need more constant supervision. He'll be intrigued with pulling out the contents of dresser drawers and cupboards, with unscrewing knobs, and with investigating everything he can reach. He'll be able to feed himself quite well with a spoon if he's had some practice, but he may not always be interested in doing so.

Toddlers like to climb up and down stairs, still holding on to a hand or railing, but not yet alternating feet as they go. Their finger dexterity is improving rapidly. They can usually pile blocks five or six high now before they topple over, put a lid on a box, unscrew a screw-type toy, and with increasing skill, fit things together, such as a peg into a hole or a ring onto a pole.

Self-help skills are also developing. In the weeks just before his second birthday, your toddler will probably be able to brush his own teeth, or at least make a try at doing so with your encouragement; turn on a faucet; help wash himself when you're bathing him; wipe his own nose with a paper tissue; undress himself completely; and unwrap a small object, like a piece of candy in loose paper. He can climb out of a crib (now is a good time to shift him to a real bed of his own) and will probably nap only once a day. He probably has developed enough control over bowels and bladder so that he can be toilet-trained without much difficulty if you are patient and gentle about it and help him see it as a marvelous new step in growing.

Your youngster is probably using both hands interchangeably now as he plays. But many toddlers are already indicating a clear preference for their right or left hand. It's advisable not to try to train your youngster to be right-handed, despite its advantages in our right-handed world. Forcing, or even actively encouraging, a child to be right-handed when he is naturally left-handed can create a variety of problems later on, most experts agree. By letting his natural handedness develop without pressure, whichever your toddler prefers, you can avoid possible difficulties that show up at school age or after.

The fun a child can have scribbling increases during the second half of his second year and his control over what he's doing improves. As a result of his intense preoccupation with objects, he will probably be able to match two identical things by the time he's two, know the difference between "one" and "more than one," and have a basic idea about ownership, especially about what is his.

TWENTY-FOUR TO THIRTY MONTHS

As your child marks his second birthday and moves into the third year of his life, his increasing control over his body and his physical activities is obvious. It's no longer an achievement that requires his careful concentration to walk, run, climb, squat, stoop, balance briefly on one foot, take off his clothes, or build a tower of blocks. Now he takes these skills for granted and is turning his restless curiosity and learning drive toward other challenges.

The gains toddlers make during this time span aren't in the obvious areas of big muscle development. Instead, they're found in more skilled use of the fingers and hands for small tasks such as drawing and manipulating toys with small parts and in learning more new words and new ways to put words together into new ideas.

By the time they are two and a half years old, three out of four youngsters can wash and dry their own hands and put on their shoes. But fewer than half can yet do a reasonably good job of dressing themselves even with supervision and only one in four can manage to get a button through a buttonhole.

But your toddler's most obvious achievement during this time span comes in talking. Every new word he learns encourages him to keep adding to his vocabulary. Now he's practicing putting words together to make important wholes. He's learning rudimentary grammar, about subjects, predicates, and objects of verbs, mostly by imitating the speech patterns he hears around him: "Bobby do it." "Give Susie ball." "Me want cookie." "Me" is probably the only pronoun he's using yet and when he doesn't refer to himself as "me," he calls himself by his own first name.

So intrigued by language is your toddler now that you may hear him talking to himself as he plays. He'll issue commands to his toys as he handles them. He'll describe to himself what he's doing. And he'll say the names of objects he's playing with to himself as a sort of labeling process, especially if you did it for him when he was younger.

The more your toddler uses words, the more he realizes their great power. In the months after his second birthday, he'll become more adept at issuing commands: "Me go out." "Up, Daddy, up." "More milk, Mommy." He'll also become more aware of the force of his "No"—probably because it's been said to him so much—and he'll use it increasingly during the next several months.

Often your child will say "No" simply because he can't yet manage to put into words what he does want or what he's feeling. If your youngster is screaming "No" when you're trying to put on his shirt, for example, it's sometimes difficult to tell whether he's resenting your help with a task he wants to do himself, whether he prefers to wear a different shirt, whether he's angry at your interrupting his play, or whether he just wants to remind you that he's insisting on a voice in what is done to him. It will be many more months before he can talk well enough to clue you in consistently to his emotions. Until then, you'll have to rely on your knowledge of his reactions and contend with his "No" as tactfully and casually as possible.

One of the most noticeable developments during your child's third year of life occurs in his behavior, his attitudes about himself, his determined drive for more independence from you, and his insistence on more control over his immediate environment. Just when your toddler grows into the stage of negativism that some child-care experts and hard-pressed parents call the terrible twos depends on his own, individual timetable of development, although it's most common about two and a half. It's characteristic of this phase of life for your child to say "No" to almost every-thing you want him to do, to insist on his own way continually, to fight you, kick, scream, run away when you want to dress him, refuse to feed himself, and deliberately ignore rules you are sure he understands.

Some of your toddler's demands and frustrations will seem rea-sonable. He may scream because you try to dress him some morn-ing when you're in a rush; he, however, is determined to dress himself, no matter how long it takes, so he can be free of his babyish dependence on you. Other times, your child may be trying desperately to make you understand something he's trying to say; when you can't comprehend his jargon, he may react with a tantrum.

But other times, your toddler may seem obstinate just for the sake of being stubborn and difficult. He may seem deliberately to seek a contest of wills with you, just to show you he no longer has to let you rule every aspect of his life. It helps to remember that being more independent of parents is a major milestone during the third year of your child's life and that his behavior is really a sign of growth.

You can also expect your toddler to become fiercely possessive about his own toys and clothes about this age. He's been told, "No, that's Daddy's" and "Don't touch, that belongs to Mommy" so often that once he discovers the idea that something belongs to him, he's ready to make an issue out of every possible violation of his personal property rights.

There are several strategies you can use to help ease your tod-dler through this phase—and make family life with your offspring easier. It helps to give your child as few orders as possible, to cut down the temptation for him to say "No" as a way of asserting his independence. A friendly "Let's have a story now before bedtime" or "I'll help you put your blocks away before your nap" is less likely to spark a revolt. There are other ways, too, to avoid a contest of wills. You can let an alarm clock signal bedtime. Or you can lure your child into shifting from play to bed with a ride on Daddy's shoulders, or a race against your countdown, or a surprise under his pillow.

Because your child is so eager to grab as much independence for himself as possible, it helps to let him make as many of his own decisions as you can. If you let him decide whether he will nap with his teddy bear or his stuffed elephant, for example, he may forget to rebel against sleeping. If you give him a choice of blue sweater or green, he may feel that is sufficient acknowledgment of his independence to let you dress him without fussing. By the time your offspring is two and a half or more, you will probably have a good idea of just how you can motivate him and encourage him, so you can avoid many of these common confrontations.

You may have to reevaluate your toddler's need for sleep during this age span or the next. Because you welcome some respite from him during his long, strenuous day, you may be tempted to put him to bed for more sleep than he really needs now. Postponing his bedtime or eliminating a nap may cut down on some of the causes of conflict.

You may also be trying to get your toddler to eat more than he needs or wants. A child gains only about four pounds between his second and third birthdays and his appetite is normally quite small. If you get into the habit of excusing him casually from the table if he refuses to eat and give him nothing between meals except for a nutritious snack at midmorning and midafternoon, you can usually avoid getting into battles over food that can become a chronic conflict between you.

Most toddlers are physiologically ready for toilet training by about their second birthday and it's a good idea to get it out of the way before a child begins saying "No" to almost everything. You can usually tell when your toddler is ready: He's dry when he wakes up from his nap. He can stay dry for at least an hour or longer. He can tell you by some sort of word that he's about to wet or have a bowel movement. And he's aware and uncomfortable when his diapers are wet or soiled.

Then toilet training really isn't any different from helping your child learn anything else new. You get a potty chair or a toddler's toilet seat that fits over a standard toilet. You explain to him that you are going to help him learn to use it, like bigger children and grown-ups do, so he will be through with the nuisance and discomfort of diapers. When he wakes up from a nap or when you think he may be about to wet or have a bowel movement, you put him on the toilet for a few minutes. If he succeeds, you praise him enthusiastically. If he doesn't in a few minutes, or if he gets restless or resists, you shouldn't insist, but try again a little later; often much of the resistance to toilet training comes from children who aren't upset about toileting, but who just hate to be told to sit still.

Once your youngster begins to have some consistent success, you should dress him in training pants, pointing out how much more comfortable they are than diapers and how easily he can manage them himself. You can encourage him to tell you when he needs to go to the bathroom, praise him consistently for staying dry, and ignore any slipups. For most toddlers, it's as simple as that. Recent studies discount completely the old Freudian theory that toilet training is somehow psychologically different from other kinds of learning and they show that rarely do youngsters develop any emotional problems centered around toilet training. If you are used to functioning as a teacher and cheerleader for your child and if he has come to see you as a guide to learning, toilet training will be just one more learning opportunity for him and its mastery another source of satisfaction and pride.

THIRTY MONTHS TO THREE YEARS

At two and a half, your child will probably still seem moody and impulsive. He'll continue to use "No" more than almost any other word in his fast-growing vocabulary. He'll resist bedtime, naptime, dinnertime, bathtime, and most everything else you try to get him to do. He'll play hard and fast until he's exhausted, then collapse in tears or a tantrum when you're trying to finish the shopping in the supermarket or just as you get dinner on the table. He'll pester you for something to do almost constantly and once he learns the word "Why?" you'll hear it almost as often as "No."

Your youngster will continue to grow more independent, although he will often feel more competent than he really is and insist on managing many self-help jobs all by himself before he's completely able to handle them. In the months before turning three, more than half of all children learn to dress themselves with supervision—and one in four can do it without supervision. Hand-washing becomes better, especially if you praise your child for doing a good job. And most youngsters can wash themselves fairly well in the bathtub, although they'd rather play than scrub.

As he becomes more confident of his abilities to be his own person and more skilled in the self-help tasks that make him feel independent, your child has less need to assert himself constantly and he seems able to enjoy his life in a more relaxed way.

As he nears his third birthday, your offspring will be much better at using words. Even adults outside his family who aren't ac-customed to his particular verbal shortcuts and pronunciations will be able to understand most of what he's saying. Almost all young-sters use plurals before age three. More than half are able to say their first and last names. And many are beginning to use preposi-tions and pronouns in their sentences and to talk about feelings and ideas as well as objects and actions. All of this makes your youngster more content with himself and less contentious in his relationships with his family.

For most young children, turning three marks a particularly happy and sunny stage of childhood, a period of calm after the stormy stresses of a few months earlier have been weathered. At almost three, your child is interested in playing more cooper-atively with other youngsters. He's ready for a great variety of experiences outside of his home and for learning in a wide variety of ways. Because his routine physical care is now much easier, you can spend more of your time together in encouraging and sharing his learning in happy and creative ways.

The age of three marks a major transition in your child's life. He is no longer a baby or a toddler, but a preschooler, a child. You have seen him change from the helpless infant he was at birth to the walking, talking, thinking, learning individualist he is at age three. Never again will your child learn so much and change so fast as he has during the first three years of his life. You have already helped your child accomplish what is probably the greatest mental task of his lifetime—learning a language. No other intel-lectual effort he will ever undertake will be as basic or as essential.

If he has spent his first three years in a loving, mentally stimulating home, you have also taught him a joy in communicating, in using words to express his ideas, to indicate his needs, to seek and give information, and to reach out in love and concern in a uniquely human way.

10. How to Encourage Your Toddler's Mental Development

What happens to your child during the second and third year of his life—what kind of home he has, how his parents treat him, the quantity and quality of his learning opportunities—indelibly shape his life. The more scientific and meticulous the data that researchers collect, the more obvious the conclusion becomes: The years between one and three are critical, probably the most important of your child's life.

At twelve months, it's difficult to detect which youngsters will do well and which won't. Developmental and intelligence tests at age one do reflect the effects of loving, stimulating parenting during the first year of life. But the differences between children at that age aren't great or necessarily permanent. A baby's progress at age one does not necessarily foreshadow his future.

By thirty-six months, however, there are enormous, measurable differences between children—usually rather accurate predictors of future development. Already, it's obvious which youngsters are competent and able to cope with their environment and the people around them in socially acceptable ways and which children are not. Already, differences in mental ability are apparent—not only the narrow kind of intelligence measured by formal IQ tests, but in a broad sense that includes creativity, imagination, social adeptness, motivation, inventiveness, and common sense. Already, it's easy to see which children will do well in school and after and which probably will not except, perhaps, with expert remedial help.

What makes the differences? Dr. Burton White, who directed the painstaking, pioneering research done by the Harvard Pre-school Project, and others have identified three general areas that are vitally important:

1. Once a child is able to move around by himself, first by crawling and then by walking and climbing, he needs an environ-ment full of fascinating things he can handle and manipulate freely and safely without constant supervision and restraint. These include not only carefully selected toys, but household objects that can be easily manipulated, opportunities to develop motor skills, and a great variety of fascinating things to look at. Successful par-ents are able to design this kind of enriched, challenging environ-ment and be tolerant of an incessantly curious toddler who is constantly into everything—while still imposing a few firm sanc-tions. They don't hover over their youngster continually, but are generally available in a casual, friendly sort of way to share a child's enthusiasms, to suggest new ideas and projects, and to let a youngster know they consider what he's learning to be important and worth cheering on.

2. Stimulating the development of language is the second major way parents help a toddler to develop optimally. This language stimulus comes in very brief snatches, perhaps no more than a few words or a sentence or two at a time, and is designed to respond to what a toddler is doing or looking at and to relate directly to his interest at the moment. For example, when a toddler sees some-thing interesting or when he gets stuck trying to manipulate a plaything, he may call his mother or go to her. Usually, but not always, mothers of toddlers who are developing well respond by talking to the child about what he is doing, by helping him, by being enthusiastic, or by suggesting an interesting, related ac-tivity. These mothers choose words for their responses that the child already knows, perhaps putting them into a longer sentence than he usually uses or adding a new word or two, to give him a

bit of challenge. The interchange may last no more than ten to thirty seconds. But because the parent's comment is directed specifically to what the youngster is doing, it expands his curiosity, teaches him when he's most open to learning, and encourages him to go on exploring his environment.

Parents needn't be with a toddler all of the time to help him develop well, says Dr. White, who notes that the mothers of some of the most competent youngsters he studied held part-time jobs. They don't have to have had teaching experience or be well educated themselves. They can be affluent or poor, young or middle-aged, married or single. They don't even have to be infinitely patient or always respond to a child seeking attention; sometimes merely telling him to wait a few minutes is sufficient because that, too, helps a toddler learn. But it's the accumulation of countless, immediate responses keyed specifically to a child's level of development and immediate focus of interest that makes a measurable, significant difference in how well he turns out.

3. How parents—especially mothers—deal with a toddler's drive for independence and with the negativism that begins when he can get around actively on his own also influences how well he develops. Parents of bright, competent children are neither overrestrictive nor overpermissive. But they seem to understand and appreciate the forces that are propelling their toddler and continue to enjoy his progress—and him—without great stress or conflict. They are firm and consistent in the limits they do set for their child, but the rules allow him plenty of freedom for exploration and for satisfying his curiosity. They see their youngster's needs as taking priority over fragile home furnishings and meticulous housekeeping. And they can generally shift from parenting a cuddly baby into a somewhat different, more strenuous relationship with a rambunctious toddler without much strain.

Other researchers whose observations and data have led them to the same general conclusions use somewhat different words to describe the role of parents—especially mothers—in helping a toddler develop well through this crucial period. Parents, the researchers say, should function as "designers of a toddler's learning environment," creating a home that is rich in opportunities for a toddler to satisfy his curiosity and to learn. They should see themselves as "learning resources" their child is encouraged to consult dozens of times a day and who volunteer bits of appropriate information specifically keyed to a toddler's activity of the moment. Parents should see themselves as "interactors" who create, guide, and expand a child's intellectual experiences, adding a learning component tailored precisely to their toddler's needs in their everyday experiences together. They should be "facilitators" who help bring the wonders and fascinations of the outside world to their learning child in appropriate ways.

Toddlers who are developing poorly spend much more time in idleness and boredom than those who are learning well, research clearly shows. They spend more time doing nothing; what one researcher called their index of emptiness is high. Their curiosity isn't encouraged and is often thwarted. And they have less opportunity to interact with an approving, loving adult who participates, at least for very brief but numerous intervals, in what they are doing.

It's possible to predict half or more of the variance on children's IQ scores at age three just by knowing their mothers' attitudes, behavior, and ways of interacting with the youngsters when they were toddlers, concludes a study made by Dr. Craig T. Ramey and others at the Frank Porter Graham Child Development Center at the University of North Carolina at Chapel Hill.

Parents whose children do best generally enjoy being parents (at least most of the time) and actively sharing with their youngster his fresh sense of wonder about the world and his relentless curiosity about how things work. They make sure he has lots of opportunities to learn. And they reinforce his efforts at learning with language that feeds him a bit of challenge and offers companionship and encouragement for what he's doing.

A few educators, toy manufacturers, and parents have misunderstood the purpose of this new emphasis on early learning for toddlers. It's not to produce superkids or seventeen-year-old college graduates or adult geniuses by force-feeding facts into the brains of one- and two-year-olds—any more than up-to-date information about nutrition is supposed to persuade parents to force-feed youngsters with vitamins to turn them into pro quarterbacks. The purpose of early learning is not to force but to foster mental development in gentle, loving ways—not only so a child becomes more intelligent, but also happier because more of his genetic potential is realized and more of his innate needs for mental nourishment are satisfied. The best guide to avoiding pressuring and pushing your child is his own reactions to what you are doing.

If you give your toddler the kinds of early learning opportunities described in this chapter, he'll be much happier than if he's frustrated and bored—and so will you. If you help your child learn to talk and increase his vocabulary, he'll be able to express his needs and emotions better and won't be so likely to collapse in tears and tantrums. If you help him develop the dexterity he needs for routine self-help, he'll feel more independent and won't be so likely to scream in rebellion because you have to feed and dress him. And if he is encouraged to come to you to share his discoveries and marvels, you'll be rewarded by having a loving and delightful companion.

The older children get, the more difficult it becomes to generalize about their behavior. Differences in youngsters become more pronounced. The effects of early experiences and environment show up more clearly. Learning styles and temperament become more evident. So the age-level suggestions for fostering your toddler's mental development in this chapter can only be approximations, intended to spur your own thinking and planning for your child, not as inflexible timetables or instruction manuals. You'll probably need to read ahead a bit and perhaps backtrack some to meet the needs and challenges of your particular toddler.

TWELVE TO EIGHTEEN MONTHS

When your toddler isn't engrossed in walking, he's busy exploring everything he can touch and grab with his hands—objects have taken on a fresh fascination now that he is able to view them from an upright position and get to them himself. By experimenting and handling, your toddler gradually learns what objects are light and which ones heavy, what's hard and what's soft. He discovers that a ball will roll but a book will not and that a crayon will roll one way but not end over end, giving him a wealth of sensory perceptions from which he can eventually draw useful conclusions—for example, about the kind of shapes associated with rolling. He learns that a pot makes a noise when banged on the floor, but a pillow doesn't. And to double-check his newly discovered fact—to verify his data as a scientist is expected to do—he feels it is necessary to bang the pot over and over again.

Because he's so intrigued with objects and can learn so much from them, toys are increasingly important during this age span. Wooden stacking rings and simple fit-together toys provide him a sense of mastery and accomplishment, even though he may need some tactful help from you at first in putting them together. He'll learn quickly by watching your hands, if you make your motions slow and easy to follow. He'll be increasingly adept at fitting nesting boxes or bowls together, absorbing the concepts of "inside of" and "outside of" and "bigger" and "smaller" as he does. Small wooden blocks in cube shape interest most youngsters this age. They are easy to carry about and to stack and they teach ideas like "above" and "below" and "beside."

Because he is still so intrigued with walking, a toddler who has become fairly steady on his feet likes to have a push toy he can propel in front of him as he goes. It's even more fun if the toy makes an interesting noise or has other moving parts that your youngster can feel he's activating all by himself.

Before he's eighteen months old, your toddler will probably be able to fit three or four or more shapes into a wooden form board or wooden inlaid puzzle. (You can get extra use out of the wooden puzzles you buy by choosing those that are a bit advanced for your child, then gluing a few of the pieces in place, leaving only two or three for him to manipulate at first. After he's learned to replace these pieces with ease, you can loosen the others and increase the challenge.)

Soft, fuzzy toys are a particular sensory joy for young children. By age one, most youngsters have decisively chosen a soft object— usually a stuffed animal, doll, or baby blanket—as a favorite. Such a toy or object gives a toddler emotional comfort when he's tired or hurt or insecure or lonesome or just drifting off to sleep. And his attachment to it will become even stronger during the months ahead. There's no reason for not allowing a young child to enjoy such a security blanket; it's not a substitute for you or an indication that he's lacking in love or bonding, but you should make sure that the soft, cuddly toys your baby or toddler is given are easily washed and durable.

If you give him a chance to play with them, your toddler will make toys out of dozens of everyday objects in your house. An empty shoe box is fun to push or carry around. Or to cover with a lid that fits. Or to hide a wooden block in. Or to fill with smaller boxes or toys. A large packing crate sets the scene for hide-and-seek or just for simple games of "in" and "out." Cardboard milk cartons that are carefully washed, dried, and covered with foil or contact paper make excellent lightweight blocks for impressive buildings.

A wide-mouth plastic bottle into which little blocks or wooden balls can be dropped and then retrieved by dumping the bottle over makes a good plaything and reminds a toddler that objects still exist even when they can't be seen immediately. Your child probably has a good grasp of this concept of object permanence by now and enjoys seeing it reinforced with the reappearance of objects he can't see for a brief time.

There are other ways you can feed important sensory information into your toddler's brain, too. You can let him play briefly bare-handed in the snow or try to catch a snowflake in a beginning storm. You can encourage him to touch the rough bark of a tree, rub his fingers in fresh-cut grass, feel a prickly evergreen, experiment deliberately with putting his finger in cold, lukewarm, and warm water.

Talking to your toddler about what he's seeing, touching, and doing is another effective way to help his mind develop. You need to supply him with words for his experiences, to say "The bark is rough." "The evergreen needles are sharp," "That water is warm and this water is cold" so that he'll have words to go with the sensations that his fingers are sending to his brain. He won't be able to repeat the words to you yet, but he should hear them from

you now in preparation for the great burst of language development that will come later.

As you continue to label objects in your toddler's environment
in words, you'll find that, increasingly, he comes to you to indicate he wants to know the name of something he's playing with or
interested in. He's learning to use you as a resource, deliberately
trying out a new way of getting information and satisfying his curiosity. That's why it's important that you respond while his interest
is focused on an object or activity. But there's more to what he's
doing than just getting verbal information. During this age span,
your child seems to have a particularly strong drive to share his
discoveries with you, to bring you objects he finds fascinating, to
persuade you to share his wonders and inventions. By getting involved, even for just a very brief time, perhaps even with just a
comment, you show him that you think what he's doing is important and you give his learning efforts a little emotional payoff.

During these months, you should continue to help lay the
groundwork for the big burst of talking that will come nearer to
your child's second birthday. You should continue talking to him
whenever you are with him, feeding him not only words for concrete objects, but for feelings as well. Nursery rhymes, simple
songs, and easy word games help give him the idea that language
can be fun as well as useful.

Reading to your toddler is increasingly important, especially
when it's associated with love and warmth and sharing. Your child
is able to turn the pages of his books himself by now, although not
usually one at a time. He'll like the game of pointing to objects on
the pages as you name them—and reversing the action by pointing
first and asking for your response. A stack of old magazines your
toddler can have for his own can provide fun and learning stimulation, too.

Music is another important way of helping your toddler learn
through his auditory sense. Toddlers quickly come to identify records they hear repeatedly and by the time he's eighteen months
old, he'll have particular favorites—and often be able to identify
the records he wants to hear by almost imperceptible markings
he's able to distinguish.

This is a difficult stage in a child's development for parents, especially for mothers. Although a toddler can understand the meaning of "No" if you use it consistently, you can't be sure he'll remember and obey that "No" every time. So he requires constant supervision. But you don't want to fence him in so much that you deprive him of opportunities he needs for a wealth of sensory experiences. And you don't want to give him the idea that he's a "good boy" or that you love him best when he's quiet and not busy investigating the world around him.

It takes three strategies to widen your toddler's world, help him to become more independent, and still keep him safe:

The safety proofing you gave your home when your baby first started to crawl needs to be reassessed to make sure it keeps pace with your toddler's expanding abilities to run and climb and explore. Your medicine bottles must have safety caps your toddler can't open and should all be stored in locked cabinets all of the time. Many detergents, furniture polishes, bleaches, insecticides, and other substances commonly used in the home are poisons and must be kept where it's impossible for even the most venturesome toddler to reach them. So are some familiar plants, including dieffenbachia (dumb cane), oleander, poinsettia leaves, hyacinth and narcissus bulbs, and mistletoe berries. You should also police your home to make sure that sharp knives, scissors, electrical appliances, cords, and other possible hazards are impossible for your youngster's exploring hands to grab.

Once you've eliminated the dangers from your child's environment, you should be serious and consistent about teaching him the meaning of "No." You do it by telling him firmly "No" when he's about to reach for something you don't want him to handle, such as the controls on the television or a pot on the stove. Then you gently, but firmly, remove his hand from reaching for the forbidden object, hold it for a moment in yours, and repeat "No." If he doesn't take you seriously, you can hold both of his hands against his cheeks so that you can turn his head to look directly at you, repeat "No" firmly, and hold him still for about thirty seconds. If you are consistent in preventing him from touching what he shouldn't, it won't be long until he remembers and reminds himself. Often a toddler will approach something he knows he shouldn't touch, shake his head, and tell himself "No" as he turns away. But he's still much too young for you to be able to count on his remembering all your prohibitions and acting on them every time.

As your toddler gets a bit older, you can add a third step to your safety program by tagging your "No" with a reason that helps him learn more about hazards. "No, it's hot," you can warn him about touching the stove. "No, they're Daddy's," you can tell him about his father's glasses. This technique gives your toddler information he can apply himself in other situations, shows him that you are not just being arbitrary and bossy, and helps him become an intelligent, self-directing individual, not just a product of obedience training.

Many independent-minded toddlers won't accept "No" at this age. But they are usually easy to distract from what they intend to do. And it's easier, usually, to offer an intriguing alternative than to get involved in a battle of wills.

If there are stairs in your home, your toddler is probably fascinated with them at this age and eager to conquer their heights. About half of youngsters learn to walk up stairs during this age span, while others are still using a combination of walking and crawling up. You'll have to keep your steps securely gated when you can't be there to watch your child during this learning stage.

If you have an apartment or ranch-type home, your toddler may be a bit slower to acquire stair-climbing skills for lack of practice. But he may be even more intrigued with steps wherever he sees them and will often insist on trying them again and again, no matter how impatient you get waiting for him. A one- or two-step ladder makes an excellent piece of play equipment from now until well into the third year of life.

EIGHTEEN TO TWENTY-FOUR MONTHS

How and how much you talk to your toddler becomes even more important during this age period and the months between now and your child's third birthday. It can make a measurable difference in his development, for example, if you talk to him frequently, using simple words and sentences about what he is doing and looking at, and answering any questions he asks immediately in the same easy-to-understand way. Your comments and replies don't have to be more than a few words and often you can keep right on with your own activities while you are talking to him; it's the immediate use of words to connect with what your toddler is doing and seeing that counts.

You should also be feeding your child words and ideas and sentences whenever you are with him—naming the clothes you are putting on him as you dress him, talking about what he is eating at mealtimes, giving him words for what he is seeing and doing when you take him with you outside your home. This isn't just an educational strategy on your part. It also increases your child's delight in playing and exploring. One study shows that a toddler will play much longer with a toy when he knows its name—even as simple a word as "train" or "truck"—than with a similar plaything for which he doesn't know an identifying word.

How much a mother contributes to her child's ability to learn language is seldom acknowledged—but it is awesome. Ernst L. Moerk, a psychologist at California State University, Fresno, tape-recorded interactions between a toddler named Eve and her mother for hour-long intervals during the eleven months when Eve was between the ages of eighteen and twenty-eight months. Then he analyzed how much verbal input Eve's mother was actually giving her daughter and found he was able to count "between 600 and 1,700 items of linguistically instructional input per hour." That added up to 300,000 bits of grammar and vocabulary per month and about 3.5 million during this critical year. Learning language was "an almost unavoidable consequence" for Eve in the home environment her mother gave her, Moerk concluded.

The verbal input Eve's mother provided for her was "overwhelmingly rich," Moerk found. It was "linguistically very informative and astonishingly well structured" so that a child could hardly fail to learn grammatical rules from it. If Eve's mother realized her toddler wasn't understanding what she was saying, she rephrased her comments, broke them down into simpler forms, or tried another approach. She used an enormous number of simple language strategies in her casual conversations with Eve (but expressions of disapproval made up less than 1 percent of the total words she said to her child).

For example, Eve was watching TV and said, "Soldier." Her mother glanced at what Eve was seeing and gently corrected her by saying, "Yes, there are soldiers on the TV. There are two soldiers." Eve then repeated, "Soldier." Again, her mother responded, "Soldiers. Uh-huh, two soldiers," in a relaxed, agreeable way without seeming to correct her daughter obviously. In the exchange, Eve's mother provided and then reinforced a small lesson about plurals, softening it with the "yes" and "uh-huh" that seemed to confirm Eve's observations and letting her know she was sharing in her experience.

In another example Moerk gives, Eve's mother told her daughter, "You must put the blocks in the box first, before you can play with the bouillon cubes." Then after a moment, she said, "You can play with the bouillon cubes if you put the blocks back in the box." The two sentences gave Eve quite a challenging message about the sequencing of activities—and about different grammatical ways to convey an idea. Yet in both cases, the language lesson was such a natural part of everyday life that its vital importance is often overlooked.

As you continue reading to your toddler, you can make it a habit to stop occasionally and talk about the pictures in his books and ask him to name the animals and people he's hearing about. This is a good time to point out to him such ideas as "up" and "under" and "beside" as they relate to pictures. Your child will probably want you to read his books to him again and again, long after you are weary of them. But it is important that you do repeat them for him. In part, your youngster is enjoying the attention he gets from you as you read to him. But he also needs to assure himself that the black marks on the pages always form the same words and that the pictures remain the same. He has to have repetition to do a thorough job of learning about the ideas he's getting from books.

Your toddler will enjoy not only imitating words you say, but copying what you do—and this imitation is an important form of learning for him. Most toddlers like to "help" with household tasks, such as wiping a table or floor with a damp cloth, trying to dry plastic dishes with a towel, and putting clothes away in a drawer. This kind of "help" can slow a busy parent almost to a standstill, but it does contribute significantly to your toddler's mental development.

Playing with toys does more than stimulate the development of your child's muscle skills and eye-hand coordination. It also helps him begin to grasp many concepts he won't be able to put into words for years: that two of this kind of block are exactly equal to one of another size, that it's easier to balance small blocks on bigger ones than the other way around, that parts of a structure can be taken apart and reassembled in a different form. Such concepts seem so obvious to adults that it's sometimes difficult to remember that every child must learn them anew. These ideas will seem obvious to your youngster, too, when he's old enough to put them into words—primarily because he's had great opportunity to experience them in operation through his play.

If your youngster has difficulty putting together parts of a toy or puzzle, you can show him how, moving your hands and fingers through the activity slowly and directly. At this stage, he can learn more easily by watching your motions than by listening to a verbal explanation. But unless he's frustrated or angry with what he's trying to do, or seems to have no idea about the possibilities of a toy, it's better to let him make discoveries for himself. It is tempting for an adult to take over a child's activity because a grown-up can do it easier and faster. But such a take-over often interferes with a youngster's learning process.

TWENTY-FOUR TO THIRTY MONTHS

All the tactful, everyday efforts you've made to feed words into your child's mind should continue during his third year of life. Now, increasingly, you'll see the results of your input coming faster and more directly, as your toddler's verbal output jumps.

Now, when you read a familiar story to your child, you can sometimes stop just before the last key word in a sentence or on a page and your child will rush to say it before you do. Now, you can recite a familiar nursery rhyme and wait for your toddler to chime in with the last, rhyming word. Now, occasionally, you can tell your youngster the name of an object and he'll repeat it after you, or try to.

All of this language teaching should be handled as a game and as a routine part of your lives together, rather than as lessons. Your role is simply to be a resource and a guide in your child's determined search for words. You can be happy and cheer your toddler on when he does say a new word. But you shouldn't get into any kind of repeat-after-me sessions and you shouldn't be upset or cross when your youngster can't say a word after you or isn't in the mood even to try.

It's time now to drop any baby words you might have been using with your toddler. These do serve some purpose earlier in helping your baby grasp the general idea that sounds have meaning and that he can create meaningful noises himself. But what your child needs from now on are correct language models to follow. Your sentence structure should be correct when you talk to your child now. And you should aim your conversation at his current level of understanding, plus adding a bit of new challenge—both in vocabulary and grammar—to keep him interested and learning.

Increasingly, your youngster will enjoy playing with words. He'll delight in sharing nonsense rhymes with you, in listening to simple records and to easy songs. Most of all, he'll want your attention in listening to him as he tries out his new abilities at speech. You'll probably find it impossible to give him all the attentive listening he'll crave during the next several months, but what you can provide will motivate him to try even harder to master talking.

This is a good age for rhymes and poetry. Too often, parents offer a toddler only the traditional nursery rhymes, many of which have a catchy rhythm-and-rhyme pattern, but few of which have words with a meaning suitable for youngsters. A few can even be scary for a small child who tries to make sense out of the words (many are actually old English political criticism disguised as nonsense for children to obscure their real purpose). It makes much more sense to give a toddler—whose chief developmental task is to learn language—rhymes with words he can understand and appreciate, along with a beat and word pattern he enjoys, than to limit him to ditties like "Three Blind Mice" and "Four and Twenty Blackbirds."

Playthings your toddler can control—by pushing, pulling, taking apart, putting together, building, dumping, and reshaping—continue to be favorites with two-year-olds. The more a child can discover for himself to do with a plaything, the longer it will hold his interest.

Water has particular play value for two-year-olds and preschoolers, especially when combined with a few plastic containers and pouring utensils. The experiments a young child can make with water are almost endless: He can pour it from one container to another, measure it, stir it, make it splash, note how the temperature changes when an adult adds hotter or cooler water, and how its color alters when a grown-up puts in a few drops of food coloring. He can squeeze water from a sponge or washcloth, stir it into bubbles with a few soap flakes, watch it disappear down the drain. He can observe an ice cube or a handful of snow as it melts into water—and how water can be turned back into ice cubes, but not back into snow.

Sand can provide the same kind of manipulative learning fun for a toddler. It can not only be poured from one container to another and run through a sieve, but can be built into castles and other shapes if there's a supply of water handy. Sand play is easier to arrange outdoors in a sandbox in warm weather. But indoor sand play is also possible, especially in a warm basement with an easy-to-clean floor, if you can find a sit-down sandbox or a stand-up sand table with legs.

Blocks continue to be a basic plaything at this age—and will for most of early childhood. Blocks take on added value for a toddler if they can be sorted by color and/or shape and if they can be fitted together in a variety of ways. As your toddler continues to experiment with blocks, he will discover for himself which ones will balance in what way on others, which ones will roll with what kind of push, and how far up they can be stacked before they topple. You can multiply the possibilities of blocks by showing your child how they can be combined with other toys—hauled about in a little wagon, incorporated into sand play, or used for the rudiments of houses for small dolls or stuffed animals.

With practice, your toddler's eye will become more accurate in recognizing shapes. He will be able to put pieces into puzzles with little wasted motion now, without the trying and changing he did earlier. But he will still get great satisfaction from fitting pieces into their proper places, a kind of self-check or immediate assurance that he is correct and has mastered the challenge. This sense of satisfaction and mastery is one reason a two-year-old likes to repeat an activity again and again.

It is not too early now to introduce your toddler to the concept of numbers. As he takes the pieces out of a puzzle or puts them back, or as he stacks his blocks into a tower, you can show him how to count them. Or, you can simply push one block after another into a pile, counting as you do so. It is important that as you count, "one, two, three, four," and so on, you put the proper number of objects together. You want to make sure your toddler gets the idea that "two," for example, means two objects—not the second object in a series.

THIRTY MONTHS TO THREE YEARS

As your child moves into the second half of his third year, he becomes more interested in expanding his activities outside your home and ready for more contact with people other than his own family. How you handle these opportunities can make a big difference in the ease with which you can help him through the rest of the terrible twos stage and the attitude with which he will approach new experiences as a school-age child and as an adult.

When you take your two-and-a-half-year-old to the supermarket with you, you can plan easy, interesting things for him to do there, rather than try to keep him imprisoned in the grocery cart when the inactivity is making him fussy and frantic. You can tell him that you need his help to find just the right items the family wants and play several different games with him as he helps.

This won't take much longer than it does to cope with a youngster who is restless and fussing while you are shopping. Yet it will give your child valuable learning experiences, let him know you appreciate his growing abilities, and make the trip a good occasion for both him and you. It also helps to set a tone to your relationship—one of friendly cooperation and mutual pleasure in each other. You'll be much less likely to slip into a scolding parent/defiant child hassle if you can find a way to satisfy your child's urgent need for learning than if you equate "being good" with being quiet and try to force him into obedience. You'll feel better about yourself as a parent—and like your child better, too.

Similarly, when you take your two-and-a-half-year-old any place where you expect to have to wait—the doctor's office, a shoe store, a car trip—it helps to take along something interesting to keep his mind occupied. Your youngster isn't old enough to sit still without this kind of aid. An inexpensive children's book you can read to him and talk about as you wait is a good choice. Simple word games work well in such situations, too—and at home when you're busy and your youngster wants your attention. If he is beginning to recognize colors by name—and many children can identify at least three at this age—you can challenge him to point to something red or blue or green. If he doesn't know the names of any colors yet, you can show him something red and ask him to find another object or picture in a book that is the same color. Or you can vary the game by suggesting he find something bigger or smaller or heavier than an object you give him for a starter.

Your child is old enough now for a few short expeditions arranged to stimulate his learning, not just to tag along on your errands. A simple walk around a block can be an adventure if you look for signs of spring: greening grass, buds on a tree, ants scurrying out of an anthill in a crack in the sidewalk. Or it can be a trip to a children's zoo or a farm or a pet store. Almost three-year-olds enjoy taking a ride on a city bus or a commuter train. They can learn from a visit to a bakery, a shoe repair shop, or a parent's office, and enjoy checking out all of the neighborhood parks within convenient distance, a fast-food shop, a greenhouse, and a children's library.

Another good game at this age is to put three or four small items into a paper bag and close it at the top with just enough room for your youngster to put his hand inside without seeing into it. Then you challenge him to pull out each item as you name it, identifying it by feel alone. When he's ready to have the game made more difficult, you can ask him to name several objects in a paper bag one by one, using his fingers alone without any verbal clues at all. You can also let him set up the game for you to play at his direction.

Your child's powers of observation are becoming increasingly acute now and he likes games that make use of them. Easy lotto-type games appeal to many two-and-half-year-olds, especially if you limit the difficulty by giving him just two pairs of cards to match at first, then adding a third set and a fourth as he becomes more adept. You can also play matching games with a variety of other objects: paint sample cards, blocks, spools of different-colored thread, and swatches of fabrics. Once your youngster can match the fabric swatches by looking at them, you can make the game more challenging by suggesting he try to match them with his eyes shut, using only his sense of touch.

Reading to your child should be a daily part of his life—as it should until he is able to read independently at his level of interest, usually about age eight or nine. Reading has many values for your youngster. It gives him input for his increasing vocabulary. It feeds information into his brain, not only about his own environment, but also about the world outside his home. And it adds to his appreciation of the use of words as symbols, laying a foundation for his own learning to read.

But you should choose with care the books you read to him. Small children, who are so eager to explore and learn about their environment, are more likely to be confused than delighted by books of fantasy; fairy tales have much more appeal for youngsters old enough to be well grounded in reality, who can then appreciate the make-believe. Young children are often confused and upset by books which use words they already know but assign them a different, puzzling meaning, such as carelessly substituting "cry" for "yell" ("'Here I come,' the boy cried"). Toddlers who are just getting the idea that pictures in books can represent real objects and actions are sometimes concerned when illustrations show only part of a person and may worry, "Daddy, where's the boy's legs?"

The broad range of toys your child can use and learn from at this age is enormous. Action toys like trike, wagon, scooter, swing, sled, slide, and climbing bars help his large muscles to grow and his coordination to improve. Dolls, dollhouses, puppets, blocks, doctor kits, costumes, trucks, trains, and cars encourage his imagination to grow and satisfy some of his need to imitate adults. Paints, paper, crayons, finger paints, clay, chalk, and marking pens with washable ink stimulate his creative feelings. And simple rhythm instruments such as a small xylophone, wrist bells, finger cymbals, bells, and drum encourage him to participate actively in music you play for him on records or tapes.

But whenever possible, it's a good idea to buy your child real things rather than toys. Real things—housekeeping implements, flashlight, magnifying glass, large-sized magnet, blackboard, simple tools—work better than most toys and give your child what he wants most, a chance to manipulate and experiment with reality.

Some of the frustrations your two-and-a-half-year-old experiences come from being unable to manage simple self-help skills like dressing himself, forcing him to remain dependent on you when he desperately longs to do things all by himself. Dr. Maria Montessori, the Italian physician who started the Montessori school program in the early 1900s, developed some exquisitely tactful techniques and equipment for helping small children through this frustrating stage. Profoundly sensitive to what young children are trying to achieve and to the importance of giving them the self-esteem that comes from real achievement, she developed methods of breaking tasks down into small parts that a toddler could master.

"Who doesn't know that to teach a child to feed himself, to wash and dress himself is a much more tedious and difficult work, calling for infinitely greater patience than feeding, washing, and dressing the child one's self," she wrote. "But the former is the work of an educator, the latter is the easy and inferior work of a servant. Not only is it easier for the mother, but it is very dangerous for the child, since it closes the way and puts obstacles in the path of the life which is developing."

Dr. Montessori, for example, developed "dressing frames" to help children master the basic steps in managing their clothing independently. Each wooden frame holds two double-thicknesses of cloth which can be fastened together in the center in one of a variety of ways—with buttons, snaps, laces, buckles, or zipper. An adult then shows the child, slowly and precisely step by small step, just how the fasteners work and lets the youngster practice as long as he wishes until he has mastered the basic movements necessary to accomplish the task. The dressing frames are available from several commercial sources or can be made easily at home.

You can use the same technique of breaking an activity down into very small components, each of which your child can learn to do, to help him develop some of the other skills he so urgently wants. But you also have to arrange your home so that he has easy and independent access to what he needs. A small child can learn to hang up his own sweater or jacket, if you provide a clothes rod low enough for him to reach and show him how. In a Montessori school, youngsters are taught to spread a jacket flat on its back on a low table. A small hanger is pushed into each shoulder and the jacket is buttoned and hung up.

Similarly, a parent who is attuned to Montessori ideas, either from reading various translations of Dr. Montessori's books or books about Montessori concepts, or visiting a Montessori school, can find many other early learning techniques that make life easier with a two-and-a-half-year-old. For example, most youngsters go through a ritualistic stage at about the age of two and a half when they insist everything be done precisely as they are accustomed, when they won't eat dinner without the same glass, spoon, and cup, or take a bath without a yellow washcloth and a green cake of soap, or go to bed without the door being precisely ajar. This is the time to teach children a sense of neatness and order, Dr. Montessori said. In Montessori schools, youngsters are taught that tasks have a beginning, a middle, and an end and that they must assemble the components they want for a playing/learning activity, use them, and return them correctly to a low shelf where they belong before going on to something else.

This won't work in a home without patient training and without arranging the environment so that a child can reach the materials he wants and put them back by himself. But the effort it takes pays off for both you and your child. In Montessori schools, all the pieces of an inlaid puzzle are marked with a bit of the same color tape and kept in a basket also tagged with matching tape. All the parts of a game are stored together in a convenient box, all of them taped in the same color to make identification easy.

The purpose of helping your child develop a sense of order isn't to turn him into a neatness nerd, but to give him the sense of independence and control over his environment that he so urgently craves and because it gives him satisfaction. For the same reason, Montessori schools teach youngsters very early to pour water, milk, and juice carefully without spilling, to serve themselves and others, and to wash and dry dishes. Montessori educators are quick to turn a routine job into an interesting challenge: "Can you spread the peanut butter all the way into every corner of the bread?" "Can you polish the shoes without getting marks on the paper underneath?" Montessori activities are usually planned to have a self-teaching, self-correcting component that helps children learn by themselves, independent of adult correction, reinforcing the feelings of intrinsic satisfaction children get from what they are doing and learning. This is a good feature to look for when you choose toys and other materials for your youngster.

Dr. Montessori (and Montessori schools) emphasized household tasks—polishing furniture, shelling peas, washing plastic dishes, scrubbing the floor, setting the table—as immensely satisfying activities for young children. But adults must respect what children are doing and take it seriously as work, she insisted. A child should be allowed to do and redo a chore as long as he wishes and an adult should never do it over in his presence, she cautioned.

Toys that encourage pretending along with imitative play are also good at this age and increasingly so during the next two or three years. A child can have weeks of fun with a big cardboard packing box he can turn into a house, a space shuttle, a fire station, or a fort, especially if you make available a few props to strengthen the illusion. A row of chairs can become an airplane, a bus, a train, or a classroom—especially if he's had a chance to see the real thing himself. Or, the pretending can be done on a smaller scale with dolls for central characters and blocks or smaller boxes to make the boundaries of a spaceship, a shopping center, or a castle.

Most two-and-a-half-year-olds aren't completely ready to play well with other children, although those who are in day care or share a sitter with other youngsters may do better than those who are cared for at home. It's quite common, even in day-care centers, for two toddlers to play in the same room, each with his own toys and each watching the other with interest, but without actually playing together.

But as your youngster grows toward his third birthday, his interest in other children usually increases. Play with other youngsters becomes increasingly important, not only because it is fun, but because it gives your child fresh mental stimulation and new ideas for activities and teaches him beginning lessons about cooperation, working together, and sharing.

As your child begins to play more with other youngsters, he becomes ready for toys that are fun to share. It's normal for a three-year-old to resist sharing his belongings sometimes, especially if a favorite toy is involved. One way to make it easier is to explain to your child when a small guest is coming that they will be playing together with his toys. You can suggest that if there are a few special possessions he can't bear to share, these should be put away in advance while other toys are brought out ready for joint use.

At this age, boys and girls play well together, without the segregation by sex that usually comes a few years later. But in their play, boys and girls usually do imitate the sex roles they see around them and on television. Boys will play with dolls, but usually only if they clearly define their role as "daddy" or "doctor." Increasingly, parents can use children's pretend and imitative play as occasions to point out to both boys and girls that girls need not be limited to being mother or nurse or teacher, but can also be doctor, pilot, truck driver, or work at any other adult occupation they choose and that boys, like fathers, now care for children and help with housework.

If you have followed the ideas and suggestions in this book, you have undoubtedly seen your child's innate curiosity and eagerness to learn expand and grow. Not only has he learned an enormous amount, he has also developed a joy and satisfaction in learning that will last him the rest of his life. Now, as he turns three, he is ready to push on into a wider world, ready to learn from a bigger circle of teachers, neighbors, and friends, ready to grow, to develop, to change, to achieve, and to build on the strong foundation you've given him.

 SECTION IV

The Years From Three to Six

IN many ways, real childhood begins at about age three. Your offspring's need for the intensive parenting of earlier stages has lessened. He's no longer quite so dependent on you; not only will he tolerate an increasing amount of independence from you, but he will begin to seek it and to savor it. The breathing space helps you both. Yet, except for an occasional outburst of temper or brief rebellion, your child is still openly, enthusiastically, uncritically devoted to you—as only a young child ever is.

The routine drudgery of caring for a baby or a toddler has lessened now. More of your time together can be spent in more interesting ways. Your child can speak your language quite competently now, although he often adds his own charming inventions—words that aren't baby talk but marvelous interplays of meaning and sound, some of them so fresh and insightful they deserve to become a part of the common tongue.

The great, remarkable gains your child can make during these three years are not only physical, but also intellectual and social. If you have started him off well, if you have been encouraging his brain to develop, if you continue to give him appropriate learning opportunities, you will be astonished and delighted at the range of his mind. In almost the same, relaxed, nonpressuring way you helped him learn to speak his native language, you can show him how to read it—a skill that depends on the same kind of brain development as talking and gives him the same satisfying feelings of competency and mastery over a bit of his environment. With a little thought, you can introduce him to numbers and guide him into some elementary math skills. You can divert his innate curiosity into some simple but quite valid experiments with science. You can spur his creativity and show him how to turn it on deliberately and happily. And you can help him sort a bewildering input of sensory stimuli into some reliable concepts about the world around him, the way it works, and the people in it.

It is even possible, some new research suggests, to deliberately create a family climate and a personal relationship that set your youngster on the road to extraordinarily high accomplishment.

Little of this learning will come automatically to your child. Much of it will depend on the planning you put into his environment and your life together. But these years give you an irreplaceable opportunity to help your child learn one to one, at his own speed, in his own way, without group pressure or fear of failure, in the company of someone he loves and admires. Chances are, you will find your changing relationship with him almost as satisfying as he does.

11. How Your Preschooler Grows

Once in your baby's life you could measure his development by days on a timetable universal to human kind: arms begin to grow on the twenty-sixth day after conception and rudiments of fingers appear for the first time on the thirty-first. After his birth, you could see him change and grow by the week, his environment and temperament nudging him only a little ahead or behind a predictable schedule. Even when he was two, you could check his progress and find much in common with other youngsters also age two and clearly see progress when he reached two and a half.

But now it is almost impossible to set up norms and timetables and write descriptive summaries that hold reasonably true for all threes and fours and fives. By now, the effects of children's encouraging environment and early learning opportunities are clearly apparent and will become increasingly obvious. In planning learning situations and daily life for your child, you will do much better if guided by your observations of him and his responses to you rather than by developmental charts, which generally underestimate the differences in children produced by differing homes and parents.

Physically, the proportions of your child's body will change considerably during these three years. He'll grow leaner and leggier, although his growth in height will be gradually decelerating, along with the slowdown in his gain in weight. He'll probably add about five pounds as a three-year-old and shoot up an average of three and a half inches. By five, even this small increase will diminish to an average of four and a half pounds and two and a half inches for the year.

Differences in the age at which young children develop particular physical skills also increase during these years, almost to the point where norms and standards lose any meaning. One child in four can balance on one foot for ten seconds by the age of three, but another one in four can't until fully five years old. A few children can catch a ball on the bounce at age three, half can do so at three and a half, and a few can't manage the maneuver until they are five. One child in four can draw a man with at least three parts before reaching the age of three and a half, while one in four still can't do so even after another year and a half. One four-year-old in ten puts six parts in a drawing of a man, half do so by five, and some still don't when they are fully six.

The same wide differences show up in language testing. Half of three-year-olds understand prepositions well enough to move a block behind, under, in front of, or on another object when asked to do so, but one in ten can't do it at age four and a half. Half of preschoolers can pick out which block is red, green, blue, or yellow by age three and one in ten still can't manage it at almost five. At three and a half, one youngster in four can define words like ball, lake, desk, house, banana, curtain, ceiling, pavement, and hedge, but one in four can't do so even when they are fully six.

Some children develop a vocabulary of about twenty-five thousand words during these years; others may know only a small fraction of that total. An increasing number of preschoolers are learning to read with considerable pleasure and are able to extract much more information and meaning from the world around them than other children by the time they start their formal schooling. The old assumption that a child had to be six years old—or at least have a mental age of six—was obviously incorrect. Learning to read, like many other intellectual skills, depends not only on the maturation of the brain and central nervous system, but on appropriate opportunities for learning that are in the environment.

Age-related stages of behavior are much less easy to identify during the years between three and six than they were earlier in your child's life; they, too, depend heavily on previous experience and environment. Parents used to be told that three-year-olds are happy and well-adjusted, that three-and-a-half-year-olds are rebellious and irritable in almost a rerun of behavior at two and a half, that four-year-olds are active and exuberant, that five-year-olds are sunny and cheerful, and that five-and-a-half-year-olds are difficult and disorganized.

Some parents do see some of these age-stage patterns in their children. But many do not. And the concepts are much less useful during this age span than they were much earlier in your child's life when his activities and learning were much more dependent on physical and neurological development than they are now.

You can expect your preschooler to be much more interested in playing with other children than he was before he turned three. Assuming that he has opportunities for supervised play with other youngsters, he'll learn to take turns and share (although he may angrily or sulkily refuse to do so at times). He is ready to go to a half-day nursery school or join an organized play group for a few hours a day; he'll need some group experiences before he starts his formal schooling.

Your preschooler will be better able to control his emotions and express his feelings in words rather than in whining and tantrums now that he is older. He may be able to understand and respect some of your feelings, too, if you share them with him.

Your child is capable of enormous mental growth during these three years—in language, reading, math, science, creativity, and social relationships. But it's development that can't be plotted specifically on a universal growth curve because it is so highly dependent on your stage setting, your planning, and your participation. The amount of enrichment you have already provided your child, the kind of life you share with him now, and the opportunities for learning you deliberately arrange for him will determine a big part of what he is like when he is six—and thereafter.

12. How to Increase Your Preschooler's Intelligence

Every few years, a new study is published that attempts to trace back into the lives of famous, achieving adults to find the roots of their abilities, to identify factors in their early childhood that predisposed them to greatness or genius later on, in hopes of garnering useful advice for a new generation of parents. Most of these reports aren't really research at all, but a collection of anecdotes. The selection of the adults included is sometimes haphazard, a mixture of people of genuine ability and those who are merely celebrities. And the studies are retrospective, depending on recollections that may be distorted by the lens of time.

These reports always show that the early lives of children who grow up to be famous are marked by a home rich in sensory and intellectual stimulation and by parents—especially mothers—deeply and actively involved with their children. In one such book, *The Roots of Success*, Dr. Cynthia S. Pincus, of Yale University, and her colleagues wrote:

"We've seen that most of our superstars were unremarkable as babies and that their backgrounds vary so much as to be inconclusive. So beyond admitting that genes play a part, we want to talk about what was striking: the evidence of what mother can contribute to raising an achiever from a very early age. Almost without exception, the mothers of our superstars took a very intense and serious interest in the child, observing and nurturing his or her talents and abilities early. Beyond cuddling and loving, they watched to see how the child responded to music, pictures, building blocks. . .

"This type of early interest crossed all socioeconomic backgrounds and always involved the mother, sometimes the father or other relatives. Instead of a group of gifted child prodigies, what we found was a group of gifted mothers. Consistencies that didn't turn up in the backgrounds or development patterns of the survey children did begin to emerge in the responses and attitudes of their otherwise diverse mothers. Basically, this gifted mothering seemed to rest on a deep commitment to the child from the beginning which was sustained throughout the child's upbringing. The mothers were also consistent in not laying their aspirations on the child, but rather in encouraging his or her own bent, often in what seemed self-sacrificing ways."

Dr. Pincus and her associates found that these gifted mothers had high expectations for their children. They shaped and enriched their home environment. They were intensely involved in childrearing during their offsprings' early years. They were enthusiastic about their youngsters' early accomplishments. And they helped them to develop their own motivations and encouraged them to want to achieve for their own satisfactions.

Somewhat the same findings emerged from a much more extensive and scientific study by Dr. Benjamin Bloom, the University of Chicago professor of education and former president of the American Educational Research Association. Dr. Bloom and his associates did considerable research on the lives of twenty-five of the top achievers between the ages of seventeen and thirty-five that they could identify in each of six different fields: research mathematicians, concert pianists, Olympic swimmers, tennis players, sculptors, and neurologists. The researchers talked for hours with the achievers themselves and with their parents and teachers. Although they had originally expected to find that these highly skilled and talented people had shown exceptional promise as young children, which in turn led to their receiving special training, this wasn't what they discovered.

Instead, the rich, encouraging, motivating environment came first, Dr. Bloom's data showed, and the children developed their ability and interest because their environment enthusiastically fostered it. The pool of talent among young children seems to be much greater than we have assumed, he suggested. But it almost always takes the right kind of parents to help the talent bud and flower.

What the parents of these extremely successful achievers did to produce such excellence in their offspring followed a typical pattern, according to Dr. Bloom, with some variations because of the particular kinds of talent involved.

When the children were very young, their parents surrounded

them with their own enthusiasms for a particular endeavor: for sports, for music, for art, or for intellectual activity. This interest was a natural part of the youngsters' lives, something they customarily saw their parents doing, although their father and mother were generally not outstanding in the field themselves. None of the parents pushed or pressured the children to achieve at an early age, Dr. Bloom found. Instead, they encouraged the youngsters to play, to experiment, and to enjoy the activity with them as a routine part of family life. When they began to show even a small sign of skill, the parents gave them lots of happy praise and loving attention.

At an early age, parents also passed on to their children their own work ethic, a feeling that they must do the best of which they were capable—and a motivation to train and practice hard that would make them favorites of their teachers later on. These parents were also alert to catch signs of talent in their youngsters and not only encourage it but reward it with enthusiasm, praise, and sometimes with gold stars or candy. The children were well aware of how to please their parents, and they learned not only because of their own growing interest in the activity, but because they liked the praise and attention it earned for them.

As signs of special ability began to emerge, parents started their children off with a private teacher, perhaps a father (as was usual for the future mathematicians), but more likely a local individual who worked with the youngsters on a one-to-one basis and used the same combination of praise and rewards and made practicing and lessons seem like fun. The parents continued to be closely and enthusiastically involved with the children and their special interest.

(The pattern by which extraordinarily talented individuals continue to develop goes beyond the age limits of this book. But generally, the children moved on to a more skilled teacher who recognized their unusual ability and strong motivation and encouraged it, again making them feel special with attention and praise, as did the parents who continued to be closely involved with the lessons. Gradually, it became evident that the youngsters had enormous potential and their teachers began to urge them to reach for the top.

(Then, somewhere between the age of ten and early adolescence, the children became hooked by the fascination of what they were doing and the satisfactions they were getting and started to devote, by their own choice, an increasing amount of time to training and lessons, pushing everything else in their lives into second place. Family dedication to these offspring also grew, as lessons became more expensive and took more time. In the final stage, in middle or late adolescence, parents helped the teenagers to find a master teacher or coach who encouraged them to even greater dedication, helped them reach an even higher level of skill and performance, and showed them how to gain entry to the top ranks in their field.)

These studies are not described to urge parents to begin trying to make geniuses or Olympians out of their children when they are only preschoolers. Many parents are uneasy about channeling a child's choices at such an early age, even though Dr. Bloom and his associates found no evidence of outright pressures in the success stories they collected. The purpose here is simply to show what an enormous influence parents have on a young child—deliberate or inadvertent, by design or neglect, for better or for worse. It's to suggest how much can be taught to a youngster by sharing enthusiasms, enriching the home environment, and providing interesting opportunities to try new activities. And it's to remind parents that the most effective way to teach and influence a child is by praise and attention.

Even if you have no interest or intention of trying to help your child become a genius or a star performer—and this book is not intended to suggest that as a goal—there are several major areas where you can help your child make significant advances in learning that will benefit him not only in the first grade but for a lifetime.

Your child's mind works so fast, his attention span is still so short, and his need for a wealth of sensory stimuli is so great that he learns best in small increments and usually on the go. Often, he is most open to new teaching when his attention is already focused on an event or an object on which an alert parent can build. One of the great advantages of helping your preschooler learn at home is that you can adapt your teaching to his immediate interests, you can shape the way you are teaching to fit his learning style, and you can work with him on a one-to-one basis which is the ideal condition for teaching.

The following will give you a brief idea of what kinds of learning a preschooler is capable of and some suggestions as to how you can go about helping. How much your child actually does learn between the ages of three and six will depend on how much he has already learned as a result of earlier enrichment, how much time you can spend with him, how closely you can cue your teaching to his interests and learning abilities, how much time he must spend with a sitter or in a day-care center, and what happens to him when you are not with him.

LANGUAGE

Your child's most stupendous intellectual achievement is learning his native language—and his command of it will increase explosively and delightfully during these three years. His vocabulary will expand enormously if you provide a rich verbal environment for him. And he will learn to use complex grammatical structures—subordinate clauses, tenses, every part of speech—not only to report information and convey ideas, but to seek new knowledge and to express emotions.

But your child's language acquisition depends on you—to an extent parents rarely realize and for which they are almost never given credit by teachers. Unless you speak well, your child will not. If your vocabulary is sparse, his will be, too, at least until he has had considerable schooling. If some of your grammatical patterns are incorrect, his will be, too, when he starts to school and perhaps for the rest of his life.

Nothing illustrates better the effectiveness of home environment on a child's learning than the acquisition of language and the critical role parents play—deliberately or unwittingly—in their child's development. Your youngster will learn to talk just from the role model you provide in the course of your lives together. But there is much you can do to increase his vocabulary, expand his verbal abilities, and help him enjoy the fun and power of language, if you are attuned to the way language is acquired during these years and the level of stimulation your child needs.

Your youngster does not simply imitate what you say. Although he probably doesn't realize it consciously, his brain is absorbing hundreds of thousands of bits of verbal input, sorting them into what seem to be patterns of word formation and grammar, forming concepts from these observations, and creating new words and sentences based on the concepts he has formulated all by himself. This is intellectual activity of the highest kind—and irrefutable evidence of the power of the young human brain to think, conceptualize, and create.

If you listen closely to what your child says during these years, you'll notice he uses words like "mouses" and "sheeps" and "foots." These are not charming little mistakes he makes because he is just learning to talk—although most parents treat them that way. They are, instead, evidence of intellectual ability at work. Your preschooler, of course, has never heard you or anyone else use words like "mouses" or "sheeps" or "foots." They are the end products of great, if subconscious, thought. Your child has come to understand, first of all, that certain parts of speech are nouns that are the names of objects. Nouns can be altered slightly to indicate quantity, and the way the English language conveys the idea of more than one is to add an *s* to the end of a noun. After he has figured out this rule for himself, he then applies it to new words—including those that are exceptions to the rule in the English language.

Your child will make other "mistakes," too. He will probably say things like "Daddy goed to work" or "Suzie runned fast." Now he has deduced that English contains parts of speech called verbs that express action or state of being and also convey a sense of past, present, or future time. He has observed that the way to make a verb past tense is to add *ed* to it. And he has applied the principle he discovered all by himself to words in which the English language makes an exception.

What's remarkable is that a young child never puts *ed* on the end of a noun, only a verb. What's also curious is how difficult many children find it to learn about parts of speech and verb tenses when they study grammar in sixth or seventh grade. Even though they figured out the grammatical rules all by themselves before they were old enough to start first grade, they often have trouble trying to learn the same rules when they are taught in a formal classroom at a much older age.

All of the ways you have already been using to help your child learn language continue to be helpful during the years from three to six. You should continue to talk companionably and extensively to your youngster whenever you are together, aiming your vocabulary and sentence structures at his current level of understanding and just a little beyond so that he is continually challenged to learn more and to absorb new vocabulary from the context in which you are using unfamiliar words.

Small trips and excursions, books you read to your child, TV shows you watch together, and other shared experiences help give your youngster new things to talk about and expand his vocabulary. Most youngsters enjoy knowing some big, multisyllable words—Potawatomi, tyrannosaur, hippopotamus, crocodile, geranium—they can roll around on their tongues and use to impress their friends. But it's more fun if they have been to a zoo, a museum, or a greenhouse and have a good idea of what the words really mean.

When your child does make a mistake in grammar or uses a word incorrectly, you shouldn't try to correct him directly; it isn't necessary and it could blunt his intense drive to learn and make him self-conscious and insecure about experimenting with words. All you need to do is casually use the correct word or sentence structure in your conversation: "Oh, Daddy went to work?" or "Where was Suzie going when she ran fast?" This provides corrective feedback without criticism and gives your youngster the information he needs to continue learning.

You should expect your preschooler to stumble over what he's trying to say, to start and stop and start again when he's talking, to use what speech therapists call disfluencies, especially between the ages of about two and a half and four. A few parents worry excessively about these hesitancies and repetitions and are afraid that their child has begun to stutter. But many speech experts theorize that a child turns into a stutterer when parents pay too much attention to the disfluencies and hesitancies that occur normally in all youngsters as they learn to talk. By calling attention to the problem and making a preschooler overly conscious of what he is trying to say and the physiological mechanism by which he produces speech, a parent may actually cause the disfluencies to increase and eventually become a habit.

It helps to listen to your child with the courtesy and consideration you would give an adult guest in your house, no matter how bored you are with three- and four-year-old talk. That way your youngster won't feel he has to rush through what he wants to say for fear of losing your attention. It also helps to structure your conversation so that you tactfully supply your child with words he may be struggling to say. The vocabulary of most preschoolers— especially the three- and four-year-olds—still isn't nearly adequate to express their thoughts, and by casually supplying your child with the words he needs, you keep him from stumbling so much.

You should expect your youngster to mispronounce a few words and one or two speech sounds even at age five or six. But you needn't be concerned unless his speech is almost completely unintelligible to others outside the family after he's reached age four.

As your child's verbal abilities grow, you can encourage him to appreciate more of the marvelous uses of language. You can talk to him in ways that make him think, that let him have choices, that require him to plan ahead, that suggest how he can avoid mistakes. You can show him how to put some of his feelings into words and use words to help him understand the emotions of others.

You can play games with language ("What word can you think of that starts with the same sound as 'Tommy'?" "How many words do you know that end in the same sound as 'trike'?") not only because the games are fun but because they tune your child's ear to phonetic elements that will be useful when he begins to read. And you can make it a shared pleasure to try to think of just the right word to describe a sunset you are watching together, or the feel of a fabric, or the scent of a flower, or the feeling of wind in the face on a blustery March day.

By holding conversations with your preschooler—when you are driving the car, waiting in the supermarket checkout line, doing housework—as if he were one of your most fascinating friends, you help him become just that sort of companion.

Your child is old enough now to begin selecting some of his own books. Trips to the children's room of the nearest library should be a regular part of your lives. And you can buy him books of his own for special occasions or celebrations. You'll find a much wider selection of books to read aloud to your youngster now that he's a preschooler and you should be helping him appreciate the variety: books of information that answer his questions and expand his horizons, books of poetry for pleasure, stories that are deliberate make-believe. You can show him how reading can enrich his life—by reading to distract him when he is ill, by stretching out on a blanket in the park to read on a summer day, by cuddling up to read together on a blustery night, by reading to ease the boredom of a long car trip, by reading as a reward when you've finished a job together. Your child also needs to see his parents reading extensively—for pleasure and for information.

By the time he's three, almost certainly by four, these happy experiences with books will probably have given your youngster a thirst to learn to read by himself. Then you can show him how, in a relaxed, nonthreatening way attuned to his interest and style of learning and for his great satisfaction.

SECOND LANGUAGE

So capable of learning language is a young child's brain—far more so than the adult brain—that your youngster can learn a second language while he is learning English, with almost no apparent effort, without mixing up the two languages, and with great lifelong benefit. He merely needs to have the second language spoken to him consistently, naturally, frequently, and well by someone in his environment who speaks the language like a native.

The most successful strategies for bringing up a child to be bilingual are variations of the total immersion plan recommended by most language learning schools. For example, one parent will speak only to the child in English and the other in a second language—beginning in the earliest months of life, if possible. The child simply comes to understand and accept that if he wants something from his father, he uses one set of words; if he's talking to his mother, he uses different ones.

If both parents can speak the second language fluently, there are other possibilities. Dr. Wilder Penfield, the late McGill University neurologist who studied the bilingual children of Canada, said bilingual parents could set aside certain areas of their home—perhaps the upstairs, or the dining area—where only the second language is to be spoken. A grandparent your child sees regularly could provide the second-language input. A preschooler can also get a good start at bilingualism in a day-care center or nursery school where the second language is used exclusively or from a neighbor who talks frequently with your child in the second tongue.

What's essential is that the second language be a natural, routine, daily part of your child's environment so that he can absorb it as naturally as he does English—and so that he must use it to get what he wants from the adult who is speaking the second language. This adult must use the second language easily and fluently. The plan doesn't work if you are trying to learn the French or Spanish or German yourself, or if you substitute language records for routine daily conversation. Attempting to teach a second language in elementary or nursery school a few words at a time once or twice a week is a waste of time.

What Dr. Penfield called "the mother's method" of teaching a second language actually programs neurons of the brain with the basic phonemes, or smallest speech sounds of the language. As the child grows older, he uses the basic language units he has built into his brain as the basis for rapidly expanding his vocabulary. His brain also forms interconnecting links between these language units and other neurons used in other kinds of thinking and brain activities, so that your child can then actually "think" in his second language as well as in English without using a mental process of translation.

However, according to Dr. Penfield, after a child has reached the age of ten or eleven, his brain can no longer be programmed so easily with the sounds of a new language. An adolescent or an adult who is trying to learn a second language is forced to use the languate units of his original tongue that are already built into his brain. No matter how intelligent he is or how hard he tries, he will always speak the second language with the accent of his mother tongue.

A child exposed routinely to a second language develops a kind of switch mechanism in his brain that allows him to shift automatically and effortlessly from one language to the other when appropriate. An adolescent or an adult is too old to build such a switch mechanism—or conditioned reflex—into his brain, Dr. Penfield said, and must depend on a less efficient, more difficult translation process in turning from one language to another.

One mother, Nancy Gail Reed, described her experiences in raising a bilingual child like this, in the *Christian Science Monitor:*

"On the day our daughter, Genevieve, was born, I began speaking French to her. Her father spoke English to her. The result: At 4½ years old, she chatters away normally in her native tongue and can carry on a pretty decent conversation in French. The learning process has been delightful for all of us.

"I was one of the early '70s European wanderers, another kid wearing jeans and a backpack. If there was anything I learned from all that seemingly pointless wandering around and 'rapping' in youth hostels with kids from other countries, it was that most European teen-agers spoke at least one language other than their own. I decided that, if I ever had children, I would give them this gift of language.

"I had a B.A. in French, had spent time in Europe, and had afterward remained involved in some teaching of French and in various cultural activities that allowed me to speak French. But before I began to teach French to Genevieve, I had to learn an entire new vocabulary. After all, who ever heard of sandboxes and swing sets in a class on Sartre?

"The process of bringing up our baby bilingual has been fun. I kept a diary of her early words, most of which were French. Later, as she expanded her world, her English slowly advanced beyond her French. Today, though I continue to speak nothing but French to her, she usually responds in English.

"For a while, I worried that she couldn't speak French, but could only understand me. Recently, however, a young American-French couple whom we'd met when they were hitchhiking paid us a visit. The French wife spoke at great length with our daughter about a book in French that Genevieve had been given. Genevieve didn't hesitate to tell her visitor the story of Titou, a little boy who was making his house all by himself because his parents were busy. Her conversation included words like hole, screwdriver, saw, wood, and spy—all in French. I had to keep myself from dancing around the room."

Genevieve's mother suggests getting children's books for a bilingual youngster in the second language. She also advocates finding other people in the community—perhaps foreign students—
who will talk with your child in the second language.

"Total immersion is the only way," Mrs. Reed explains. "You
may encounter a lot of opposition to your plan and you are going
to need a fair amount of confidence. People may tell you that your
child will have trouble with English or will lisp or will feel left out
of the play group. However, if you've ever met any offspring of
non-English-speaking parents, you know that it will all come out
just fine."

It's curious how much evidence has surrounded us for decades
about the astonishing language learning abilities of young children
and how blatantly we have ignored it. We have known—at least
since the nation's founding—that when immigrant families came
to this country, their young children learned to speak English
much faster and better than the parents. No matter how motivated or how bright the adults, they never learned English as well
as their offspring, and when they did speak English, it was always
with the accent of their native land.

Yet even with this ample and obvious evidence, we have made
it educational policy not to introduce a second language in school
until high-school level—or perhaps junior high in some pro-
gressive communities. Yet by this time, the built-in neurological
ability of the brain to pick up a new language easily is almost
gone. Most of us who learned a second language starting as a high-
school requirement—even if we studied it two years or more in
college—lose it quickly after the last exam in the course. Yet
many adults who learned a second language in their home as
young children—even if they haven't used it for decades—can still
recall it automatically and speak it adequately if they need to.

Dr. Penfield suggested that the mental stimulation involved in
learning a second language as a young child also seems to foster
other kinds of intellectual development as well; he noted that the
bilingual children of American immigrants and the French-En-
glish-speaking children of Canada often do unusually well in
school and after. This observation, however, depends on both languages being spoken fluently and well. Studies show that children
from disadvantaged homes where neither English nor a parents'

native language is used correctly may indeed be handicapped when they start to school.

Unfortunately, for families where neither a parent nor an at-hand grandparent speaks a second language well, giving a child the gift of bilingualism seems almost impossible. The nation has lost a priceless heritage in not preserving and handing down from one generation to another in families the languages immigrants originally brought to this country.

READING

The same language learning abilities your preschooler's brain possesses also make it easy for him to learn to read—to understand written words that reach his brain through his eyes just as he does spoken words that reach his brain through his ears. He can also learn to reproduce words with his hand, using pencil and paper as well as through his vocal apparatus. It is his brain, after all, that is making the connection and deciphering the symbolism of the words—whether they come in the form of auditory or visual signals, from the ear or the eye.

In fact, it's probably easier for a four- or five-year-old to learn to read at his own pace, in his own way, in his own home, when he's in the mood to learn, with the loving one-to-one help of a parent than it is for a six-year-old to try to learn in a classroom at the time the teacher selects by a method the school system decrees should be used, and at a pace that may be too slow or too fast to be comfortable.

Today, hundreds of thousands of preschoolers are learning to read—taught by parents, by nursery-school teachers, by TV programs, by psychologists in experimental programs—and by six-year-old sisters who like to play school. (In one study of California youngsters who were able to read when they entered first grade, the largest number were taught by a sister about two years older in the course of playing school.) They are learning to read by phonetic methods, by sight-word methods, by the Montessori method, by writing-first methods, by eclectic methods, and by no method at all—using newspaper comic strips, first-grade primers, sandpaper letters, how-to books, and homemade assortments of paper and pencils, blackboard and chalk.

What makes almost any sustained teaching effort successful is the enormous language learning capabilities of a young child's brain—and the loving involvement of a parent.

There are at least five good reasons for making the effort to teach your preschooler to read: (1) His brain may be better attuned to language acquisition in any form before age six than after, so he will learn easier and better. (2) Bright children profit from the added mental stimulation of reading; studies show that preschool readers did better after five years of schooling than bright youngsters of similar IQ did after six years of school. But children of average or lower IQ benefit even more by being introduced to reading at a slower, individual pace at home, without the pressures to keep up with a first-grade class, according to research. (3) Reading expands a child's command over his environment and his ability to extract information from his surroundings. (4) It's fun for your child and cuts down on "Mommy, what can I do now?" (5) Parents who have tried it say it is enormously satisfying. As one mother put it, "It's like seeing my child take her first steps toward me, only better." Commented another, who had taught her son to read, "It is a true pleasure to be able to be his parent in this new adventure. It definitely enhances the parent-child relationship."

Considerable research over the last two decades shows clearly that the best and easiest reading method is one that begins by teaching phonics, not sight words, so that a youngster gets the idea first of all that words are simply sounds written down that he can learn to decode. Once a preschooler has learned to recognize several sounds and a few phonetic rules about how to combine them, he should be able to begin reading words independently. Then, he'll pick up the rest of the common letter and letter-combination sounds and his reading will take off. (If you weren't taught to read by a phonetic method, you may be surprised to discover how logical and sensible such a system is. The *Chicago Tribune* put together a series of daily comic strips parents could use to teach preschoolers to read at home using phonics and ran it for thirteen weeks in 1964. Parents tried it with so much success and delight that it was repeated in 1969 and 1973 and reprints are still widely used. The *Tribune* has received thousands of enthusiastic letters from parents whose offspring have learned to read joyously and well with its help.

The easiest way to teach a preschooler to read is to make a game of letting him in on the secret knowledge of how to decode the written letters and words he can see into sounds he can recognize. You can write a letter *m* for him, for example, tell him it makes the "m-m-m-m-m-m" sound he can hear in the word "Mommy" or "milk" or "meat," and practice saying it with him. You can point out the *m*'s in the stories you are reading to him and on signs you see in the supermarket, and you can ask him to dictate words you can write for him that start with the *m* sound. Your child may want to try writing the letter himself, or you can write it for him on a blackboard or with crayons. Montessori schools use letters cut out of sandpaper several inches high and pasted on a cardboard square to help youngsters learn the shape of the letter by involving their tactile sense as well as eyes and ears.

During these early lessons, you should not tell your child the name of the letters he is learning, only the sounds the letters make, because you want him to automatically associate the letter with its sound, not its name. He can learn the names of the letters later on. You shouldn't spend more than two or three minutes a day showing him letter sounds, unless he pushes you to teach him more. You shouldn't push him or urge him to sit still for a lesson, or act disappointed if he doesn't seem interested. All you need to do is act as if you were telling him a fascinating, powerful secret.

Next, you should teach him several more of the consonants that make a consistent sound, such as *t*, *d*, *h*, *s*, *p*, *b*, and *l*, in the same low-key way, praising him happily when he shows interest and being matter-of-fact when he doesn't. Then you can tell him that there are a few magic letters—magic because they help other letters roll up into a word and because every word must have at least one. You can explain that these magic letters can make more than one sound—their own name and at least one other slightly different sound—and that sometimes he may have to experiment, trying one sound and then another to get the word just right.

After you have taught him the short sound of *a*—as in the word *at*—you can begin helping him learn whole words, rolling the consonant sounds he already knows with his first vowel in words like *dad* or *hat*. This stage may take several repetitions, over several days, until he finally gets the idea of rolling the sounds together quickly into a word. When he does, you can show him how to substitute other consonant sounds he knows for those in the words he has learned to make, for example, words like *sad, bad, pad,* and *had,* or *sat, bat, cat,* and *pat*. You can play the same kind of games as you teach him the short sounds of other vowels: *e* as in *egg, i* as in *it, o* as in *pot,* and *u* as in *put*.

As you go along, you can make up simple games to play with your child, to give him practice in recognizing the letters and words you've taught him. For example, you can draw up a bingo card, using sixteen to twenty easy words or letters, and let him mark them with raisins or jelly beans as you call them out. When he gets "bingo," he wins the markers to eat.

When you teach your child the remaining consonants, you will have to explain that *g,* for example, sometimes makes a hard sound, as in *get,* and sometimes a softer sound, as in *germ,* and that *c* sometimes sounds as it does in *cat* and sometimes the way it does in *cent*. If one sound doesn't make sense in a word, you can tell your child, he'll just have to try the other. Most youngsters accept this idea as a way of using an alternative decoding strategy, not as mere guesswork.

Next, you can show your child how two letters stick together to make a single sound, in common digraphs like *sh, ch, ph,* and *th*. And you can tell him that as a shortcut he can read certain groups of letters together because they almost always sound the same: *ight, atch, ank, ing, er, aw,* and *oy,* for example. By adding a consonant he already knows to these groups of letters, he can quickly expand his reading vocabulary with words like *sing, ring, king, fight, sight, light,* and *night*.

After your youngster has become comfortable using the short vowel sounds, you can teach him the long ones—the sounds vowels make when they say their own name. And you can tell him one easy rule: When there are two vowels together in a word or when only one other letter comes between them in a short word, the first vowel says its own name and the second one keeps quiet.

Then you can show him how this simple rule dramatically expands the words he is able to decode: *ate, eat, meat, neat, coat, cute, bite, boat, note, goat.* There are a few common words that don't follow phonetic rules a preschooler can easily learn and it's easiest just to tell your child that these words break the rules and he will have to learn them one at a time. Such words include *said, shoes, there, to, very, where, you, could, were, friend, one, pretty,* and *says.* Most youngsters rather enjoy the idea of words breaking rules and they don't have any trouble learning a few sight words.

It is important, however, not to start out teaching your child with sight words—as do some primers and most of the easy-to-read books written for young children. It's unnecessarily difficult for a youngster to have to learn every new word as an individual shape, a word at a time, without the help of phonetic decoding clues. Although sight-word advocates say they are teaching children to "read for meaning," or to use "context clues" in deciphering new words, what they are really doing is encouraging a child to guess. By starting with phonetic decoding principles, you can help your child get the idea that reading is a logical, orderly process, a puzzle he knows how to go about solving, and you help him get into the habit of thinking logically about reading and writing. Of course, after your child has sounded out a new word several times, you should urge him just to say it right off if he recognizes it. Sounding out letters is a decoding strategy for learning; with practice, your youngster will automatically shift into reading the way good readers do—in whole words and phrases.

After your child has gotten into the habit of associating letters with sounds, you can teach him their names. You can also help him learn the alphabet with the familiar alphabet song that's set to the "Twinkle, Twinkle, Little Star" tune.

As soon as your preschooler has begun to sound out a few words, you should fill his life with interesting opportunities to read. You can write him notes. Encourage him to read signs to you. Ask him to look for products with names he can sound out when you are shopping. Print name cards for familiar objects in your house. Write stories and letters at his dictation for him to read back. Let him read sounds and words to you from the TV screen.

If you weren't taught phonics yourself as a child, you may want to find some phonetic primers to use as a guide to the basic principles your child should know. Usually parents find they don't have to work all the way through advanced phonetic rules with a preschooler before he is reading happily on his own with only occasional assistance.

It's important to remember that the reading instruction you give your preschooler should be considered a fascinating game he and you play by choice, not a lesson he must do to get your attention and approval. He may need to have a sound or a word presented to him several times before he remembers it; this shouldn't be a surprise when you recall how much verbal input he had as a baby before he was able to produce a word himself in speech. Some authorities on early reading theorize that if young children have as much exposure to words in written form as they do in speech, they would learn to read at about the same time they learn to talk. Both spoken and written words are symbols that are fed into the brain by electrochemical impulses and interpreted by the brain; in theory, it should make little difference whether the original impulses come via the eye or the ear. Reproducing words should actually be easier with the hand, which a child can monitor with his eyes, than with all the complex coordination of vocal cords, lips, throat, and breathing that is necessary to talk.

Even if you are able to give your child only a small start at reading before he begins school, it will benefit him enormously. You will be setting him up to succeed in first grade and giving him not only self-confidence but logical tools to use in going about further learning. Studies show early readers aren't confused if teachers use different reading methods than parents. Early readers are more likely to do well in school later on. And they have been encouraged to acquire one of life's most useful pleasures at an age and in a way that made it a game rather than an assignment.

MATH

Even if you are the kind of adult who suffers from math anxiety, you can give your preschooler a useful introduction to some essential mathematical concepts and operations—again in a way that makes math seem like an absorbing game rather than something he is forced to do by classroom pressures later on.

You begin by teaching your child the numerals from 1 to 9 and helping him understand in concrete ways what the numbers mean. If you just let him learn to count by rote, he may confuse the concept of quantity (five children in a set, for example) with the idea of order in a series (the fifth child in a line). He'll grasp the concept of quantity more easily if you move the correct number of checkers or small blocks or big buttons into a group as the two of you count together.

You can write out a set of numbers from 1 to 9 on large index cards and paste the correct number of gold stars or red hearts on each card, or draw the right number of circles or squares or rabbits or smiling faces. Then, your child can play matching games, lining up the correct number of checkers or buttons to equal the number on the card. As he becomes more adept, you can give him a new set of cards with just the numbers for him to use.

Next, you should introduce your preschooler to the number zero, making sure that he understands zero is a number. It's not the same as "nothing," as your child will have to learn when he works with larger sums. In the number 705, the second digit is zero. If it were nothing, the number would be 75.

To give your preschooler practice, you can conceal two checkers in one fist and keep the other empty and ask him to choose one and tell you the correct number when you open it up: two or zero. You can also play simple math games: "How many apples in the bowl?" "How many forks on the table?" "How many dinosaurs in the sink?" "How many stuffed animals in your bed?" "How many Indians riding horseback in the bathroom?"

You can usually find wooden inlaid puzzles that have cutout numerals with a corresponding number of dots or pegs or other objects that can be removed; these are particularly helpful to a child because they are so easily self-correcting and give him independent practice in number concepts. Montessori schools use several elegant devices for making number concepts concrete and self-correcting, some of which you can adapt for use at home. One is a box with ten sections numbered from 0 to 9. (An egg carton with two sections taped over is a good substitute.) A preschooler is given forty-five pennies, dried beans, or buttons to distribute correctly in the sections.

The index number cards and buttons (or beans or beads) can also be used to give your preschooler concrete experiences with the idea of "odd" and "even." This time, after he has counted out the correct number of buttons to correspond with a number card, you can show him how to arrange them in pairs. If the pairs come out even, the number is "even"; if not, the number is "odd."

If you make a second set of number cards and get more buttons or beans, you can use the same kind of teaching strategy to help him play with the concepts of "equal," "more," and "less."

Introducing your preschooler to simple addition and subtraction is also easy with number cards and buttons. You start your child off with two small numbers which total less than 10, helping him lay out both number cards and buttons for, say, 4 and 5. Then, he combines the buttons into a single pile, counts them, and finds the matching number card. As a final step, you can show him how to use the number cards and + and = signs to write out what he has done: 4 + 5 = 9.

Subtraction is just as simple to learn, as a reverse sort of operation, using a − sign. Your child will need lots of practice with both operations until he's comfortable doing them.

To teach your preschooler the rather difficult concept of the place value of numbers, you need 200 small objects you can conveniently fasten together in groups of 10. Popsicle sticks you can buy at a craft store or tongue depressors from the drugstore can be rubber-banded together by 10s. Buttons can be tied together in strings of 10. Or sticky-backed tape with a small, repeatable design can be pasted on a strip of cardboard in a row of 10. Montessori schools use golden beads wired together in strips of 10 and in squares of 10 strips that make 100. Cubes painted to resemble 10 squares of 100 are also available to give children a concrete sense of what the number 1000 means. You also need 10 sets of number cards.

Now, you teach your child how to write the number 10 and to count out the right number of buttons or popsicle sticks to match the number cards 1 and 0 that you place together for him to make 10. You point out to him that when two numbers are written together in that way, the first one means the number of groups of 10 and the second one the number of single things. Then, you can help him lay out other two-digit numbers and arrange the corresponding number of groups of 10 and individual objects; 21, for example, would be two 10-units and one single; 43 would be four 10-units and three singles. As you go along, you can teach him how to count by 10s and the correct names of the numbers up to 100.

Your child may need considerable practice before he develops a comfortable understanding of place value. Again, it helps to play simple games with him, for example, asking him to set up for you the two-digit numbers you call out at random for him, using both number cards and the 10-units and single objects. For another game, you can write a dozen two-digit numbers on single slips of paper and put them into a small paper bag, then challenge your child to shut his eyes, draw them out one at a time, and set up the 10-units and single objects they represent.

After your preschooler is comfortable with two-digit numbers, you can go on to show him three digits, linking together 10 of the 10-unit stacks of sticks or strings of buttons to demonstrate concretely what 100 really means. If your preschooler continues to be intrigued, you may want to round up enough sticks or buttons or sticky-paper designs to put together ten 100-unit packages so that he can actually produce any number up to 1000 in concrete form. In Montessori schools, sometimes, a child will line up enough 10-bead strings in a long row to make 1000, putting together the correct number cards beside them at intervals so he can keep track of his accumulating total. Montessori schools have enough beads, bead strings, and cubes so that children can construct any number up to 9999 and can add, subtract, and divide four-digit numbers.

Now your preschooler should be ready for another difficult mathematical idea: carrying and borrowing. This time, when you give him a problem in addition to solve, it can be one with a two-digit answer: 5 + 6, for example. As a first step, your child should assemble the number cards and corresponding groups of 5 and 6 single objects, say the popsicle sticks. Then the next step is to combine the two piles of sticks to make 11. Next your youngster should lay out the number 11 with his number cards. Now, you point out to him that this number really means one 10-unit package and 1 single popsicle stick and have him trade in 10 of his single sticks for a package of 10. So he ends up with a 10-unit and a single stick.

It may take several weeks of playing occasional adding games that require carrying before your child feels he has mastered the idea. Then you can reverse the process and show him that when he wants to take away a number in which the digit in the singles place is larger than the digit from which he is subtracting, he will have to trade in one of the 10-units from the 10s place to get enough single objects so that the operation can be carried out. You'll find that the process is much easier to demonstrate to your child than to explain. In Montessori schools, preschoolers often add and subtract four-digit numbers that involve carrying and borrowing.

It helps a child enormously in understanding the function of numbers and basic mathematical operations if he can also see them in concrete form and manipulate them tangibly. Once he gets to school, he'll learn to add, subtract, multiply, and divide by memorizing number facts as shortcuts. But he'll have a much better idea of what he's really doing than children who just learn arithmetic by rote.

Four- and five-year-olds with a bit of experience with numbers usually enjoy playing games commonly considered appropriate for older children, such as Sorry, Parcheesi, and bingo. A child's desire to play with adults and to win usually provides a strong motivation for him to learn to count and recognize numbers. Dice can also make a good math game; you or your child simply rolls the dice, then he writes down the numbers they represent, and adds them up, using the cards and sticks if necessary.

If your preschooler is interested in money or confused about why you get money back when you buy something, you can adapt some of these strategies to help him learn about monetary values. If he understands about "equal," you can help him construct monetary equivalents: matching five pennies with one nickel, ten pennies or two nickels with one dime, five nickels or twenty-five pennies or other combinations with one quarter, and ten dimes or a hundred pennies with a dollar. If he understands place value, he can learn that a penny is a single object, a dime is a 10-unit, and a dollar is a 100-unit. Having a small allowance to spend for practice also encourages a preschooler to learn about money.

SCIENCE

Scientists start, essentially, as children whose relentless curiosity and insatiable drive to learn have been bolstered by specialized knowledge and focused in a specific direction. Whether or not you ever progressed past high-school chemistry, you can do several things to nurture the innate scientist in your preschooler and to encourage the questioning, exploring, manipulating, testing, experimenting nature with which he comes equipped.

For example, you can sensitize him to the everyday marvels and small miracles of chemistry, physics, and biology around him and share his fresh sense of wonder about what he sees, hears, touches, and figures out. You can show your child how to watch for signs of spring in the chill of March. Keep track of a twig as it buds and unfolds into a leaf, turns color and falls. Try to count the stars as they come out on an August night when it's too hot to sleep or a December twilight when the dark comes before dinner. Look for a bird's nest. Watch for bees and butterflies. Scan the skies and try to guess whether they mean rain or storm or shine. Grow peas in the backyard or a narcissus bulb on a windowsill or mold on bread.

Take a walk together and keep tabs on how many bicycles or roller skates or red coats or strollers you see or how many smells you can smell or how many sounds you can identify. Look for bugs and count their legs (a hand magnifying glass is a magical tool for a preschooler). Visit a dinosaur's bones in a museum. Set out a dish to catch the snow, bring it inside, and see how fast it melts. Watch for seeds and speculate on how they travel. Observe the principles of physics in operation in a swing or a teeter-totter on the playground.

Along with a sense of wonder, another gift you can give your preschooler is a scientific attitude. Often, he'll ask questions that can lead to simple scientific experiments: "Why is the mirror in the bathroom all foggy?" "Where do flowers come from?" "Why does the toy duck float in the bathtub and the soap doesn't?"

Most libraries have books of science experiments intended for elementary-school children. But many of the activities are suitable for preschoolers with adult aid. There are dozens of simple experiments you can rig up for your child to try using just air, water, and ordinary household utensils. Your child can spend a fascinated half hour experimenting to see what floats and what doesn't, and trying to figure out why. You can help him understand the rudiments of evaporation and condensation and appreciate the power of the air that floats toy ducks, gives lift to balloons, and can be blown through a bubble pipe or straw. Growing things make good science projects, too, if your child isn't too impatient to wait several days for some results. Large dried beans, radish seeds, birdseed, and other fast-growing seeds can yield at least a dozen experiments on the effects of water, sunshine, temperature, and time on growing things—even if you have no larger place to garden than a windowsill or a sunny table corner.

What's important is the scientific attitude you can encourage your preschooler to take toward experiments. When you begin, you can talk about what you are trying to find out, how you are going to set up an experiment to get an answer, what things you should be looking for. After the experiment, you should review together what your youngster observed, why he thinks it happened, and whether the same thing would occur again if he tried it a second time.

Science experiments won't answer more than a small fraction of the endless, relentless questions preschoolers like to ask. "Why" usually replaces "no" as the most-used word in a child's vocabulary when he turns from a toddler into a preschooler and often becomes an attention-getting whine rather than a serious attempt to get information. Nevertheless, if you can give your child some interesting help in answering even a fraction of his questions—even if you field them yourself or look with him for the answers in books or other sources—you'll help his mind to grow and encourage him to keep learning.

It's even more important to encourage a daughter's scientific interests than a son's. Too many girls are still closed out of careers in science—and their considerable rewards—because they are made to feel long before high school that girls just aren't good at science and somehow aren't supposed to be concerned about it.

Yet research clearly shows girls have as much innate scientific aptitude and interest as boys before social pressures subtly turn them off. One great advantage of helping your preschooler learn at home during these early years is that you can catch and build on these innate interests and aptitudes before your child is influenced by peer pressures and obsolete sexist assumptions of others.

CONCEPTUAL THINKING

Whether all theorists on child development realize it or not, young children are constantly formulating concepts, sorting out and trying to fit together little bits of information, sensory impressions, and observations they have accumulated into an understandable picture of the world around them. Some of the concepts they form, consciously or subconsciously, are right. (It hurts to fall down, so it's best to avoid doing so if possible.) Some are delightfully off track. (Anyone who goes to the hospital comes home with a new baby.) Some can stunt development if they are not corrected. (Women are weak, men are strong.) Some are emotionally destructive. (Daddy doesn't live here anymore because I was bad.) And some are downright dangerous. (Anything that comes in a bottle is good to drink.)

Too often, a child's conceptualizations are misinterpreted as deliberate fantasizing rather than highly creative attempts to make sense by piecing together little bits of reality. So adults often deliberately feed youngsters more fantasy ("Oh, did the nasty floor come up and hit you?" "Is Mr. Wind trying to freeze your fingers?") when what preschoolers crave is solid, relevant facts. Even when young children play pretend games, they try to reconstruct reality, to play that they are daddies and mommies, or astronauts or cowboys; they play house and reenact what is for them the realities they have seen on television. Only when they have a firmer grounding in reality—at age six or seven or older—do most children fully enjoy and appreciate fantasy.

There are three reasons parents should be aware of the kinds of concepts a child is forming—not only about the physical world but about social relationships. Forming concepts is a handy way to organize random bits of information so that it begins to make sense. For example, a child who has an accurate concept of air as a reality can put together observations—about wind, beach balls, balloons, and sucking juice through a straw—into meaningful context. So helping your child form accurate concepts helps him learn more efficiently.

A second reason is that much of your child's behavior, just as yours, is based on his developing concepts of how and why things happen. For example, a child who has some concept of how and where cars and trucks move in streets and how traffic flow is regulated by stop signs and lights will be less likely to dart off the curb after a ball—and will be better able to take care of himself when he's old enough to go to school alone—than a youngster who just follows orders because he's afraid of a spanking.

The third reason parents should be aware of the concepts a child is constructing is that he is often mistaken—not because his thinking process is faulty but usually because he lacks sufficient data to form accurate conclusions. These incorrect concepts, however, can have unhappy consequences. For example, a child who believes that her father left home because she was a naughty girl is likely to behave quite differently from a youngster who has at least a little understanding that the complex reasons for his parents' divorce had nothing to do with him. A four-year-old girl who notices the differences between her body and a boy's and concludes she has lost a vital body part isn't likely to feel the same about herself as a little girl with a more accurate, if rudimentary, idea of how boys and girls differ physically.

Preschoolers formulate so many concepts and revise them so often that it can be difficult for parents to know when their children have some worrisome misconceptions. This is particularly true of young children who watch inappropriate television programs. Cartoon shows rarely disturb even young children, studies show, because they are clearly not a representation of reality. But soap operas, in particular, can cause emotional upsets in youngsters because they seem so real and it is easy for children to read the social pathology of the characters into the routine activities of their own family. One study found that sometimes school-age children who watched soap operas for a week or longer when they were home from school sick became so upset about what they were seeing that their illness was prolonged.

There are several things you can do to help your preschooler develop accurate and useful concepts. One of the most important is to listen to what he talks about, so you can understand the basic ideas he's developing and detect any misinformation he may have picked up. If he's wildly off track, you can look for ways to set up new experiences he can use to reshape his thinking. If your child is confused about where babies come from, you can find books in the library to give him some background explanations. You can visit baby animals in a zoo or a pet store. There may be an exhibition in a nearby science museum that shows how babies grow inside their mother. And you can talk, discreetly, about a family you know that is expecting a baby.

A trip to a parent's office may help correct some highly imaginative ideas a child may have about what a mother or father does at work. A visit to a dairy or a bakery or a pick-it-yourself orchard or a shoe repair shop or a neighbor's garden can provide useful data for concept building. So can watching a new building under construction and talking about what's happening. (Why is there such a big hole in the ground? Why are machines used to dig it? What part of the building is put up first? Why? How do the workers know what to do?)

Playacting is another useful way to feed a child information he needs for accurate concept formation. You can act out in advance with your child what will happen when he takes an airplane trip, starts to school, goes to the dentist, or must be hospitalized. Trying out a role before he actually has to take it on in public gives a preschooler practice in figuring out how to behave, helps correct any mistaken ideas he may have about what is to happen, and lets him have a chance to deal with his fears on a basis of reality.

It's particularly important to make sure your child understands what's real and what isn't on television. You can begin by talking about the programs he watches and identifying them to him as news that shows what's actually going on, as made-up stories being playacted by actors and actresses in front of a camera, and as commercial messages that try to get someone to buy something or do something. When your youngster sees an actor being shot in a Western movie on TV, you can talk about what a good job of pretending he is doing. When the shooting is an accident or part of an armed confrontation in a foreign country, you can explain to him what is occurring and express your sorrow about the reality. The average youngster is witness to an estimated fifteen thousand killings on TV before he's through high school, and your child needs some active guidance from you to keep what he's watching in perspective. You don't want him to be callous to killing, but neither do you want him to become excessively fearful and distrustful of other people.

Your child will see tens of thousands of televised commercials during his childhood, and preschoolers, especially, need assistance in understanding what commercials are in learning to react to them as an informed and wary consumer. You can explain to him how you yourself check out the advertising claims made in a commercial before you buy a product, and you can help him do the same with a few items that catch his attention. He's going to be the target of a lifelong barrage of commercial messages and needs assistance early on in sorting them out and evaluating them.

If you can manage it, it helps to take a four- or five-year-old to a TV studio where you can watch a program being filmed. Later on, you can suggest to him and a few playmates that they set up a pretend-TV studio from which they can "broadcast" real news programs about what is happening in their neighborhood, act out make-believe dramas, and produce convincing commercials for products from your kitchen shelves.

Preschool children can understand a surprising amount about such vast subjects as geography, history, ethics, sociology, and morality, given an appropriate introduction, studies show. Observers who have sat quietly in the corners of nursery schools listening to children and taking notes on what they talk about list scores of subjects and ideas that catch their attention. Rather than assume your preschooler isn't capable or interested in big ideas and sweeping concepts, it's better to look for ways to introduce them to him in a meaningful way.

Many four- and five-year-olds, for example, can grasp the idea of what a map is and how it works—and with it a sense of geography. You can begin by helping your youngster draw a map of his room on a sheet of wrapping paper, marking off the location of bed, chair, bureau, closet, lamp, windows, door, and toy shelf. Then, you can spread a big sheet of wrapping paper on the floor and together map out your block, sketching in the streets, intersections, buildings, driveways, empty lots, and other features, perhaps using blocks to construct the houses and toy cars to make traffic on the streets. Once he grasps the idea of how maps represent reality and has some concept of scale, you can try mapping the familiar streets of your community or the drive to grandmother's house, or a weekend trip you make. Many four- and five-year-olds can put together an inlaid wooden puzzle map of the United States and enjoy having pointed out to them where cities and states they hear talked about on TV are located.

Most preschoolers lump together anything that happened in the past—from a grandfather's childhood to cavemen and dinosaurs—as somehow occurring in the same "olden days." One way to help your child develop a better idea of time and the relation of his own life to history is to make him some "time lines" to talk about together. You can take a piece of string about six feet long and at intervals of about one foot tie a knot to mark each of your child's birthdays. Then you can explain that each segment between the knots represents a year of his life and you can talk about what happened to your family each of those memorable years.

You can also make a time line for yourself and point out to your child the segments of string that mark your own childhood, the year you finished school, the time you met the person you married, and the year your child was born. The next time your youngster needs a reference about the past—to the years John Kennedy was president, for example, or when men first walked on the moon—you can make an appropriate time line. If he wants to know when this country got started, you can tell him that the time line would stretch from his front door to the street and back again. When you are talking about dinosaurs, you can explain that a time line to show how long ago they lived on the earth would extend from his home to his aunt's house and back again ten times.

For most of his life your child will be building on the concepts he's starting to form during his preschool years. By helping him fit into usable patterns the great masses of sensory data he is accumulating, and introducing him to sources and ways of getting additional information he needs, you help him to learn more effectively and to form fewer misconceptions about the world.

CREATIVITY

As you become adept at observing how your child's mind grows, you'll notice that he thinks and learns in many different ways— some of them surprisingly adventuresome and original. This fresh, inventive kind of intelligence—whether it shows itself as artistic or musical talent or as imaginative thinking in other areas—is usually referred to as "creativity" and is mental activity of the highest and most satisfying order.

Creativity is considered an essential element in genius of every kind—in breakthrough scientific reasoning, in exploration, in invention, and in pioneering discovery in every field. Researchers who have studied creativity, trying to pinpoint how it differs from more standard components of intelligence and how it can be fostered, conclude that it stems naturally from the intense curiosity and drive to explore and experiment that all young children have, although it is often blunted by childrearing practices and pressures to conform to a group. Although by definition "creativity" can't be taught, parents can build an environment where creativity can flourish and encourage its development by their relationship with their youngster.

Starting at about age three, children naturally seem to begin thinking more creatively, studies show. This gradual increase in creativity drops markedly at about five or six when youngsters start formal schooling (presumably because of pressures to conform to group learning), then rises slowly again until another sharp decline occurs at about grade four. How creative your child will be thereafter depends to a large extent on how much encouragement he has at home for creative thinking and how much satisfaction he gets from using his mind in these special ways.

It's particularly important to encourage your child's creativity at home because creative youngsters are often turned off by classroom pressures at school. Their insatiable curiosity, their itch to experiment, their unwillingness to accept pat answers to their questions, their unusual sensitivity to people and discrepancies, and their offbeat ideas that may sometimes seem silly or smart-alecky, often make them a problem to a teacher who prizes conformity and rote learning. Once your child has started going to school—or to a day-care center or day-care home—the requirement that he act and learn with a group, at group speed and in group ways, can blunt whatever creative talents he has unless parents make deliberate efforts to nurture them at home.

There are several ways you can nurture your child's creative abilities. Some of them have been suggested as strategies for fostering other components of intelligence, but are also important for stimulating creativity as well, such as (1) encouraging your child to be sensitive to his environment, to experiment, to manipulate, to ask questions; (2) being enthusiastic about your child's achievements, projects, and ideas; (3) letting your youngster make as many of his own decisions as possible and realize their consequences; and (4) talking companionably with your child about his ideas and experiments.

In addition, you can do what one educator called creative calisthenics with your offspring, challenging him to be deliberately inventive and original in his thinking—for the pure joy of doing so. One commonly used test of creativity is to ask a child how many uses he can think of for a brick besides building a wall or a house; a highly creative youngster may be able to think of two or three dozen. You can vary the game by taking turns thinking up new ways to use an empty milk carton or a plastic bottle or a pie tin.

You can also encourage your youngster to think originally by tossing him challenges like, "If you could take only three things with you for a month on a desert island what would they be?" "How could we help Maggie not to feel so shy?" "How many things can you think of to do with wrapping paper?" You should be openly enthusiastic about your child's inventiveness, praise him happily, and avoid pointing out why you think some of his ideas wouldn't work.

There are other incentives you can give your child for being creative, too. If he knows that you'd welcome some new art to post on your refrigerator door, he'll be more likely to produce it than if you merely glance at his creations and say something perfunctory. If you write down the stories he makes up and collect them in a scrapbook, his output of fiction will jump. If you suggest that a favorite book needs a new dust jacket and cut one to size out of plain paper that he can illustrate with crayons, he's likely to try his hand at designing. Some five-year-olds enjoy pretending they are professional designers and getting an assignment from you to create "the most beautiful car in the world" or "a new play area to go in the park."

Part of fostering a creative environment in your home is giving your youngster what one psychologist called psychological safety to voice new ideas and original thoughts without being afraid you'll laugh at him or put him down. He also needs to know that it's all right to experiment with an idea that doesn't turn out well. You can help by talking about your own creative efforts and how you feel about them and about what you learn when something doesn't give you quite the results you anticipated. Most highly creative children try to tackle projects that are too difficult for them and may need some help in accepting frustration and discouragement as an occasional part of trying to do challenging new things. Sometimes you can show your youngster how he can avoid failure (and you must be sure he is physically safe). But it's important that he learn to accept the fact that not all experiments succeed and not all efforts work out as intended and that trial and error are also valuable ways to learn.

As you encourage your child's creativity efforts, you'll develop a sort of sense about when he needs direction and encouragement and when he should be left to work out his own ideas by himself. You should show him, for example, how to use a paintbrush without spattering, but not line by line what to color, and how to use tools and craft materials, but not precisely what to create with them. He may also appreciate a suggestion or tactful comment if he's stuck on a project, but you should avoid trying to take over his work so that it becomes yours and not his.

If your child's life is tightly scheduled around a day-care center and intense family activities in the early evening and on weekends, you may have some difficulty finding time when your child can have the privacy and freedom from interruption to be creative. It just doesn't work to schedule a "creative hour" for 3:30 P.M. Saturday and expect him to be in the mood for adventuresome thinking. It's also difficult in many families to prevent the omnipresent television from usurping time that a child could use to be creative by himself, on his own. Children who are in group care a large part of their waking lives may rarely have an ideal atmosphere for being creative; teaching a child to "share" is such a traditional tenet of preschools and day-care centers that it rarely occurs to a teacher or an assistant that a child may urgently need uninterrupted time and access to materials to work on his own. Montessori schools are an exception and try to protect the irreplaceable moments of discovery and creative thinking by following the dictum of Dr. Maria Montessori: "Don't interrupt a child who is working even to praise him."

Creativity and adventuresome thinking in many fields seem to be related, and one way you can help your child get into the habit of expressing his ideas with inventiveness and originality is to see that he has plenty of art materials and props for playing imaginative games. (You can find lots of ideas you can adapt for your youngster in craft books intended for older children.) You can also help him find inspiration in one creative area for another by suggesting he make up a dance to go with a favorite record or draw to music or invent a tune to go with a few lines of a favorite poem.

SECTION V

Combining Child Care and a Job

CAN a mother hold a full-time job away from home during the first few years of a child's life—while helping him develop in the best way possible? Can a father, a grandmother, a sitter, or a day-care worker not only provide traditional nurturing for a youngster while a mother works, but optimal mental nourishment, too?

It's difficult to separate tradition and maternal mystique from scientific evidence to find the answer. It's tough to avoid tripping over feminist rhetoric, family sentimentalities, psychological theory, and assumptions that have solidified into accepted "facts." And it's almost impossible to trace the single influence of a mother's working on her child as he develops into an adult because how he turns out is affected by so many other environmental and genetic factors and by so many other people.

Most child-care books take it for granted that a youngster's primary caregiver will be his mother and don't give serious attention to a forty-hour-a-week alternative. Most publications for "working mothers" concentrate primarily on the mother's needs and time-management problems and conveniently assume that almost any arrangement she makes for the physical care of her child will be all right. You can find appealing case histories, anecdotes, and "expert" opinion to back almost any conclusion you want about child care. Some authorities even change their views—not so much because of new research as because of new pressures to give popular answers. But there are almost no long-range studies done with scientific objectivity to show how well children turn out after being reared by loving parents who care intelligently about their offspring, but both of whom work full time away from home during their youngster's infancy and early childhood. Research on the effects on a child of being reared by a single working mother or father is even less helpful and results are often distorted by socioeconomic factors and the education level of the parents.

The most useful way to answer the question is to look at a child's specific needs during the early years of his life and see whether—and how—they can be adequately met if neither parent is able to be with him most of the time.

The physical well-being of your child is the easiest to provide— and to monitor. It doesn't take much training or experience to care for a youngster's physical needs. You can tell if your infant is sick too often or if a red, rashy bottom testifies that his diapers aren't being changed often enough. It quickly becomes obvious if your toddler's nose is allowed to run without being wiped or his toilet training is permitted to lapse.

It's more difficult to make sure your child is developing a secure emotional foundation for his life. A baby or a toddler can't tell you when he is unhappy with the caregiver with whom you've left him. You can't always know from his reactions whether he is content with the situation or has become so discouraged about changing anything with his objections that he's lapsed into a kind of hopeless resignation. And when you have to leave him crying in the arms of a sitter or a day-care worker five days every week, you can't always get accurate reports on whether his distress is short-lived and normal or so prolonged that you should make other plans for him as quickly as possible.

It's most difficult of all to make sure your child is getting optimal mental stimulation. Although you can check his mental development against some broad norms for his age group, you will never know for sure if more attention from his parents might not have boosted his IQ by a measurable amount.

Here are the chief areas of concern you should consider during the early years of your child's life—and a summary of the best information available to help you make the best possible choices for your child and yourself.

BREAST FEEDING

There is no scientific doubt that breast feeding gives your baby a better start in life than formula, for several reasons. Breast milk contains an ideal balance of nutrients for a human infant—and shifts subtly and specifically as your baby grows and his needs change. Recent research also shows that breast milk has an arsenal of antibodies to protect a baby against infections, some of which a mother's body develops to order in specific response to the needs of an individual infant. Other substances in breast milk are now thought to help prevent obesity and arteriosclerosis throughout life, to lessen the risk of allergies, and to spur the development of the baby's intestinal tract and immunological system. Some research suggests babies who are breast-fed are less likely to have serious illnesses or have to be hospitalized than other infants, although other factors may also be involved as well.

The more pediatricians and nutritionists learn about breast milk, the more strongly they recommend that a mother nurse her baby for at least the first four to six months of his life without adding extra formula, cereal, or solid foods. La Leche League, the international organization that promotes breast feeding, urges mothers to keep on nursing until a baby, in effect, weans himself—which may be at about nine months or perhaps not until well into the second year of life.

What may be even more important is that breast feeding an infant creates an emotional foundation for bonding between mother and child, as the newborn learns to look to his mother to satisfy his most basic needs and the mother discovers the satisfactions of fulfilling those needs in a way that obviously makes her baby deeply content and happy. Breast feeding almost forces a mother to attune herself to her infant's needs, to adapt to her baby's innate rhythms, and not only to feed him when he fusses with hunger, but to take her cues from him as to what else he needs. This loving sensitivity to the baby's needs spills over into other areas of the new relationship and continually reinforces the emotional bond between parent and child.

But nursing a young baby puts inordinate demands on a mother's time and energy. Especially during the earliest weeks of life, an infant often needs to nurse every two or three hours, day and night. It may take weeks, or even longer, to nudge him gently into a predictable schedule of nursing every three to four hours, and still longer for him to sleep through the night without needing to nurse. A mother's supply of milk is maintained and regulated by her baby's sucking; without regular and frequent nursing, it is difficult to sustain.

In recent years, a few women with jobs have been experimenting with ways to combine nursing with employment. Susan Catainia, a state representative from a Chicago district, took a nursing daughter with her to Springfield while the Illinois General Assembly was in session; the baby napped in a bassinet under her desk during legislative sessions. Firefighter Linda Eaton had to go to court to compel the Atlantic, Iowa, fire department to let her nurse her baby between alarms at a fire station (but she eventually quit her job because of the problems she encountered). Michele Bertrand, a Manhattan bank vice-president, kept an electric breast-milk expresser in her office to collect milk for her infant while she was away at work.

It is difficult to breast-feed an infant while holding a full-time job away from home. But it is possible, as a group of eight mothers—most of them pediatricians or nurses themselves—wrote in a letter published in *Pediatrics*, the professional journal of the American Academy of Pediatrics. In part, they said:

"We are working mothers who are writing to bring to the attention of practicing pediatricians some practical aspects of combining breast-feeding with employment outside the home. We have learned that the nursing problems encountered by mothers who work outside the home include all those encountered by mothers who remain at home and several others. We hope our experiences may contribute to more constructive discussions of this aspect of infant care.

"A working mother who returns to work before her child is weaned will, of course, have to rely on bottles for her infant's nourishment during her working hours, unless arrangements can be made for her to nurse her baby at frequent intervals during her work day—an ideal situation only rarely available in this country at this time. It has been our experience that the earlier the bottle is introduced, the easier is the transition to this form of nourishment. In general, late introduction of the bottle is likely to be associated with some resistance on the baby's part, whereas introduction of the bottle after several weeks of exclusive breast-feeding but before five weeks of age is not.

"After it is introduced, the bottle needs to be used regularly (once daily) to maintain the baby's acceptance of it. Some mothers find that once the bottle is introduced, their infants lose interest in the breast, but this is unusual; it is generally no problem to continue to nurse the baby when the mother is home. On the other hand, if introduction of the bottle is postponed until the baby is several months old, the mother may be unable to return to work until the infant is weaned or able to drink from a cup because the baby absolutely refuses to take the bottle. Some mothers feel that atypical bottle nipples facilitate combining bottle and breast-feeding and these, on occasion, overcome an older baby's resistance to the bottle.

"Because of the superiority of breast milk, many working mothers choose to express milk for bottle feeding during their working hours. Others, however, find this process difficult, unpleasant, or inconvenient, and choose to use formula for bottle feedings.

"Mothers who have expressed milk for their babies have used clean rather than sterile techniques. The mechanical devices mentioned in many books are inefficient at best and ineffective at worst. Most of us therefore rely on manual expression of milk, sometimes using a pump to initiate the letdown reflex. The technique for manual expression of milk requires practice. It involves compressing the areola in a repetitive fashion, either pressing it back against the rib cage or not, depending on what works better for the individual mother. It usually takes at least 15 to 20 minutes to empty both breasts. Mothers who express milk while at work store it in a refrigerator until they leave for home. At home, the milk is kept in bottles or plastic nurser liners and stored in the refrigerator (for up to 24 hours) or in the freezer (for up to several weeks) for later use; the milk is thawed by placing it under tepid water immediately prior to use.

"A mother who chooses not to introduce formula at all must build up a supply of frozen milk before she returns to work, generally expressing small amounts of milk (0.5 to 1 ounce) before or after the baby's feeding for several weeks before she starts back to work.

"If the choice is made to combine breast and formula feedings, it is necessary to replace one or more breast feedings with formula feedings. This must be done gradually to avoid uncomfortable engorgement and the risk of mastitis. It generally takes five to seven days when the mother and baby are not 'in sync' and manual expression may be necessary to relieve the mother's discomfort.

Child care arrangements that include the mother's arrival at a specific time for a scheduled feeding greatly facilitate maintenance of the breast-feeding routine.

"As the baby grows, the mother's milk supply must keep pace with the baby's needs. This occurs naturally when the mother is nursing full time, but some provision must be made if the mother is combining formula and breast feeding. One way to do this is to maintain the weekday bottle feeding schedule during the weekends except for one additional breast feeding. This may sometimes lead to discomfort on Monday, but it reduces the likelihood of inadequate milk supply which is so frustrating to both the baby and the mother.

"The most important point is that it is indeed possible to combine breast feeding and employment outside the home. The unique pleasures of breast feeding and the resultant bonding with the new baby may be especially precious to mothers who share the infant's care with others (fathers, grandparents, sitters). At this time in history, many mothers are, through career choices or economic circumstances, returning to work while their children are very young. Mothers who wish to combine breast feeding and employment should be provided with the information they need and should be encouraged to continue nursing, just as are mothers who stay home."

The single best source of practical information and emotional support for a breast-feeding mother and her family is the La Leche League International, Inc., 9616 Minneapolis Avenue, Franklin Park, Illinois 60131. The league has instructional material about nursing, can send lots of loving testimonials to its role in family bonding, and can put a mother in personal contact with a local leader (there are more than 12,500 in fifty countries) and mothers' groups (there are almost 5000 around the world) for moral support, help, and friendly sharing of practical child-care information.

Of all the substitutions the mother of an infant might be tempted to make so she can return to a job, the use of formula instead of breast milk is probably the safest and most scientifically tested. Formula isn't as good for a baby as breast milk, but most manufacturers have changed and upgraded their products in response to new nutritional data and when properly used and stored in clean conditions, it's difficult to show that the substitution is harmful. A majority of two full generations of American children have been nourished with formula and it is impossible to look at them now as adults and tell whether they had the advantages of breast feeding as infants or not.

ATTACHMENT

Psychologists, psychiatrists, physicians, and educators have been paying great attention in recent years to what they call bonding or attachment. What they mean is basically love—the development of mutual love between parents, especially the mother, and an infant; the development of a baby's trust in his parents; and their loving acceptance of a kind of I'd-lay-down-my-life-for-my-child responsibility for his well-being.

Love between a parent and a baby seems so fundamental and automatic that it's usually taken for granted. But it shouldn't be. Babies who aren't loved—because they have been institutionalized or neglected, for example—often fail to thrive and they can wither away emotionally and even die. Some experts in child development suspect that inadequate attachment between a child and his parents accounts for a wide variety of persistent emotional disturbances, school failures, and other problems later in childhood and adulthood. They have been trying to answer the questions raised by the enormous increase in mothers of very young children who now work full time away from their offspring: How much time must a mother spend with an infant to avoid jeopardizing the process of attachment? At what age is it safe to leave an infant with a sitter or in a day-care center to return to a job? Will a baby's attachment to his mother be inadequate if she's not around during the day five days a week? Is the process and strength of attachment the same for fathers as for mothers?

Like many other issues in child care, the answers still aren't completely clear. Some tests have been developed to measure how firmly a baby is attached to his mother and to his father—how he reacts to a strange person or in a strange situation, for example. But the assumptions behind the tests are theoretical. The samples of children who have been evaluated are very small. And many factors other than attachment may be involved in what the researchers are observing.

The attachment—or bonding—process is most easily seen and understood in animals and birds. Often called imprinting, it seems to be biologically programmed, to occur quite quickly after birth, and to be essential for normal development in the offspring.

The process isn't nearly so clear, so quick, or so immutable in humans, although it almost certainly does have some biological basis. Biologists see attachment as an evolutionary survival strategy; they view it as a way an infant successfully secures protection and attention during his dependent years and also as a reinforcement of a mother's biologically programmed effort to make sure her genetic stake in the infant survives.

Some observers assume that a kind of imprinting, or bonding, occurs during a particularly sensitive, irreplaceable few hours after birth for human babies, too. They urge that hospital routines be changed to allow time for a new mother—and a father, too—to bond with their newborn infant while they are still in the delivery room. In 1977, the American Medical Association gave support to this idea when its policymaking House of Delegates adopted a statement urging hospitals to change their policies and practices to allow time for bonding contact between mother, father, and newborn immediately after birth. During such a bonding time, a new mother—and a new father if he is in the delivery room—is urged to hold her baby, to stroke him, to have eye-to-eye contact, and to talk softly to him.

But for decades, hospital routines in the United States have called for just-born babies to be whisked away from the delivery room to a central newborn nursery. Although some hospitals have liberalized their practices in response to pressures from parents and as a result of new research, tens of millions of mothers have had very little contact with their new offspring during their entire hospital stay, except to nurse them or give them a bottle. These parents and children seem to have suffered no apparent permanent disruption of the attachment process.

Longer hospital stays, however, can be hazardous. Many studies show that premature babies kept in isolation in incubators—sometimes for weeks—can suffer from subsequent emotional disturbances. More obvious and easier to attribute to a lack of opportunity for bonding is the fact that some mothers of prematures emotionally reject them when they are ready to go home; although only a few women actually abandon such babies, studies show that a substantial percentage of others find mothering to be unusually difficult and unrewarding. Many newborn intensive care units now make it a policy to encourage mothers of their tiny patients to visit often, to stroke and handle their babies as much as possible, and to talk to them and have lots of eye contact.

Attachment is probably much more like falling in love than love at first sight for humans, most research now suggests. Like falling in love, it's such a natural process, it's difficult to analyze. What encourages attachment is, first of all, touching. Your baby needs to be held, cuddled, stroked, patted, rocked, back-rubbed, soothed by your touch, given abundant skin-to-skin contact (it's also effective sensory stimulation for his brain as well). He needs time for ample eye contact with you; face-to-face, eye-to-eye gazing between mother and infant is such a common, natural activity it is probably based on biological instinct. A baby nursing at the breast or taking milk from a bottle while being held almost always stares intently at his mother's face and it is a mother's natural impulse to gaze intently back—unless she lets herself be distracted. Some biologists think it's not just coincidence that the distance between the eyes of a baby nursing at the breast to his mother's face is approximately the distance at which the eyes of a newborn focus most clearly.

You can also encourage attachment by talking to your baby—right from the first time you hold him. But vocalizing should be a two-way exchange with your infant—a kind of verbal Ping-Pong one researcher called it—with each of you responding to the other, building a lifelong relationship between you sound by sound, word by word.

When you respond to his fussing, his crying, his attempts to communicate, you build his sense of trust and love. When he responds to you by smiling, laughing, holding up his arms to be picked up, by stopping his crying, he builds your sense of self-esteem and your love. As the relationship between you develops and grows in the days and weeks after his birth, the bond strengthens into permanent attachment. Your baby learns, gradually, that he can count on you to be there when he needs you, that you will ease his discomforts, satisfy his hunger, make him feel secure. You discover the satisfactions of being a good parent and of being loved with a rare and surprising intensity.

This attachment—love really is a better name for it—also gives your child the security and confidence to take on new learning tasks, to cope with new experiences, and eventually to begin to move into independence. Eleanor Maccoby, professor of psychology at Stanford University, suggests that a secure attachment between parent and child predisposes a youngster to learn from a parent by gentle pressure and friendly persuasion, so that misbehavior is rare, discipline is not a problem, and punishment of any kind is unnecessary.

Although the biological imperatives may be less, attachment also occurs between father and infant—to the benefit and joy of both. The few studies that have been done on father-baby bonding show that, if carefully nurtured, it isn't much different from mother-child relationships.

How long does it take to establish a firm attachment between a parent and an infant? There is no clear consensus among researchers. But the process is certainly much slower in human babies than in animals and requires much more consistent, reciprocal interaction. In studies on attachment, assumptions about the time required range from a few weeks to three years or more.

How much time and attention must you give your baby to be sure you two are well bonded? Again, there are no reliable answers. The ill effects of poor attachment are obvious in instances where newborns are left without mothering in intensive care units for more than several days or when babies are placed in institutions without close, consistent mothering care. But incomplete or inadequate attachment is much more difficult to define and to prove, although some experts in child development say it shows up in insecurity, unhappiness, anxiety, and emotional problems all during childhood. Temperamental differences in babies may affect the length of time it takes to bond completely with a parent; some babies seem to relax into a contented, trusting relationship with parents more easily than others. The quality of time you give your baby is also a major factor; it's often difficult for a busy father or mother who is used to being efficient and fast-moving to relax and move at an infant's pace in a loving give-and-take that encourages bonding.

What can a parent do to build a firm attachment to a baby? There are several things. You can give your baby a great wealth of contact—by holding him, rocking him, stroking him, cuddling him close. You can talk to him, beginning the very first time you hold him after his birth, pausing to let him vocalize in response and then responding to his efforts to communicate with you. You can make him feel secure with you, by comforting him when he cries, coming when he attempts to call you, smiling at him when he smiles, seeing that he is dry, fed, rocked, and given mental stimulation and human contact when he signals that he needs them. And you can create a consistent, dependable environment that seems safe and familiar to him. In other words, you can simply be there for him—and help him learn to count on it.

SUBSTITUTE CAREGIVERS FOR A BABY

A mother who wants to work full time during the first year of her baby's life has only a few choices for substitute care: a relative or nonrelative who baby-sits either in the baby's home or the sitter's, a day-care home that may or may not be licensed by the state, and a nonprofit or for-profit infant day-care center. Availability and cost may reduce even these small choices. Of these, only infant day-care centers have been the subject of any research and that has been limited mostly to a few experimental programs in university settings.

Traditionally, women who worked while their children were babies left them with a relative—a live-in grandmother or aunt, or a sister or cousin who lived nearby and was staying home with a small child of her own. There were few serious worries about the arrangement. The substitute mother was likely to be loving and devoted to the baby, more likely than not to reflect the same kind of philosophy about child care as the baby's parents, and likely to be available consistently for years. The cost was minimal. Perhaps the most serious worry a mother had was that her baby might come to love the grandmother or mother substitute more than his own mother.

Day care by a relative, especially in your home, still seems like the best arrangement for a baby younger than age one—if you're lucky enough to have a loving and willing relative available. About 44 percent of care is still provided by relatives, according to a 1978 survey.

You can almost always count on a relative who mother-substitutes for you to take good care of your baby physically—and to do so even when your infant is sick. But a grandmother, especially, may not be aware of the enormous amount of new evidence about the need for mental stimulation during early childhood. Because you'll be gone during most of your baby's waking weekday hours, you should discuss these findings with your sitter, leave appropriate playthings and learning materials, and suggest specific activities you want her to provide for your baby. Once she sees how well your baby responds, she'll probably want to keep on helping him learn—just for the fun of it and because it makes caring for him easier.

Your baby will almost certainly become attached to a relative who cares for him forty or more hours every week. A loving attachment will make it easier for him to bear separation from you five out of every seven days. But that shouldn't affect his attachment to you, research suggests, if you have established a strong bond before you go back to work. You should expect to feel a little jealous, however, even of your own mother, when she—not you— gets to hear the baby's first intelligible word and to watch him pull himself upright for the first time. It will also hurt when your sitter begins telling you what your baby needs or what works best with him, when you can't help but feel it should be the other way around. You may also have a few bad moments when your baby turns to the sitter for comfort or help when you are there.

But such incidents will happen and such feelings will be triggered, no matter with whom you leave your baby. The more secure both of you are in your relationship, the less such incidents will matter. That's an important reason for staying at home with your infant as long as you can after his birth.

Child development experts differ somewhat as to precisely when a baby recognizes his mother as his mother, but most of them suggest it occurs between the ages of three and five months. At about seven months, a baby begins to show a definite aversion to strangers and a discomfort in unfamiliar surroundings, in part because he's gotten so good at identifying his parents and his own home that he can now recognize what isn't. At this age, he can't be sure that what's out of his sight even still exists and he can't be assured that yes, his mother will come back to him at 5:00 P.M. He will be well past his first birthday before he can be told in words and can remember that you'll return after you are through working.

A few experts on child development suggest that if a mother is going to go back to work, she should do so before her baby is seven months old or perhaps wait until he's at least fifteen months old. But there is little research to back up or contradict this opinion other than a baby's normal apprehension about strangers during this time span.

The second least disruptive child-care arrangement is the mother substitute who comes to your home. This plan means your baby need only get used to the sitter and not to a whole new environment. You won't have to bundle him up in every kind of weather to deliver him to a caretaker. The sitter will probably still come if your baby is sick. And with the sitter in your home, you'll probably feel more in control than if you are delivering your child to someone else's house or to a day-care center.

The greatest problem with this plan is finding a good mother substitute. The more jobs that open up for women, the fewer women there are who are willing to baby-sit full time—to do essentially for someone else's child what that baby's own parents don't want to do. Few parents are able to pay even minimum wages for a full-time baby-sitter or to offer the benefits that now go with most other employment, and the arrangement becomes, essentially, a way of exploiting a woman who needs a job.

This raises some hard questions about why a woman you can afford would take the kind of job you are offering. There are some obvious reasons—she can't speak English well, she is an illegal immigrant, she is elderly and has little energy but wants something to do or needs money—that should immediately disqualify an applicant. At a minimum, the mother substitute you choose should speak English adequately without an accent; she will be a

major language model for your child during the vital years when
he is mastering his native tongue. She should have enough energy
and inclination to take active care of your baby, not to keep him
confined to a crib or playpen as much as possible. She should have
had some experience in child care. She should be in good health,
not only to protect your baby but to avoid disruptions in your
schedule if she doesn't show up. She should be dependable, so
tension doesn't build up the mornings she is late because you are
worried about getting to your job on time. It should be likely that
she'll be available for two or three years at least, so your baby
won't have to keep getting used to new caregivers. And she should
be intelligent and loving because she will, after all, be parenting
your baby for as many or more hours of his waking time as you will
be.

The best kind of candidate for your job are mothers whose own
children are grown or almost so, who may not have other marketable skills or want to take the time for training, and who need
to earn some money but aren't necessarily totally dependent on
what you can pay. Some women like this are still available in
some areas. If you can find one, she should be treated with as
much businesslike consideration as you expect from your employer. You should pay her as much as you can and give her as
many fringe benefits as possible. You should make it clear that she
is to be an active substitute for you, not just a passive baby-sitter.
And you should work with her closely in sharing your information
about your child's development and in making sure she gives your
baby the amount and kind of mental stimulation that's as important for his optimal development as his physical care.

If you can't find or can't afford a good substitute mother who
will take care of your baby in your home, you will have to explore
options away from it—as do 69 percent of families with working
mothers, according to a 1978 count. These choices include dropping your baby off at a sitter's house, putting him in a day-care
home, or enrolling him in an infant day-care center. All of these
alternatives mean your baby must be up, dressed, fed, and out of
the house on your schedule, even when he's sleepy or cranky, and
that he must get used to a strange environment as well as an unfamiliar caregiver. He'll have to share an adult's attention with at
least one and possibly several other young children. And he'll al-

most certainly be exposed to a variety of new infections and diseases against which he hasn't yet built up much resistance.

Most women who care for babies and toddlers in their own home do so because they need to earn money and for some reason—usually because they have young children of their own—want to work at home. Many of these mothers simply agree to take on an extra baby. Others organize a more formal day-care home for several children, which may require a state inspection and licensing. Usually, the cost is less than any other day-care arrangement except a live-in grandmother.

Besides the criteria already mentioned, there are other checks you should make before settling for this kind of arrangement. You'll need to look carefully at the physical environment in which your child will be spending so much of his waking time: Will he have a crib of his own? Are the standards of cleanliness equal to yours, especially when your child will begin to crawl on the floor? Have dangers like exposed electrical outlets, open stairs, slippery rugs, and poisonous cleaning supplies and insecticides been eliminated? Are there plenty of playthings your baby can safely handle without being told "No" constantly? Will your child be stuck in one small area all day or will there be opportunities to move about and have a change of scenery?

You'll also want to make sure the day-care mother's philosophy of child care is close to yours, especially with regard to the importance of mental stimulation. You'll probably feel less free to make suggestions or insist on certain routines or activities with a mother into whose home you are bringing your baby than with a sitter who comes to your place. So you'll want to be sure you are comfortable with her way of doing things before you decide to leave your baby in her care.

Another thing you should try to evaluate is whether the day-care mother has enough energy and enthusiasm for what she's doing. Studies show that twins and children who are born close together in age grow up to have, on the average, a slightly lower IQ than others from similar backgrounds who are only children or not so close in age to siblings—presumably because their parents didn't have the time and energy to give them as much individual attention and mental stimulation as other youngsters. You may be putting your baby into just such an environment.

A day-care mother is often on the job from 6:30 or 7:00 A.M. until 5:00 or 5:30 P.M. Usually, she has no one to relieve her even for lunch or a coffee break. She may be trying to get some housework done as well as look after children. It's understandable that she could run out of patience and strength and be tempted to leave your child in a crib or a playpen or propped up in front of a television set for far too long.

You really have no way of knowing what happens to your child in a day-care home. State licensing usually is concerned primarily with the physical environment of the home, not the personality and characteristics of the mother. Usually, there are no follow-up inspections after the initial approval. Almost no research has been done on the effects of day-care homes on babies or toddlers or preschool children. So you—and your baby—are highly dependent on your evaluation of the woman in whose care you are considering leaving your offspring.

Depending on where you live, you may have access to a formal infant day-care center—run by a university as a training program for early childhood educators, or by a nonprofit agency with or without government funding, or by a for-profit corporation or chain, or rarely, by an employer as a service to workers. Of all the arrangements parents make for babies, a day-care center is the only kind that even pretends to be of benefit to the children instead of merely a help to working mothers. It is the only type that has been studied carefully by researchers. And it is the only one where the care your child gets will be professionally supervised.

Generally, the research findings on infant day-care centers are reassuring. They show that children in such centers don't progress more slowly in social or emotional development than comparable youngsters who stay at home. Their mental development seems to be about the same. They continue to be firmly attached to their mothers and obviously and consistently prefer them to other caregivers when they have a choice.

But the research has been done on only the very best of infant day-care centers—almost always those in prestigious university settings run by educators with national reputations in early childhood development. Furthermore, the evaluations are almost always made by the center itself—by those who have a professional stake in proving that what they are doing is sound. The designs of some of these studies have been questioned as inadequate. The methods of evaluating attachment to mothers and to others are controversial and may not be accurate or adequate for this purpose.

Physicians connected with infant day-care centers where research is done report no serious health problems associated with group care—although other doctors often disagree sharply. Studies show that infants in day-care centers have an average of 9.6 episodes of illness per year (8.4 for all center age groups) and significantly more flu, colds, and minor problems like diaper rash than children who stay at home. Because most centers accept sick children—again, their major aim is to help parents, not children—infectious diseases spread quickly through the group, although center doctors say they also occur at about the same rate in children of similar age who stay at home. Still, statistics aren't much comfort to a sick baby who must be dressed and delivered to unfamiliar caregivers in surroundings where he may not yet feel at home—or to mothers whose own pediatricians strongly recommend against exposing their baby to infections they may not be mature enough to fight adequately.

Some of the child development experts who head university-based infant day-care programs view their own statistical successes with great caution. Some of them are concerned about the extreme emotional and physical fatigue shown by very young children as the long day drags on. They cite examples of the obvious longing that babies and toddlers have for absent parents, the reactions of anxiety and apathy at separation and the great—sometimes angry—relief at the arrival of a parent in late afternoon. All of them worry that without the financial support of a university or a foundation or a government grant, and without university-based expertise, others who try to run infant programs will cut too many vital corners.

Dr. Jerome Kagan, professor of psychology and social relations at Harvard University, says, "During the infant's first three years of life, a caretaker should not be responsible for more than three infants. Our day-care project [the Tremont Street Infant Center in Boston] found that responsibility for more than three infants placed a serious psychological burden on the individual caretaker. Moreover, in environments where the ratio is much greater, children suffer temporary retardation in cognitive and affective development." Yet in many infant day-care centers, the ratio is one staff worker to four or five babies.

One national survey found that 51 percent of for-profit day-care centers provided only "poor" quality programs and an additional 35 percent offered only "fair" care. Among for-profit programs, 40 percent were rated good or better, but 50 percent were considered fair or poor. Another survey found that 25 percent of day-care centers listed themselves as "custodial" and didn't even pretend to be giving children any kind of educational program.

If you have access to an infant day-care program, there are several aspects to check in addition to the obvious concerns about safety, sanitation, spaciousness, and equipment. In particular, you'll want to know precisely who will be taking care of your baby most of the time. Even when the ratio of staff to children is the recommended one to three, your baby may be handled by a bewildering number of inexperienced caregivers. In a university-based program, for example, students may rotate through the centers for six- or eight-week periods, using your baby, in effect, to practice on and interfering with his attachment to a special individual. Many nonprofit centers are required by the terms of a government grant to hire unemployed women with no marketable skills, such as welfare mothers, and to provide training—again using your baby to do so. Most for-profit franchises and centers can pay only a minimum wage for caregivers if they are to keep their costs down enough so that working couples and single parents can afford them; but that means high turnover and again, insecurity for your baby.

You should be sure the center you are considering uses early learning principles, not pushing the children into precocious achievements, but offering an abundance of stimulating activities from which a baby can choose freely. You don't want your baby shoved into a schedule that's uncomfortable for him, unable to nap when he needs it or forced to spend hours in a crib when he isn't sleepy. You—and your baby's doctor—should be satisfied with the center's policy about sick children. And you should feel a rapport with the center's staff that makes you all partners in working together for the good of your child.

Day care, especially for infants, is in drastically short supply compared to the number of mothers with children under age six who are in the labor force. Year-around, day-long day care for a young child, done with adequate attention to acceptable standards, costs much more than public schooling for an older child. There continues to be strong political opposition to publicly financed day care, except for disadvantaged and handicapped children and the offspring of welfare mothers. And some development experts who have done comparison studies of day care in other countries suggest that group childrearing may produce a somewhat different type of adult—less competitive, more compliant, more peer dominated, less independent—than most Americans want their children to become.

Enthusiasm for day care as an employment benefit offered by corporations has not increased in recent years, except where the need for young women workers is acute, such as in hospitals and on military bases. Day care has limited appeal as a fringe benefit, is expensive, and even when offered, many young parents prefer to leave their babies at home with a sitter rather than commute to work with them, surveys show.

There has been some growth in for-profit day care, especially centers operated by chains or franchisers. But child development experts worry about the fundamental incompatibility between the efficiencies required of, say, a fast-food outlet and the care of very young children. It is difficult to provide an adequate number of skilled and caring staff plus the play equipment, learning materials, food, and health care babies need at a price young parents can afford—and still make a profit on the necessary investment. Some kindly educators who have tried to turn their teaching expertise into managing a day-care center have been forced into bankruptcy because they simply lacked the hardness of heart to tell a mother—for example, a recently divorced woman whose child support check failed to arrive, struggling to keep a new job— that her baby could no longer come to the center until she could pay up.

Some for-profit centers apparently count on young parents being so desperate to find care for their children that they won't look closely at its quality. One day-care chain that took several surveys of middle-income parents says they want convenience first, then they are concerned about price, and only after that do they consider the quality of the center. Another chain cynically makes it a policy to try to locate new centers on the side of the street convenient for most parents on their way to work.

No child development expert will dispute that the best start in life for a baby comes from being cared for at home by a loving mother who uses principles of early learning individually attuned to his interests and development. But a good day-care center can't be proven to do harm to young children—and can be shown to be better than a home where a baby is abused or neglected.

How can you tell if your day-care plan is hurting your baby? There are a few obvious signs. Your baby may be sick too often or have trouble getting over respiratory infections. He may have diaper rash or a runny nose most of the time. Your child's doctor may express some concern about his frequent exposure to illness or his general lack of resistance to repeated infections.

But other signs are more subtle and hard to interpret, especially for young, inexperienced parents who can't easily compare their infant with many others. Your baby may find the long day away from you too emotionally and physically exhausting, especially if he's trapped in the hectic, frenetic atmosphere of some day-care centers; and he may react by being cranky, tense, unhappy, or apathetic. But most young children are cranky, tense, unhappy, or unresponsive on occasion, especially in the late afternoon. It's often hard to know what is normal and what should be considered a warning that you should make other arrangements for him. If your baby is too tired to eat at night and too tired to relax and be soothed to sleep too often and too tired to arouse and get going in the morning, or if he doesn't seem to have much energy or enthusiasm generally, you should make a change as soon as you can. Child-care experts used to insist that youngsters weren't ready for a full five-hour day at school until they were six, yet many infants and toddlers are expected to put in nine- and ten-hour days in day care. Few workers put in forty-five or fifty hours a week on the job, yet day-care children are required to spend that long, or longer, in a single room or two, reacting to the same people, unable even to get away for a coffee break.

The long separation of all-day care may put strains on your baby's attachment to you and he may show it by fussing when you leave him in the morning, by hanging on to you, by turning away from his sitter or the day-care worker, and by greeting you with anger or indifference when you pick him up at night. But these signs are also difficult to read because somewhat similar behavior is assumed by child-care workers to mean he is well attached to you and simply wants to maintain that loving relationship without interruption.

In the absence of definite signs that your baby is not doing well, your evaluation will have to be largely intuitive and based on your feelings about how happy your baby is generally, how eager he seems to be for new experiences, and how well your relationship seems to be going. He should seem to enjoy being himself, at least most of the time. And you should enjoy being his parent, at least most of the time.

One of the most deceptive rationalizations about mothers—and fathers—who hold jobs is that it's not the quantity of time they spend with their children, but the quality. The older a child is, the easier it is for him to wait for his share of your quality time— until after dinner, or after the Saturday errands, or after everyone has slept late on Sunday. The younger a child is, the more urgent is his need for loving reassurance or a bit of mental stimulation. These teachable opportunities, these loving moments, may not last more than a minute or two. But they must come when your baby is ready to respond to your teaching or your loving. They can't be lumped together into quality time in the evening.

Late afternoon is down time for almost everyone: for tired workers hurrying home from jobs, for mothers who are trying to get dinner for a hungry family, and for small children, even when they have been at home all day. Very few mothers can work all day at a job, pick up a tired baby, fix dinner, perhaps do some essential laundry, and still give a baby a full day's worth of concentrated quality time before he goes to sleep.

Another factor many mothers don't anticipate when they sign up for a maternity leave and plan to return to a job a few weeks after a baby's birth is the change that may occur in their own feelings and values.

"My priorities are different now, since Jamie was born," commented an account executive, twenty-nine, who has an M.B.A. degree from a prestigious university. "My competitive edge isn't as sharp as it was before the baby was born and getting a new account just doesn't seem as vitally important as it used to. I'm softer and more loving than I used to be and I like myself better this way."

Despite the great jump in the number of working mothers, more than two out of three women don't go back to work the first year of a baby's life, according to a 1978 survey. A slightly larger percentage goes back to work during the second year and the number increases rapidly after that.

SUBSTITUTE CAREGIVERS FOR A TODDLER

For many parents, the toddler years are the most difficult. A toddler's energy level is so high it can readily exhaust a conditioned athlete. His reckless mobility and incessant curiosity necessitate constant supervision. His quick emotional swings between sunny companionship and screaming obstinacy are psychologically wearing. His lack of verbal skills to express his wants and feelings is enormously frustrating to him and to you. His attention span is short. His need for fresh stimuli is innate and real. And so arduous is his care that some child development experts, like Dr. Burton White, urge parents not to plan to have a second child until their first is about three years old.

All of these toddler attributes make it harder for two-job couples and single parents to find satisfactory caregivers to cover a full-time working schedule than it is to get parent substitutes for a baby or a preschooler. Even the best-known authorities on day care, who head university-based centers with optimal staffs and good financial support, point out how much more difficult it is to care for toddlers than babies or older children. The better the centers and the more qualified their directors, the more reservations they tend to express about the effects of regular day care for one- and two-year-olds.

Still, it is difficult to assess whether or not it is actually harmful to toddlers to do without both parents for five full working days a week. There are several concerns about toddlers who are away from both parents all day—considerations that are more acute for one- and two-year-olds than for babies and for older preschoolers and that apply to all kinds of substitute care. For example, can a caregiver provide the kind of immediate, appropriate verbal stimulation in the same loving abundance that a mother does when she is with a toddler most of the time? Without this stimulation, will his verbal abilities develop adequately?

Can any other combination of place and caregiver offer a toddler the same kind of well-designed, learning-inducing environment that a good home and a caring mother who is attuned to the principles of early learning can? How many other toddlers can a caregiver supervise and still do an adequate job with your child? Between the ages of one and three, is a toddler well enough attached to his parents emotionally so that he can weather the long day away from them without suffering undue distress? How worrisome is the stress that is commonly reported among toddlers in day-care centers?

Generally, the choices you have for all-day care for your toddler are roughly the same as for a baby: a sitter in your home or hers, family day care, or a formal day-care center. The problems and benefits balance out much the same, as well.

A sitter who comes to the house is the kind of daily caregiver most parents prefer for a toddler as well as for a baby—for much the same reasons. But finding the right person is harder for a toddler than for a baby. Toddlers are much more difficult to manage than infants. They take more energy, more alertness, more ingenuity, more effort, more tolerance for lightning swings in mood and behavior. You must have someone who speaks English well, who won't yield to the temptation to watch soap operas on television while your toddler sucks his thumb in boredom, who will go to the extra trouble of enhancing your child's learning opportunities day after day without fail, and who you can reasonably expect will be available for the next two or three years. If you can find such a wonderful person, you should ask some hard questions about why she is willing to work for a sitter's salary.

As with an infant, chances are you can find a better baby-sitter if you are willing to pack your toddler off to the sitter's house. Then you need to be extra careful to be sure your inquisitive, investigative tyke will be safe, that the sitter really will give him the constant, individually attuned language feedback he should have, and that he won't be spending hours sucking on a pacifier or a tepid bottle while staring at the television. The sitter who lets a toddler tag along while she does housework and talks companionably to him all day about what he and she are doing may be a better choice than other day-care arrangements. But a sitter who simply puts up with him, pressures him to quell his exploratory drives, and teaches him not to bother her would be a disaster. The problem is, it may be difficult for you to tell what really goes on during the long day and your child is still too young to tell you.

A day-care home, or family day care, can also be the best or the worst of your options, for much the same reasons it can be bad or good for a baby. It is even more essential for a toddler than for a baby that a woman who runs a day-care home have time to give him individualized language feedback all day long and to have the energy and facilities to let him work off some of his energy and curiosity.

Toddlers are the most difficult age group to fit into formal day-care centers, too. Toddlers can't be kept in cribs, as is common with babies, or corralled into convenient clusters for a while, as preschoolers usually are. They don't play well together, are likely to fight over toys, and are too young to take turns reliably without fussing. Their emotions are volatile and unpredictable. They are alternately dependent and independent, sunny and sullen, clinging and running off. They must be toilet-trained. And no matter how a center is set up, it is difficult to make sure a toddler gets the one-to-one personal attention he needs precisely when it is most effective. Some candid day-care directors admit it is particularly difficult to find good staffers to work with toddlers; most prefer the cuddly, less demanding babies or the older preschoolers who are easier and less exhausting.

A good day-care center does have benefits to offer a toddler, however. It can give him a far greater selection of toys and equipment than his home, help him get used to playing with other children, and accustom him to cooperating with adults outside his family. With luck, the staff will toilet-train him without much stress on him or his parents. He may learn to feed himself rather neatly, to fend for himself with others, and to participate in a few more activities than he might at home.

Research shows rather clearly that young children develop better in a good day-care center than in a disadvantaged home with an abusive, neglecting parent. Studies also seem to indicate that a good day-care center does not do any measurable harm to children from good, stable homes who feel secure in their parents' love and get lots of good mothering and fathering after day-care hours. But it should be emphasized again that almost all of this research is done on the best day-care centers—either those connected with a university or those funded with government or foundation money, guided by professional consultants, and intended to be demonstration projects.

Many of the best-known day-care directors and consultants still have serious concerns about the effects of long hours of group care on one- and two-year-olds. Some of these reservations are obviously rooted in pre-1970s concepts about what young children need and in studies that seem to show youngsters had to be fully five years old to be ready for half-day kindergarten and fully six for a five-hour day of first grade. Perhaps some of these concerns will turn out to be unwarranted, as research increases on the effects of day care on children and when a generation has grown up which takes day care for granted as the norm. But a parent who is considering putting a toddler in a day-care center should be aware that there are still several serious unanswered questions—all of them voiced by some of the nation's best-known authorities on the issue.

Is it too stressful and tiring for a toddler to be forced to interact with five or six or a dozen or more one- and two-year-olds and several adults for eight to ten hours a day? Signs of strain are often obvious during the long day and especially in late afternoon when exhausted children and staff wait out the dragging last hours before parents come. Even high-school and college students don't put in as long a day in one place as children in day care. Neither do most adults. No age group has as much restless energy and as short an attention span as toddlers do, or as much need for fresh stimuli. Yet in many day-care centers, they must play, lunch, nap, and interact with each other in the same room all day long with no break at all except for the bathroom. And toddlers have developed far fewer emotional resources to cope with stress than older children.

Can a day-care staff be large enough and so organized that someone can give a toddler quick attention most of the times he needs it? What happens when an almost-toilet-trained two-year-old suddenly has to have bathroom help immediately and a caregiver is busy settling a squabble between two older toddlers, and a fourth child is resignedly sucking his thumb in the corner and staring ahead at nothing? Even though toddlers urgently need someone to talk to them at their own level about what they are doing or seeing at a given moment, reports abound of caregivers who rarely say anything to their charges, are clearly bored with two-year-old talk, or, in some cases, are unable to speak much English.

In order to keep their prices within a range that single parents or working couples can afford, many day-care centers charge considerably less per week than government agencies estimate costs should be or that is spent in centers which get financial subsidies of some kind. One common way to save money is to have a higher ratio of staff to children than the one to two recommended by some experts or the one to four assumed to be an essential minimum. (Only caregivers who actually deal with children all day long are supposed to be counted in these ratios—not administrators, cooks, or office help.) Another way to shave expenses is to hire caregivers who will work for minimum wages, whether or not they have any training or interest in young children, or to use volunteers, students, or senior citizens. Without ample, trained caregivers, many toddlers are likely to suffer. Not only do they get insufficient mental and verbal stimulation, but they are upset and angry or miserable and withdrawn too much of the time. Toddlers usually don't play well together and without alert staff, they are likely to take out their angry feelings and their aggressive energy on each other, while those who are timid and shy by temperament may become more so, not less.

While a day-care center may seem to offer a stimulating environment with a surfeit of playthings and a cluster of playmates, it may not, in fact, be as enriching a place as the average home with a mother or a father in it. Even the most energetic and conscientious of good caregivers can't provide four or five toddlers in her care as much immediate feedback as a parent who is interacting one to one with a child. And no matter how caring a staffer is, her conversations with a toddler don't have the special overlay of emotional involvement and love that seem to promote rapid and enthusiastic learning between toddlers and their parents. Unless caregivers are trained and particularly alert to intervene, a small

child who is shy, placid, or undemanding by nature may be ignored too often by caregivers who are frantically intent on stopping disputes, maintaining order, and getting the two-year-olds to
the toilet on time.

The wealth of toys and equipment may also be misleading.
Much of it merely substitutes for the welter of household objects
most toddlers play with at home. Children in day-care centers are
often forced to share what they are playing with before they are
ready to do so. They tend to be discouraged from feeling possessive
about anything. And the elaborate equipment may do less for
their mind and muscles than the playthings they find for themselves at home, because they can manipulate and investigate them
without interruption. Because it is so difficult to corral toddlers
into group activities, in many centers they are rarely taken outdoors. As a result, they spend the whole long day in an artificial,
contrived environment where the level of stress can be painfully
high—even for the adults—and there is no refuge from fatigue and
commotion—even for the adults.

Are toddlers still too vulnerable physically to be exposed to
group care? Toys in day-care centers are communal and habitually
mouthed by small children as they are passed around. Most play is
done on the floor. And many centers make it a policy not to
exclude children who are ill. ("After all, we try to function as an
extended family; where else could a sick child go?" asked one center director.) Knowing your sick child will be cared for as usual
may be a relief to a busy working mother. But knowing your toddler is likely to be ill tomorrow because he is being exposed to a
sick classmate today isn't much comfort to other parents.

Are toddlers still too young to be away from home and parents
all day? Experts' answers vary. What research there is shows that
toddlers will remain firmly attached to their own parents and
rarely if ever turn even to a favorite caregiver if a parent is present. The problem is just the opposite: the intense longing that
day-care children show for their absent parents. Signs that toddlers miss their parents acutely are everywhere. Often they cling
to cherished reminders of home, like tattered scraps of blanket.
Many of them call their caregivers "Mommy." Many compete,
almost desperately, for extra hugs and physical contact with
staffers, who are trained not to "spoil" their charges with too

much attention. Some centers are organized so that one caregiver is usually responsible for the same three or four or five children— who often compete aggressively for her attention and often insist on her help at the same time. Other centers are organized around staffers who each take responsibility for a certain physical area or activity; the children must interact with several adults, including any volunteers or students who are helping out. However a center is set up, the toddlers' relief when parents finally arrive in the late afternoon is often almost tangible, although the way they show it may range from squeals of joy to the eruption of a tantrum that has been building all day and can only be released in the security of a parent's presence.

The weight of the questions raised in this chapter may tip unfairly against day care for children as young as one and two years old. But the case for day care for toddlers, as for infants, has yet to be proved. As of now, the preponderance of evidence still indicates that toddlers, just like infants, do best being reared in their own homes by a mother (or father) who is away no more than a part-time job requires.

SUBSTITUTE CAREGIVERS FOR A PRESCHOOLER

After a youngster has passed his third birthday, it becomes much easier for a mother to combine his care with a job. A preschooler is much more able—physically and emotionally—to tolerate the absence of his parents for long stretches of the day than is a baby or a toddler. And many more kinds of day-care centers and nursery schools are available for three- to six-year-olds so it's easier to find a facility that will encourage his mental development.

If there is a logical time between birth and first grade when a mother can shift the bulk of daily child care to others so she can hold down a full-time job, it probably comes at about age three. A three-year-old is much more resistant to infections than a baby or a toddler (although some physicians are concerned about the rapid spread of respiratory and other diseases among preschoolers in group care, just as they are about infants and toddlers). He is toilet-trained, making him eligible for many day-care centers and nursery schools that will not cope with diapers. He is old enough to understand that the absence of his parents is only temporary and that he can rely on his mother or father to pick him up in the late afternoon.

A preschooler is more interested in playing with other children than a baby or a toddler and is beginning to develop a few of the social skills, like sharing and cooperative play, that make group care work better for three- to six-year-olds than it does for younger children. He can talk well enough so he can alert parents to possible problems and relieve some of his frustrations. And his bedtime can be pushed back a little later at night so he can have more time with his family before the day is over.

The same basic choices in child care—a sitter at your house or hers, a day-care home, or a day-care center—all work more easily with a preschooler than with a baby or a toddler. Sometimes the day care is less expensive as well. That's because one child-care worker is considered enough for every ten preschoolers, compared to a one-to-two ratio recommended for babies and a one-to-four ratio for toddlers.

The criteria for choosing a good sitter or center for a preschooler are essentially the same as finding care for a baby or a toddler—with a few exceptions. Three- to six-year-olds need more outdoor play space, more toys, more playground equipment, more books, and a greater variety of arts and crafts materials than younger children.

Still another option becomes available once your child is two and a half or three: a nursery school. In contrast to day-care centers, which are primarily intended to free parents from child care during the working day, nursery schools offer two- or three-hour programs designed to help prepare preschoolers for kindergarten or first grade. You may find several types to choose from in your community (or may be able to start a cooperative if you can't find what you think your child and your friends' offspring need).

A traditional nursery school offers a rather standard variety of group games, outdoor play, art, reading aloud, housekeeping play, juice-and-cracker time, and playing with toys. It gives preschoolers experience in being away from home in readiness for school, encourages them to play together cooperatively, and is generally aimed at fostering social and emotional development. A variation is the all-male "sports club" that concentrates on outdoor play, except in the most severe weather, and in teaching small boys the rudiments of team games. If you choose this type of nursery school, you'll have to take more responsibility yourself for encouraging your child's mental development when you are together.

Several other kinds of nursery schools now deliberately foster mental development as well as social adjustment. These include some of the Head Start programs (which differ markedly in how much emphasis they put on learning and how much on traditional nursery-school activities), some of the nursery schools run by university departments of education or child development, and some prekindergarten programs for four-year-olds run by public school systems.

Montessori schools offer the best opportunities for a child to learn. The rich array of Montessori learning materials is ingeniously designed to help preschoolers teach themselves to read, to understand basic mathematical relationships, and to become independent in their own self-care. Montessori schools protect a child's right to concentrate on his own learning independent of group activities and to take great pride in his increasing mastery of skills. Most Montessori schools enroll two-and-a-half- to six-year olds for a half-day program, but some have an all-day schedule, take toddlers and infants, and/or offer an elementary-school curriculum as well.

While two or three hours of nursery school five times a week isn't enough help for a mother to work full time away from home, it can give her enough freedom to take some part-time jobs nearby or to do some work at home. Or she can combine a morning nursery school with an afternoon baby-sitter to give a preschooler more learning stimulation and variety while she works full time.

The most useful way to choose a nursery school is to consider all of your preschooler's needs—for enormous amounts of learning opportunities, for playmates, for experience in being away from home prior to school, for activities that exercise his large and his small muscles, and for some creative challenge—decide which you can give him most easily, and find a nursery school set up to provide the rest.

OTHER OPTIONS

Many parents who aren't satisfied with the child-care choices available and who don't want to miss out on a major share of their offspring's earliest years of life are looking for other options than working full time or not working at all. Essentially, they are trying to change traditional ways of working—as well as traditional parenting—and to make the workplace bend and bear part of the brunt of the changing American life-styles rather than placing all the burden on vulnerable children.

Such options should increase rapidly in the future. Women have become a major economic and political force in the nation's life. Their earnings and expertise are critical to the nation's economy. Their tax dollars are essential to both state and federal government. When it is necessary to see that children get adequate care, women have the right—and increasingly the power—to insist on altering the forty-hour, five-day work week that was set up for the convenience of men.

The 1980 White House Conference on Families made as one of its top-priority recommendations a call for employers to devise ways to adapt the work week and the workplace to the needs of families—in particular, mothers of young children—by such strategies as flexible working hours, shared jobs, part-time opportunities, and negotiable leaves.

What makes the arguments for flexibility in work patterns even stronger is that it has also proven to be good for business. Companies which have tried a part-time "mothers' shift," for example, draw better, more effective workers. Businesses that allow two employees to share a job find they get the good ideas of both for half the cost. Those offering flexible hours attract more responsible, self-directing employees who work more productively at their choice of hours, with less absenteeism and fewer stress-related accidents. Companies with generous options for leaves—whether for child care, education, or simply to prevent burnout—draw higher quality employees and have less turnover.

Although some of the most attractive options are negotiated individually by a working mother (and/or occasionally by an employed father), most of them fall into one or another of these patterns:

• *Working at home* used to be limited to jobs like typing, baby-sitting, and sewing. But in recent years, the opportunities have expanded almost as rapidly as the number of women in the job market.

Telecommuting—information processing involving a telephone hookup between a home terminal and a company-based computer—has opened up a whole new range of possibilities for working at home. Home terminals can be used not only for secretarial and clerical tasks, but for a whole variety of high-level programming and information processing work—jobs that could include at least half of the workforce, according to one estimation. Several banks and insurance companies, for example, have put terminals in the homes of young mothers who want to stay at home with babies for a few years, but still plan long-term careers in business.

An Oakland, California, computer company employs two-hundred computer professionals, all of whom work at home with terminals. The business was organized specifically to take advantage of the pool of talented young women who don't want to be away from their young children full time. A similar British company was started by a mother who left her computer-programming job to raise her children and assumed many other women also wanted high-level, work-at-home choices. The company now has six-hundred employees—95 percent of them mothers with small children—and almost all of them work at home. The company's headquarters office contains little except its main computer. A few men, some of them fathers of young children, people who don't like to commute, and handicapped workers are also choosing to set up their own "work stations" in their homes with the help of computers.

Like most alternatives to the five-day workweek, telecommuting and other work-at-home arrangements benefit employers as much or more than employees. Companies know that such options help them keep valuable workers, avoid the costs of training replacements, and give them a huge pool of capable, well-motivated, intelligent women to draw on as workers, both for routine office jobs and for high-level professional assignments. It is also cheaper, some companies have discovered, to install a computer terminal in a worker's home and to pay telephone charges than to build additional office space for an expanding business. (One company even sweetens its telecommuting jobs by programming its terminals so at-home employees can also use them for computer games.) Some financial analysts estimate that ten million people—men as well as women—will be telecommuter employees by the mid-1990s.

It's sometimes possible for a mother who has been a valued employee before her baby was born to spin out a work-at-home arrangement with an employer on an individual basis. But usually it's up to her to make a specific proposal, to explain precisely what she can do, and to demonstrate that the plan is feasible. It helps if the company has made a similar deal with other women, or if she has a mentor who did the same thing.

Even though she's home, a work-at-home mother may hire a baby-sitter for several hours a day to clear some uninterrupted time to concentrate on the job. Even so, she's home for the important moments of her baby's life. She knows what happens to her child during the day. Her baby isn't exposed unnecessarily to infectious diseases or forced to spend a long day away from home and parents. And both she and the baby save commuting time to work and day care.

• *Part-time jobs* are easier to find for women whose major purpose in working is to earn money than for those whose chief motivation is to keep a career advancing, or at least on hold. But more than two million people—men as well as women—have part-time jobs as professionals, managers, and administrators. It's sometimes possible for a mother with long-range career plans to arrange with an employer to shift to a reduced schedule for a year or two after the birth of a baby. Altogether, about 30 percent of women who work have part-time jobs.

Sometimes, a young mother who can't find good day care for a baby—or who can't afford it—can fit a part-time job in around a husband's workweek, so he can take at least a turn at being parent-in-charge. Or she can schedule work for hours when she can find a good sitter, such as a college student who wouldn't be available full time. Part-time day care is easier for an infant to tolerate than full time, and the emotional strain of being away from both parents is reduced.

Mothers who want to work part-time shouldn't feel they are asking an employer to do them a favor. Many businesses, by their very nature, need part-time workers, such as waitresses and bus drivers for rush hours. Hospitals, which are often seriously short of nurses and other health care workers, find part-time shifts ease the problem. Mothers' shifts solve more problems for employers than for women. And an employer who agrees to a career woman's request to work part-time usually finds she contributes a full-time quota of good ideas.

• *Shared jobs* are primarily a career woman's version of part-time work and are being used by physicians, college professors, social workers, secretaries, lawyers, government employees, and almost every other kind of jobholder. Most of the arrangements are set up initially on the initiative of a woman who wants to hold onto a job and yet not be away from her baby long enough to work a forty-hour week. Typically, she finds a colleague in the same situation, with the same kind of professional skills, and they approach an employer offering to split the job—and the salary and benefits—in a variety of ways. One woman may work mornings, the other afternoons. They may take alternative days, rotating over a two-week cycle, or agree on a three-day, two-day split every week. They may even switch weeks or months. In a few instances, a husband and wife have shared the same job—a college teaching post or work in a real-estate office—alternating with child care. Job-sharing arrangements have also been worked out between young mothers and older workers who want to ease into retirement and between executives and trainees who are learning a job. In at least one instance, a working woman has shared a job with her mother.

Like other alternatives to working nine to five, job sharing helps employers as well as mothers. Depending on the salary level, Social Security costs may be slightly higher for two workers instead of one, and some companies may opt to give full benefits to both workers. But basically, an employer is getting the good ideas and enthusiasms of two people for the salary of one, and is able to keep well-motivated employees who have a strong commitment to their employer.

• *Flexitime,* scheduling full-time work at other than standard nine to five hours or regular shifts, is another way young parents can earn money, keep up two careers, and still reduce the amount of time a very young child must spend with a sitter or in day care. Most flexitime plans permit employees to start and end their work-day whenever they choose, provided they put in a required num-ber of hours and are in the office during specified core periods, usually between midmorning and midafternoon. Some allow a four-day work week of nine or ten hours. A few, like some in-flight airline jobs, let employees schedule their own hours by the month. This flexibility gives two-career parents more leeway in working out child-care arrangements, perhaps staggering their days at work so both of them are gone only three or four days a week instead of five, or juggling daily hours so one parent can give a youngster a leisurely start in the morning while the other can take over in the late afternoon to reduce the stress and fatigue of a too-long day with a substitute parent.

In some ways, this book may seem to be prodding caring parents to spend more time with their young children—when what they really want are ways to shortcut child care. But the scientific evi-dence is irrefutable: parents can make a lifelong difference in how well their children turn out, particularly in the level of their intel-ligence. And the rewards for parents who do give a child the best possible beginnings in life are also lifelong and enormous. Giving your young child the opportunities to learn described in this book will almost certainly help him to become brighter, happier, more productive, and easier to live with than he would have been oth-erwise. He—and you—will have fewer problems. Your child will be a joy to know and love. And the chances are that you will regard the time you have spent helping him start out well as more important than anything else you might have done with that time.

Bibliography

Abelson, John. "A Revolution in Biology." *Science*, vol. 209, September 19, 1980.

Adams, Judith, and Craig T. Ramey. "Structural Aspects of Maternal Speech to Infants Reared in Poverty." *Child Development*, vol. 51, December 1980.

Ainsworth, Mary Salter. "The Development of Infant-Mother Attachment." Washington, D.C.: Office of Child Development, Department of Health, Education, and Welfare, 1974.

————. "The Development of Infant-Mother Attachment." In *Review of Child Development Research*, vol. 3, edited by B.M. Caldwell and H.N. Ricciuti. Chicago: University of Chicago Press, 1973.

————. "Infant-Mother Attachment." *American Psychologist*, vol. 34, October 1977.

Almay, Millie; Edward Chittenden; and Paula Miller. *Young Children's Thinking*. New York: Teachers College Press, 1966.

American Academy of Pediatrics, Committee on Drugs. "Anticonvulsants and Pregnancy." *Pediatrics*, vol. 63, February 1979.

————, Committee on Fetus and Newborn and Committee on Infectious Diseases. "Perinatal Herpes Simplex Virus Infections." *Pediatrics*, vol. 66, July 1980.

————, Committee on Genetics. "Prenatal Diagnosis for Pediatricians." *Pediatrics*, vol. 65, June 1980.

American College of Obstetricians and Gynecologists. *Adolescent Perinatal Health*. Chicago, 1979.

Apgar, Virginia, and Joan Beck. *Is My Baby All Right?* New York: Simon and Schuster, 1972.

Arco, Christina M. B., and Hatleen A. McCluskey. "A Change of Pace: An Investigation of the Salience of Maternal Temporal Style in Mother-Infant Play." *Child Development*, vol. 52, September 1981.

Aslin, Richard N., and others. "Discrimination of Voice Onset Time in Human Infants: New Findings and Implications for the Effects of Early Experience." *Child Development*, vol. 52, December 1981.

Auerbach-Fink, Stevanne. "Mothers' Expectations of Child Care." *Young Children*, vol. 32, May 1977.

Bakeman, Roger, and Josephine V. Brown. "Early Interaction: Consequences for Social and Mental Development at Three Years." *Child Development*, vol. 51, June 1980.

Banks, Martin S. "The Development of Visual Accommodation During Early Infancy." *Child Development*, vol. 51, September 1980.

Barrera, Maria E., and Daphne Maurer. "Discrimination of Strangers by the Three Month Old." *Child Development*, vol. 52, June 1981.

Bates, John E., and others. "Dimensions of Individuality in the Mother-Infant Relationship at Six Months of Age." *Child Development*, vol. 53, April 1982.

Baum, J. D. "Parent-Offspring Relations in Man," from "Parental and Environmental Influences on Pre- and Post-Natal Development." *Journal of Reproduction and Fertility*, vol. 62, July 1981.

Beck, Joan. *Effective Parenting*. New York: Simon and Schuster, 1975.

————. *How to Raise a Brighter Child*. New York: Simon and Schuster, 1967.

Belsky, Jay; Mary Kay Goode; and Robert K. Most. "Maternal Stimulation and Infant Exploratory Competence: Cross-Sectional, Correlational, and Experimental Analyses." *Child Development*, vol. 51, December 1980.

Bikales, Gerda. *Day Care: A Program in Search of a Policy*. The Center for Analysis of Public Issues, Princeton, N.J., 1978.

Blanton, William E. "Preschool Reading Instruction: A Literature Search, Evaluation, and Interpretation." National Center for Educational Communication, Department of Health, Education and Welfare, Washington, D.C., June 1972.

Blehar, M. C. "Anxious Attachment and Defensive Reactions Associated with Day Care." *Child Development*, vol. 45, September 1974.

Bloom, Benjamin S. *Stability and Change in Human Characteristics*. New York: John Wiley & Sons, 1964.

Boegehold, Betty D., and others. *Education Before Five: A Handbook on Preschool Education*. New York: Bank Street College of Education, 1977.

Bowlby, John. *Attachment*. New York: Basic Books, 1969.

————. *Separation*. New York: Basic Books, 1973.

Bradley, Robert H., and Bettye M. Caldwell. "Early Home Environment and Changes in Mental Test Performances in Children from Six to 36 Months." Paper given at the American Educational Research Association meeting, Washington, D.C., 1975.

————. "The Relation of Home Environment, Cognitive Competence, and IQ among Males and Females." *Child Development*, vol. 51, December 1980.

Brazelton, T. Berry. "A Comparative Study of the Behavior of Greek Neonates." *Pediatrics*, vol. 63, February 1979.

————. "Importance of New Techniques of Neonatal Assessment." Paper given at the American Association for the Advancement of Science meeting, Denver, February 1977.

————. "The Joint Regulation of Infant-Adult Interaction." Paper given at the American Association for the Advancement of Science meeting, Denver, February 1977.

————. *On Becoming a Family: The Growth of Attachment*. New York: Delacorte Press/Seymour Lawrence, 1981.

Bronfenbrenner, Urie. "Is Early Intervention Effective?" Washington, D.C.: Office of Child Development, Department of Health, Education, and Welfare, 1974.

Browder, J. Albert. "The Pediatrician's Orientation to Infant Stimulation Programs." *Pediatrics*, vol. 67, January 1981.

Brown, Nancie Mae. *Bonding: The First Basic in Education.* Bloomington, Ind.: Phi Delta Kappa Educational Foundation, 1978.

Browning, Dominique. "Waiting for Mommy." *Texas Monthly,* February 1982.

Brunell, Philip A. "Prevention and Treatment of Neonatal Herpes." *Pediatrics,* vol. 66, November 1980.

Brzeinski, Joseph E., and John L. Hayman. *The Effectiveness of Parents in Helping Their Preschool Children to Begin to Read.* Denver: Denver Public Schools, September 1962.

Bureau, M. A., and others. "Carboxyhemoglobin Concentration in Fetal Cord Blood and in Blood of Mothers Who Smoked During Labor." *Pediatrics,* vol. 69, March 1982.

"The Potential for Telecommuting." *Business Week,* January 26, 1981.

Burton, Barbara K., and Henry L. Nadler. "Antenatal Diagnosis of Metabolic Disorders." *Clinical Obstetrics and Gynecology,* vol. 24, December 1981.

Carew, Jean V. "Experience and the Development of Intelligence in Young Children at Home and in Day Care." *Monographs of the Society for Research in Child Development,* vol. 45, 1980.

————. "Predicting IQ from the Young Child's Everyday Experience." Paper given at the symposium "Soziale Bedingungen fur die Entwicklung der Lernfahigkeit," Bad Homburg, West Germany, October 1975.

————, and others. "Observed Intellectual Competence and Tested Intelligence: Their Roots in the Young Child's Transactions with His Environment." Paper given at the Eastern Psychological Association meeting, New York, April 1975.

Center for Systems and Program Development, Inc. "Policy Issues in Day Care: Summaries of 21 Papers." Washington, D.C., November 1977.

Chall, Jeanne. *Learning to Read: The Great Debate.* New York: McGraw-Hill, 1967.

Chapman, Patricia A.; W. Keith Blenkinsopp; and B. Victor Lewis. "The Detection of Neural Tube Closure Defects by Exfoliate Cytology of Amniotic Fluid." *Obstetrical and Gynecological Survey,* vol. 37, 1982.

Chedd, Graham. "Who Shall Be Born?" *Science,* vol. 2, January/February 1981.

Clarke-Stewart, Alison. *Child Care in the Family: A Review of Research and Some Propositions for Policy.* New York: Academic Press, 1977.

Clarren, Sterling, and David W. Smith. "The Fetal Alcohol Syndrome." *The New England Journal of Medicine,* vol. 298, May 11, 1978.

Cohen, Leslie B. "Our Developing Knowledge of Infant Perception and Cognition." *American Psychologist,* vol. 34, October 1979.

Cohen, Sarale E., and Leila Beckwith. "Preterm Infant Interaction with the Caregiver in the First Year of Life and Competence at Age Two." *Child Development,* vol. 50, September 1979.

Consortium on Developmental Continuity. "The Persistence of Preschool Effects: A Long-Term Follow-up of 14 Infant and Preschool Experiments." Washington, D.C.: Department of Health, Education, and Welfare, September 1977.

Corbett, Thomas H. "Cancer, Miscarriages, and Birth Defects Associated with

Operating Room Exposure." Paper given at the Conference on Women and the Workplace, Washington, D.C., June 1976.

Corey, Lawrence, and others. "A Trial of Topical Acyclovir in Genital Herpes Simplex Virus Infections." *The New England Journal of Medicine*, vol. 306, June 3, 1982.

Davidson, Jane. "Wasted Time: The Ignored Dilemma." *Young Children*, vol. 35, May 1980.

De Chateau, Peter. "Early Post-Partum Contact and Later Attitudes." *International Journal of Behavioral Development*, September 1980.

Dharamraj, Claude, and others. "Observations on Maternal Preference for Rooming-in Facilities." *Pediatrics*, vol. 67, May 1981.

Douglas, Jane T. "Dollars and Sense: Employer-Supported Child Care: A Study of Child Care Needs and the Realities of Employer-Support." Washington, D.C.: Office of Child Development, Department of Health, Education, and Welfare, 1976.

Drash, Philip W., and Arnold L. Stolberg. "Acceleration of Cognitive, Linguistic, and Social Development in the Normal Infant." Tallahassee, Fla.: Florida State Department of Health and Rehabilitative Services, 1977.

Durkin, Dolores. "Children Who Learned to Read at Home." *Elementary School Journal*, vol. 62, October 1961.

————. "Children Who Read Before Grade 1: A Second Study." *Elementary School Journal*, vol. 63, December 1962.

————. *Children Who Read Early.* New York: Teachers College Press, 1966.

————. "An Earlier Start in Reading?" *Elementary School Journal*, vol. 63, December 1962.

————. "A Six-Year Study of Children Who Learned to Read in School at the Age of Four." *Reading Research Quarterly*, International Reading Association, vol. 10, 1974-75.

Earls, Felton. "The Fathers (Not the Mothers): Their Importance and Influence with Infants and Young Children." In *Annual Progress in Child Psychiatry and Child Development*, edited by Stella Chess and Alexander Thomas. New York: Brunner Mazel, 1977.

Elardo, Richard; Robert Bradley; and Bettye M. Caldwell. "The Relation of Infants' Home Environment to Mental Test Performance from Six to 36 Months: A Longitudinal Analysis," *Child Development*, vol. 46, March 1975.

Escalona, Sibylle K. "Basic Modes of Social Interaction: Their Emergence and Patterning During the First Two Years of Life." *Merrill-Palmer Quarterly*, vol. 19, July 1973.

Eveloff, Herbert H. "Some Cognitive and Affective Aspects of Early Learning Development." *Child Development*, vol. 42, December 1971.

Factors Associated with Low Birth Weight, United States, 1976. Hyattsville, Md.: Public Health Service, Department of Health, Education, and Welfare, April 1980.

Fantz, Robert L., and Joseph F. Fagan III. "Visual Attention to Size and Number of Pattern Details by Term and Preterm Infants During the First Six Months." *Child Development*, vol. 46, March 1975.

Farrell, Mona. "Familiar Factors: A Critical Dimension of Early Identification." Paper given at the Council for Exceptional Children meeting, Kansas City, Mo., May 1978.

Featherstone, Helen. *A Difference in the Family.* New York: Basic Books, 1980.

Federation CECOS; D. Schwartz; and M. J. Mayaux. "Female Fecundity as a Function of Age." *The New England Journal of Medicine,* vol. 306, February 18, 1982.

Ferguson, Patricia; Thomas Lennox; and Dan J. Lettieri, eds. *Drugs and Pregnancy.* Rockville, Md.: National Institute on Drug Abuse, Department of Health, Education, and Welfare, November 1974.

Ferry, Peggy C. "On Growing New Neurons: Are Early Intervention Programs Effective?" *Pediatrics,* vol. 67, January 1981.

Field, Jeffrey, and others. "Infants' Orientation to Lateral Sounds from Birth to Three Months." *Child Development,* vol. 51, March 1980.

Field, Tiffany, and Reena Greenberg. "Temperament Ratings by Parents and Teachers of Infants, Toddlers, and Preschool Children." *Child Development,* vol. 53, February 1982.

Flavell, John H. *Cognitive Development.* Englewood Cliffs, N.J.: Prentice-Hall, 1977.

Fletcher, John C. "Ethics of Amniocentesis for Fetal Sex Identification," *The New England Journal of Medicine,* vol. 301, Sept. 6, 1979.

Fowler, William. "Structural Dimensions of the Learning Process in Early Reading." *Child Development,* vol. 35, December 1964.

———. "Teaching a Two-Year-Old to Read: An Experiment in Early Childhood Learning." *Genetic Psychology Monographs,* vol. 66, 1962.

Fraiberg, Selma. "Children and Child Care Industries, Incorporated." *The Phi Kappa Phi Journal,* vol. 61, Fall, 1979.

———. *Every Child's Birthright: In Defense of Mothering.* New York: Basic Books, 1977.

Frankenburg, William K., and Josiah B. Dodds. *Denver Developmental Screening Test.* Denver, Colorado: University of Colorado Medical Center, 1966.

Gallas, Howard B., and Michael Lewis. "Mother-Infant Interaction and Cognitive Development in the 12-Week-Old Infant." Paper given at the Society for Research in Child Development meeting, New Orleans, March 1977.

Gelman, Rochel. "Preschool Thought." *American Psychologist,* vol. 34, October 1979.

Glass, Robert H. "Sex Preselection." *Obstetrics and Gynecology,* vol. 49, January 1977.

Glickman, Beatrice Marden, and Nesha Bass Springer. *Who Cares for the Baby?* New York: Schocken Books, 1978.

Golden, Nancy L.; Robert J. Sokol; and I. Leslie Rubin. "Angel Dust: Possible Effects on the Fetus." *Pediatrics,* vol. 65, January 1980.

Goodman, Norman, and Joseph Andrews. "Cognitive Development of Children in Family and Group Day Care." *American Journal of Orthopsychiatry,* vol. 51, April 1981.

Gordon, Ira. "The Florida Parent Education Early Intervention Project: A Longitudinal Look." Paper given at the Merrill-Palmer Conference on Infant Education, Detroit, February 1973.

———. "Parent Oriented Home-Based Early Childhood Education Program: Research Report." Gainesville: Florida University, Institute for Development of Human Resources, May 1975.

Green, James A.; Gwen E. Gustofson; and Meredith J. West. "Effects of Infant Development on Mother-Infant Interactions." *Child Development*, vol. 51, March 1980.

Greenberg, David J., and William J. O' Donnell. "Infancy and the Optimal Level of Stimulation." *Child Development*, vol. 43, June 1972.

Greenblatt, Augusta. *Heredity and You.* New York: Coward, McCann & Geoghegan, 1974.

Guerrero V, Rodrigo, and Oscar I. Rogas. "Spontaneous Abortion and Aging of Human Ova and Spermatozoa." *The New England Journal of Medicine*, vol. 293, Sept. 18, 1975.

Gurren, Louise, and Ann Hughes. "Intensive Phonics vs. Gradual Phonics in Beginning Reading: A Review." *The Journal of Educational Research*, vol. 58, April 1965.

Haber, Julian S. "Long Term Speech and Language Outcomes in High Risk Neonates." Paper given at the American Academy of Pediatrics meeting, Honolulu, March 1982.

Hanson, James W.; Ann Pytkowicz Steissguth; and David W. Smith. "The Effects of Moderate Alcohol Consumption During Pregnancy on Fetal Growth and Morphogenesis." Paper given at the Fifth International Conference on Birth Defects, Montreal, August 1977.

Harlap, Susan. "Gender of Infants Conceived on Different Days of the Menstrual Cycle." *New England Journal of Medicine*, vol. 300, June 28, 1979.

Harvey, Mary Ann Sedgwick; Marcella M. McRorie; and David W. Smith. "Suggested Limits to the Use of Hot Tub and Sauna by Pregnant Women." *Obstetrical and Gynecological Survey*, vol. 37, 1982.

Henig, Robin Marantz. "Saving Babies Before Birth." *The New York Times Magazine*, February 28, 1982.

Hertz, Thomas H. "The Impact of Federal Early Childhood Programs on Children." Washington, D.C.: Department of Health, Education, and Welfare, July 1977.

Hill, Reba Michels. *Breast Feeding.* Evanston, Ill.: American Academy of Pediatrics, 1981.

Hobbins, John C.; Roger Freeman; and John T. Queenan. "The Fetal Monitoring Debate." *Pediatrics*, vol. 63. June 1979.

Hock, Ellen. "Alternative Approaches to Child Rearing and Their Effects on the Mother-Infant Relationship—Final Report." Washington, D.C.: Department of Health, Education and Welfare, 1976.

———. "Working and Nonworking Mothers and Their Infants: A Comparative Study of Maternal Caregiving Characteristics and Infant Social Behavior." *Merrill-Palmer Quarterly*, vol. 26, April 1980.

———, and Joyce Brookhart Clinger. "Behavior Toward Mother and Stranger of Infants Who Have Experienced Group Day Care, Individual Care, or Exclusive Maternal Care." *Journal of Genetic Psychology*, vol. 137, September 1980.

Hoffman, Lois Wladis. "Maternal Employment: 1979." *American Psychologist*, vol. 34, October 1979.

Holzman, Mathilda. "The Verbal Environment Provided by Mothers for Their Very Young Children." *Merrill-Palmer Quarterly*, vol. 20, January 1974.

Howes, Carollee, and Joanne Krakow. "Effects of Inevitable Environmental Pollutants." Paper given at the American Psychological Association meeting, San Francisco, August 1977.

Hunt, J. McV. *Intelligence and Experience*. New York: Ronald Press, 1961.

――――. "The Prospects of Early Education in Social Evolution." Paper given at a symposium, Xavier University, Cincinnati, Ohio, June 1973.

Hunter, Rosemary S., and others. "Antecedents of Child Abuse and Neglect in Premature Infants: A Prospective Study in a Newborn Intensive Care Unit." *Pediatrics*, vol. 61, April 1978.

Hurst, Marsha, and Ruth E. Zambrana. *Determinants and Consequences of Maternal Employment*. Washington, D.C.: Business and Professional Women's Foundation, 1981.

Infante, Peter F., and Joseph K. Wagoner. "The Effects of Lead on Reproduction." Paper given at the Conference on Women and the Workplace, Washington, D.C., June 1976.

Johnson, Richard T. "Mechanisms of Virus-Induced Birth Defects." Paper given at the Fifth International Conference on Birth Defects, Montreal, August 1977.

Kagan, Jerome. "Continuity and Change in Behavioral Inhibition." Paper given at the American Association for the Advancement of Science meeting, Washington, D.C., January 1982.

――――. "The Effect of Day Care on the Infant." Paper prepared for the Department of Health, Education, and Welfare, Washington, D.C., June 1976.

――――. "The Effects of Infant Day Care on Psychological Development." Paper given at the American Association for the Advancement of Science meeting, Boston, February 1976.

――――, and Margaret Hamburg. "The Enhancement of Memory in the First Year." *The Journal of Genetic Psychology*, vol. 138, 1981.

――――; Richard B. Kearsley; and Philip R. Zelazo. *Infancy: Its Place in Human Development*. Cambridge, Mass.: Harvard University Press, 1978.

Karger, Rex H. "Synchrony in Mother-Infant Interaction." *Child Development*, vol. 50, September 1979.

Kierscht, Marcia. "Correlates of Early Infant Competence: A Multivariate Approach, Final Report, Part I." Washington, D.C.: Department of Health, Education, and Welfare, August 1975.

Kilmer, Sally. "Infant-Toddler Group Day Care: A Review of Research." Paper sponsored by the National Institute of Education, Washington, D.C., December 1977.

King, Charles R. "Genetic Disease and Pregnancy." *Obstetrical and Gynecological Survey*, vol. 37, 1982.

Knobloch, Hilda. "Considerations in Evaluating Changes in Outcome for Infants Weighing Less than 1,501 Grams." *Pediatrics*, vol. 69, March 1982.

Krekel, Sylvia. "Placement of Women in High Risk Areas." Paper given at the Conference on Women and the Workplace, Washington, D.C., June 1976.

Lamb, Michael E. "Development and Function of Parent-Infant Relationships in the First Two Years of Life." Paper given at the Society for Research in Child Development meeting, New Orleans, March 1977.

————. "The Effects of Ecological Variables on Parent-Infant Interaction." Paper given at the Society for Research in Child Development meeting, New Orleans, March 1977.

————. "Second Thoughts on First Touch." *Psychology Today*, vol. 16, April 1982.

Leib, Susan A.; Gary Benfield; and John Guidubaldi. "Effects of Early Intervention and Stimulation on the Preterm Infant." *Pediatrics*, vol. 66, July 1980.

Leonard, Claire O. "Serum AFP Screening for Neural Tube Defects." *Clinical Obstetrics and Gynecology*, vol. 24, December 1981.

Levin, Ann Aschengrau, and others. "Association of Induced Abortion with Subsequent Pregnancy Loss." *The Journal of the American Medical Association*, vol. 243, June 27, 1980.

Lewkowicz, David J., and Gerald Turkewitz. "Intersensory Interaction in Newborns: Modification of Visual Preferences Following Exposure to Sounds." *Child Development*, vol. 52, September 1981.

Linn, Shai, and others. "No Association Between Coffee Consumption and Adverse Outcomes of Pregnancy." *The New England Journal of Medicine*, vol. 306, January 21, 1982.

Lipper, Evelyn, and others. "Determinants of Neurobehavioral Outcomes in Low-Birth-Weight Infants." *Pediatrics*, vol. 67, April 1981.

Longo, Lawrence D. "Maternal Smoking: Effects on the Fetus and Newborn Infant." Paper given at the American Association for the Advancement of Science meeting, San Francisco, January 1980.

Lucey, Jerold F. "Retrolental Fibroplasia May Not Be Preventable." Paper given at the American Academy of Pediatrics meeting, Honolulu, March 1982.

McAnarney, Elizabeth R., and others. "Obstetric, Neonatal, and Psychosocial Outcome of Pregnant Adolescents." *Pediatrics*, vol. 61, February 1978.

McKee, Paul, and Joseph E. Brzeinski. *The Effectiveness of Teaching Reading in Kindergarten*. Denver: Denver Public Schools, 1966.

Macri, James N.; David A. Baker; and Roger S. Baim. "Diagnosis of Neural Tube Defects by Evaluation of Amniotic Fluid." *Clinical Obstetrics and Gynecology*, vol. 24, December 1981.

Radiation and Birth Defects. March of Dimes Science News Information File, March of Dimes Birth Defects Foundation, August 1979.

Marijuana and Health. Rockville, Md.: Eighth Annual Report to the U.S. Congress from the Secretary of Health, Education, and Welfare, National Institute on Drug Abuse, 1980.

Metzl, Marilyn Newman. "Teaching Parents a Strategy for Enhancing Infant Development." *Child Development*, vol. 51, June 1980.

Meyer, Mary B. "Smoking and the Developing Fetus." Paper given at the American Association for the Advancement of Science meeting, San Francisco, January 1980.

Miller, Herbert C. "Intrauterine Growth Retardation: An Unmet Challenge." Paper given at the American Academy of Pediatrics meeting, Washington, D.C., April 1981.

Miller, Louise B., and Jean L. Dyer. "Four Preschool Programs: Their Dimensions and Effects." *Monographs of the Society for Research in Child Development,* vol. 40, October 1975.

Milunsky, Aubrey. *Know Your Genes.* Boston: Houghton Mifflin, 1977.

————. *The Prevention of Genetic Disease and Mental Retardation.* Philadelphia: W. B. Saunders, 1975.

Moerk, Ernst L. "The Mother of Eve—As a First Language Teacher." Paper given at the Society for Research in Child Development meeting, San Francisco, March 1979.

Montessori, Maria. *The Absorbent Mind.* New York: Holt, Rinehart and Winston, 1967.

————. *The Discovery of the Child.* New York: Ballantine Books, 1972.

————. *A Montessori Handbook.* Edited by R. C. Orem. New York: G. P. Putnam's Sons, 1965.

————. *The Montessori Method.* Cambridge, Mass.: Robert Bentley, 1964.

————. *The Secret of Childhood.* New York: Ballantine Books, 1972.

Murray, Ann D. "Maternal Employment Reconsidered: Effects on Infants." *American Journal of Orthopsychiatry,* vol. 45, October 1975.

Naeye, Richard L. "Influence of Maternal Cigarette Smoking During Pregnancy on Fetal and Childhood Growth." *Obstetrics and Gynecology,* vol. 57, January 1981.

————. "Teenaged and Pre-teenaged Pregnancies: Consequences of the Fetal-Maternal Competition for Nutrients." *Pediatrics,* vol. 67, January 1981.

Neel, J. V., and Schull, W. J. "Current Status of Genetic Follow-up Studies in Hiroshima and Nagasaki." Paper given at the American Association for the Advancement of Science meeting, Toronto, January 1981.

Noble, Ernest P. "Evaluation of Programs and Policies for the Fetal Alcohol Syndrome." Paper given at the American Association for the Advancement of Science meeting, Houston, January 1979.

Nutrition Committee of the Canadian Paediatric Society and the Committee on Nutrition of the American Academy of Pediatrics. "Breast Feeding." *Pediatrics,* vol. 62, October 1978.

Nyhan, William L., and Edward Edelson. *The Heredity Factor,* New York: Grosset & Dunlap, 1976.

O'Brien, Marion, and others. *The Toddler Center.* Baltimore: University Park Press, 1979.

O'Connell, Martin; Ann C. Orr; and Marjorie Lueck. "Recent Child Care Trends in the United States." Paper given at the American Association for the Advancement of Science meeting, Washington, D.C., January 1982.

Ogbu, John U. "Origins of Human Competence: A Cultural-Ecological Perspective." *Child Development,* vol. 52, June 1981.

Omenn, Gilbert. "Eco-genetics: Human Variation in Susceptibility to Environmental Agents." Paper given at the American Association for the Advancement of Science meeting, Toronto, January 1981.

Orem, R. C. *Montessori for the Disadvantaged.* New York: G. P. Putnam's Sons, 1967.

Overall, James C. "Persistent Problems with Persistent Herpesviruses." *The*

New England Journal of Medicine, vol. 305, July 9, 1981.

Oviatt, Sharon L. "Inferring What Words Mean: Early Development in Infants' Comprehension of Common Object Names." *Child Development,* vol. 53, February 1982.

Palmer, Francis H. "The Effects of Early Childhood Intervention." Paper given at the American Association for the Advancement of Science meeting, Denver, February 1977.

Pass, Robert L., and others. "Outcome of Symptomatic Congenital Cytomegalovirus Infection: Results of Long-Term Longitudinal Follow-up." *Pediatrics,* vol. 66, November 1980.

Patterns of Employment Before and After Childbirth. Hyattsville, Md.: National Center for Health Statistics, Department of Health, Education, and Welfare, January 1980.

Penfield, Wilder. *The Second Career.* Boston: Little, Brown, 1963.

———, and Lamar Roberts. *Speech and Brain Mechanisms.* Princeton, N.J.: Princeton University Press, 1959.

Phillips, John L. *The Origins of Intellect: Piaget's Theory.* San Francisco: W. H. Freeman, 1969.

Piaget, Jean. *The Language and Thought of the Child.* Cleveland: World Book, 1955.

———. *The Origin of Intelligence in Children.* New York: International Universities Press, 1952.

———. *Psychology of Intelligence.* Paterson, N.J.: Littlefield, Adams, 1963.

Pincus, Cynthia S.; Leslie Elliott; and Trudy Schlachter. *The Roots of Success.* Englewood Cliffs, N.J.: Prentice-Hall, 1980.

Pines, Maya. "Baby, You're Incredible." *Psychology Today,* vol. 16, February 1982.

———. "A Head Start in the Nursery." *Psychology Today.* vol. 13, September 1979.

Pleet, Helaine; John M. Graham; and David W. Smith. "Central Nervous System and Facial Defects Associated with Maternal Hyperthermia at Four to 14 Weeks' Gestation." *Pediatrics,* vol. 67, June 1981.

Portnoy, Fern C., and Carolyn H. Simmons. "Day Care and Attachment." *Child Development,* vol. 49, March 1978.

Powell, Louisa Feldman. "The Effects of Extra Stimulation and Maternal Involvement on the Development of Low-Birth-Weight Infants and on Maternal Behavior." *Child Development,* vol. 45, March 1974.

Provence, Sally; Audrey Naylor; and June Patterson. *The Challenge of Daycare.* New Haven, Conn.: Yale University Press, 1977.

Rabinowitz, R. Michael, and others. "The Effects of Toy Novelty and Social Interaction on the Exploratory Behavior of Preschool Children." *Child Development,* vol. 46, March 1975.

Ragozin, Arlene S. "Attachment Behavior of Day Care Children: Naturalistic and Laboratory Observations." *Child Development,* vol. 51, June 1980.

Ramey, Craig T.; Dale C. Farren; and Frances A. Campbell. "Predicting IQ from Mother-Infant Interactions." *Child Development,* vol. 50, June 1979.

Redmond, Geoffrey, P. "Drugs as a Cause of Intrauterine Growth Retardation." Paper given at the American Academy of Pediatrics meeting, Detroit, October 1980.

Reeves, William C., and others. "Risk of Recurrence After First Episodes of Genital Herpes." *The New England Journal of Medicine*, vol. 305, August 6, 1981.

Ricciuti, Henry N. "Effects of Infant Day Care Experience on Behavior and Development: Research and Implications for Social Policy." Washington, D.C.: A review prepared for the Department of Health, Education, and Welfare, 1976.

Rosenweig, Mark R., and others. "Heredity, Environment, Learning and the Brain." Paper given at the American Association for the Advancement of Science meeting, Berkeley, Calif., December 1965.

Rothbart, Mary Klevjord. "Measurement of Temperament in Infancy." *Child Development*, vol. 52, June 1981.

Royster, Eugene C., and others. "A National Survey of Head Start Graduates and Their Peers." Cambridge, Mass.: Abt Associates, 1978.

Rubenstein, Judith L., and Carollee Howes. "Caregiving and Infant Behavior in Day Care and in Homes." *Developmental Psychology*, vol. 12, January 1979.

Ruddy, Margaret G., and Marc H. Bornstein. "Cognitive Correlates of Infant Attention and Maternal Stimulation Over the First Year of Life." *Child Development*, vol. 53, February 1982.

Rush, David. "Nutritional Services During Pregnancy and Birthweight: A Retrospective Matched Pair Analysis." *Canadian Medical Journal*, vol. 125, September 15, 1981.

————; Zena Stein; and Mervyn Susser. "A Randomized Controlled Trial of Prenatal Nutritional Supplementation in New York City." *Pediatrics*, vol. 65, April 1980.

Rutter, Michael. "Social-Emotional Consequences of Day Care for Preschool Children." *American Journal of Orthopsychiatry*, vol. 51, January 1981.

Sabbagha, Rudy E.; Ralph K. Tamura; and Sharon Dal Compo. "Antenatal Ultrasonic Diagnosis of Genetic Defects: Present Status." *Clinical Obstetrics and Gynecology*, vol. 24, December 1981.

Saigal, Saroj, and others. "Observations on the Behavioral State of Newborn Infants During the First Hour of Life: A Comparison of Infants Delivered by the Leboyer and Conventional Methods." *The American Journal of Obstetrics and Gynecology*, vol. 139, March 15, 1981.

Sameroff, Arnold J.; Ronald Seifer; and Penelope Kelly Elias. "Sociocultural Variability in Infant Temperament Ratings." *Child Development*, vol. 51, February 1982.

Schachter, Frances Fuchs. "Toddlers with Employed Mothers." *Child Development*, vol. 52, September 1981.

Schneider, Meier. "Mercury: A Health Hazard Associated with Employment of Women as Dental Assistants." Paper given at the Conference on Women and the Workplace, Washington, D.C., June 1976.

Schubert, Jan Basom; Sharon Bradley-Johnson; and James Nuttal. "Mother-Infant Communication and Maternal Employment." *Child Development*, vol. 51, March 1980.

Schull, William J.; Masanori Otake; and James V. Neel. "Genetic Effects of the Atomic Bombs: A Reappraisal." *Science*, vol. 213, September 11, 1981.

Seitz, Victoria. "Long-Term Effects of Intervention: A Longitudinal Investigation." Paper given at the American Association for the Advancement of Science meeting, Denver, February 1977.

Siegel, Linda A. "Infant Tests as Predictors of Cognitive and Language Development at Two Years." *Child Development,* vol. 52, June 1981.

Simpson, Joe Leigh. "Antenatal Diagnosis of Cytogenetic Abnormalities." *Clinical Obstetrics and Gynecology,* vol. 24, December 1981.

————. "More Than We Ever Wanted to Know About Sex—Should We Be Afraid to Ask?" *New England Journal of Medicine,* vol. 300, June 28, 1979.

Smith, Allen N., and Carol M. Spence. "National Day Care Study: Optimizing the Day Care Environment." *American Journal of Orthopsychiatry,* vol. 50, October 1980.

Stagno, Sergio, and others. "Comparative Study of Diagnostic Procedures for Congenital Cytomegalovirus Infection." *Pediatrics,* vol. 65, February 1980.

————. "Congenital Cytomegalovirus Infection." *The New England Journal of Medicine,* vol. 306, April 22, 1982.

————. "An Outbreak of Toxoplasmosis Linked to Cats." *Pediatrics,* vol. 65, February 1980.

Strobino, Barbara Reiber; Jennie Kline; and Zena Stein. "Chemical and Physical Exposures of Parents: Effects on Human Reproduction and Offspring." *Journal of Early Human Development,* vol. 1, February, 1978.

Thompson, Ross A.; Michael E. Lamb; and David Estes. "Stability of Infant-Mother Attachment and Its Relationship to Changing Life Circumstances, in an Unselected Middle-Class Sample." *Child Development,* vol. 53, February 1982.

Tierney, Gene, with Mickey Herskowitz. *Self-Portrait.* New York: Wyden Books, 1979.

Toner, Ignatius J.; Laura P. Moore; and Bruce A. Emmons. "The Effect of Being Labeled on Subsequent Self-Control in Children." *Child Development,* vol. 51, June 1980.

Torrance, E. Paul. *Guiding Creative Talent.* Englewood Cliffs, N.J.: Prentice-Hall, 1962.

————. *Rewarding Creative Behavior,* Englewood Cliffs, N.J.: Prentice-Hall, 1965.

Truss, Carroll V., and others. "Parent Training in Preprimary Competence." Paper given at the American Psychological Association meeting, San Francisco, August 1977.

Tulkin, Steven R., and Jerome Kagan. "Mother-Child Interaction in the First Year of Life." *Child Development,* vol. 43, March 1972.

Tyler, Bonnie, and Laura Dittman. "Meeting the Toddler More than Halfway: The Behavior of Toddlers and Their Caregivers." *Young Children,* vol. 35, January 1980.

Uzgiris, Ina C. "Patterns of Cognitive Development in Infancy." *Merrill-Palmer Quarterly,* vol. 19, October 1973.

Verp, Marion S., and Albert B. Gerbie. "Amniocentesis for Prenatal Diagnosis." *Clinical Obstetrics and Gynecology,* vol. 24, December 1981.

Vlietstra, Alica G. "Full- Versus Half-Day Preschool Attendance: Effects in Young Children as Assessed by Teacher Ratings and Behavioral Observations." *Child Development,* vol. 52, June 1981.

Wagoner, Joseph K.; Peter F. Infante; and David F. Brown. "Genetic Effects Associated with Industrial Chemicals." Paper given at the Conference on Women and the Workplace, Washington, D.C., June 1976.

Wann, Kenneth D.; Miriam Selchen Dorn; and Elizabeth Ann Liddie. *Fostering Intellectual Development in Young Children.* New York: Teachers College Press, 1962.

Whelan, Elizabeth. *Boy or Girl?* New York: Bobbs-Merrill, 1977.

White, Burton L. "Critical Influences in the Origins of Competence." *Merrill-Palmer Quarterly*, vol. 21, October 1975.

————. "Early Stimulation and Behavioral Development." In *Genetics, Environment, and Intelligence*, edited by A. Oliverio. Elsevier/North Holland: Biomedical Press, 1977.

————. "Guidelines for Parent Education, 1977." Paper given at the Planning Education Conference, Flint, Mich., September 1977.

————. *Human Infants: Experience and Psychological Development.* Englewood Cliffs, N.J.: Prentice-Hall, 1971.

————. "Should You Stay Home with Your Baby?" *Educational Horizons*, Fall, 1980.

————, and Peter Castle. "Visual Exploratory Behavior Following Postnatal Handling of Human Infants. *Perceptual and Motor Skills*, vol. 18, 1964.

————, and Jean Carew Watts. *Experience and Environment.* Englewood Cliffs, N.J.: Prentice-Hall, 1973.

————, and others. "Child Rearing Practices and the Development of Competence, Final Report." Cambridge, Mass.: Harvard University Graduate School of Education, 1974.

Whitley, Richard J., and others. "The Natural History of Herpes Simplex Virus Infection of Mother and Newborn." *Pediatrics*, vol. 66, October 1980.

Willerman, Lee. "Effects of Families on Intellectual Development." *American Psychologist*, vol. 34, October 1979.

Williams, Ronald L., and Peter M. Chen. "Identifying the Sources of the Recent Decline in Perinatal Mortality Rates in California." *The New England Journal of Medicine*, vol. 306, January 28, 1982.

Wilson, Christopher B., and others. "Development of Adverse Sequelae in Children Born with Subclinical Congenital Toxoplasma Infection." *Pediatrics*, vol. 66, November 1980.

Wilson, James G., and F. Clarke Fraser, eds. *Handbook of Teratology.* New York: Plenum Press, 1977.

Wright, Ellen E., and Margery W. Shaw. "Legal Liability in Genetic Screening, Genetic Counseling, and Prenatal Diagnosis." *Clinical Obstetrics and Gynecology*, vol. 24, December 1981.

Yaffe, Sumner J. "Drugs and Pregnancy." Paper given at the American Association for the Advancement of Science meeting, San Francisco, January 1980.

Yurchak, Mary-Jane H., and others. *Infant-Toddler Curriculum of the Brookline Early Education Project.* Brookline, Mass.: Brookline Early Education Project, November 1975.

Zelazo, Philip R., and others. "Fathers and Sons: An Experimental Facilitation of Attachment Behaviors." Paper given at the Society for Research in Child Development meeting, New Orleans: March 1977.

Zeskind, Philip Sanford, and Craig T. Ramey. "Preventing Intellectual and Interactional Sequelae of Fetal Malnutrition: A Longitudinal, Transactional, and Synergistic Approach to Development." *Child Development*, vol. 52, March 1981.

Zigler, Edward F., and Edmund W. Gordon, eds. *Day Care: Scientific and Social Policy Issues*. Boston: Auburn House Publishing, 1982.

———, and Jeanette Valentine, eds. *Project Head Start: A Legacy of the War on Poverty*. New York: Free Press, 1979.

———, and others. "Is an Intervention Program Necessary in Order to Improve Economically Disadvantaged Children's IQ Scores?" *Child Development*, vol. 53, April 1982.

Index

Radiation, and birth defects, 82–83
Ramsey, Dr. Craig T., 164
Reading
  to 9 to 12 month old, 144
  to preschooler, 195, 197
  preschooler learning, 126,
      187–188, 201–206
  teaching, 202–206
  to toddler, 168, 172, 174
  value of, 178
Recessive gene, 25, 36, 37
Red meat, and pregnancy, 78
Reed, Nancy Gail, 199–200
Repetition
  in reading books, 172
  and 3 to 6 month old, 138
Rh disease, 17, 25, 97–98
Rh vaccine, 98
Right-handedness, 154–155
Rocking baby, 133
Rolling a ball, 118, 143, 150
Rolling over, 108, 113, 135
Rosenzweig, Dr. Mark, 122
Rubella
  dangers of during pregnancy,
      53–54
  protection against, 53–56
  vaccine, 54–55
Rubeola vaccine, 54, 55

Safety, home and child's, 139, 169
Sand, play value of, 175
Sauna bath, and pregnancy, 92
Schizophrenia, 31
Science, learning, 211–213
Scribbling, 155
Second language, learning, 122,
      126, 197–201
Security blanket, 167
Self-help skills
  frustrations with, 179
  at 12 to 18 months, 151
  at 22 to 24 months, 154
  at 24 to 30 months, 155
  at 30 months to 3 years, 159–160
Self-image of child, 130
Sentences, talking in, 153
Sex, baby's

  amniocentesis to determine, 39,
      47
  choosing, 41–47
  preferences, 41
Sex characteristics, growth of, 67
Sex chromosomes, 28, 38, 41–42
Sex roles, 182
"Shadowing" mother, 152
Sharing, 168, 182, 188, 220
Shettles, Dr. Landrum, 42–44
Sibling rivalry, 52
Sickle-cell anemia, 36, 73
Sight words, teaching reading with,
      202, 205
Single-parent family, 22
Sitting up, 113, 115
Sleeping, 70–71, 111–112
Smallpox, 56
Smiling, 112, 137
Smoke detector, 83
Smoking, and pregnancy, 17, 87–89
Soap operas, 214
Sociability of child, 112, 131–132,
      137, 251
Sounds, baby producing, 111, 114,
      116–117
Speech, foundation for, 137
  see also Language
Sperm
  and conception, 27, 42, 56, 57
  production of, 27–28, 51
Spina bifida, 39, 40, 73, 74
  detection of, 96–97
Spinal cord disability, *see* Spina
      bifida
Stairs, climbing up and down, 154,
      170
Standing, 116, 118, 142
Staring, 119–120
  see also Vision
Stillbirth
  fathers over 45 and, 51
  infectious diseases and, 55
  marijuana and, 87
  Rh disease and, 97
  smoking and, 88
Stomach, placing baby on, 133
Strangers, and baby, 235
Stubbornness, 157